C0 1 72 52605 2E

G000278737

H M S
BELLEROPHON

H M S
BELLEROPHON

C. A. PENGELLY

With a Preface by
PROFESSOR CHRISTOPHER LLOYD

Pen & Sword
MARITIME

First published in Great Britain in 1966
by John Baker Publishers Ltd.

Reprinted in this format in 2014 by
PEN & SWORD MARITIME
An imprint of
Pen & Sword Books Ltd
47 Church Street
Barnsley
South Yorkshire
S70 2AS

Copyright © C.A. Pengelly, 1966, 2014

ISBN 978 1 78346 240 7

The right of C.A. Pengelly to be identified as Author
of this work has been asserted by him in accordance with
the Copyright, Designs and Patents Act 1988.

A CIP catalogue record for this book is
available from the British Library

All rights reserved. No part of this book may be reproduced or transmitted in
any form or by any means, electronic or mechanical including photocopying,
recording or by any information storage and retrieval system,
without permission from the Publisher in writing.

Printed and bound in England
By CPI Group (UK) Ltd, Croydon, CR0 4YY

Pen & Sword Books Ltd incorporates the Imprints of Pen & Sword Aviation,
Pen & Sword Family History, Pen & Sword Maritime, Pen & Sword Military,
Pen & Sword Discovery, Pen & Sword Politics, Pen & Sword Archaeology,
Pen & Sword Atlas, Wharncliffe Local History, Wharncliffe True Crime,
Wharncliffe Transport, Pen & Sword Select, Pen & Sword Military Classics,
Leo Cooper, The Praetorian Press, Claymore Press, Remember When,
Seaforth Publishing and Frontline Publishing

For a complete list of Pen & Sword titles please contact
PEN & SWORD BOOKS LIMITED
47 Church Street, Barnsley, South Yorkshire, S70 2AS, England
E-mail: enquiries@pen-and-sword.co.uk
Website: www.pen-and-sword.co.uk

Durham County Council
Libraries, Learning
and Culture

C0 1 72 52605 2E

Askews & Holts

359.32

Preface

BY PROFESSOR CHRISTOPHER LLOYD

Professor of Humane Studies, Royal Naval College, Greenwich

THE biography of a ship is often more interesting than the biography of an admiral. If, like the *Bellerophon*, she has a long record of service and a distinguished list of battle honours, her story serves as the history of a war. This, more or less, is what Mr Pengelly gives us in his very detailed account of the 'Billy Ruff'n', as her men used to call her when they could not get their tongues around her proper name.

In 1965 we commemorated the bicentenary of the launching of H.M.S. *Victory*. It is an odd coincidence that Sir Thomas Slade, her designer, also designed the *Bellerophon* in the same year, though she was not built for some time to come. Like the *Victory*, the *Bellerophon* made her reputation in the twenty years of war against the French Revolution and Napoleon. Like her, her most distinguished service was as a unit of Nelson's fleet at Trafalgar. Like her, she was painted 'Nelson fashion', that is to say, black with yellow strakes, her gunports being painted black to give her a chequer-board appearance. Like the *Victory*, the *Bellerophon* (one of Collingwood's division) lost most of her masts at Trafalgar and her captain was killed on board.

She was, of course, a much smaller ship than the 100-gun three-decker. She was the first of the seventy-fours, or two-decker third rates, the backbone of the fleet because of their strength and versatility in all types of operations.

The *Bellerophon*'s record proves what an excellent national investment she was. Her area of service ranges from the Mediterranean and the Baltic to the West Indies and the North American station.

Her battle honours include the Glorious First of June, the Nile (where she was dismasted after an hour's action

5

with the French flagship), Trafalgar, and the surrender of Napoleon off Rochefort in 1815. She had an honourable record of service in fleets commanded by such men as Howe, St Vincent, Cornwallis, Saumarez, and of course Nelson.

By using the details provided by her logs and by the journals kept by officers serving on board, Mr Pengelly can give us a detailed account of her life at sea and the conditions under which men served in her. He is fortunate in being able to draw on two journals in particular—that of Matthew Flinders, later the circumnavigator of Australia, who served in her as a lieutenant, and that of Pryce Cumby, who gives a vivid idea of the conditions under which the battle of Trafalgar was fought.

Better known to past generations is the story told by her last captain, Sir Frederick Maitland, of the surrender of Napoleon. His book is now almost forgotten, and the collection of letters about the event which I printed in my edition of the *Keith Papers* is not known to a wide circle, so we can welcome Mr Pengelly's continuous narrative of that curious and epoch-making episode.

On their way to Plymouth, Napoleon complained to Maitland that 'wherever there is water to float a ship, we are sure to find you in our way'. The *Bellerophon* is a good example of this, because she spent so much of her time in what one of her captains called 'the dismal drudgery of the Bay', meaning the naval blockade off Ushant and in the Bay of Biscay which was, in the last analysis, the reason for the defeat of Imperial France. She was, in fact, to use the better known and more colourful language of Mahan, a fine example of 'those far distant, storm-beaten ships, upon which the Grand Army never looked, which stood between it and the dominion of the world.'

It is only fitting that her figurehead should be preserved in the Victory Museum at Portsmouth and that she should now have found a devoted biographer.

CHRISTOPHER LLOYD

Contents

LIST OF ILLUSTRATIONS

Author's Foreword

IN choosing to write the story of the first *Bellerophon*, I was influenced by the fact that, with the exception of the *Victory*, no other single ship of the Royal Navy has ever had a book written solely about herself. It seemed to me that such a story as that of the *Bellerophon* was worth recording in detail.

The late Edward Fraser wrote a book on the whole line of *Bellerophon*s, and his work is valuable to the present-day writer for the task of collating together the references which are gathered from other sources and especially that of manuscript material. The other two works which are invaluable to any naval historian of the Revolutionary and Napoleonic Wars are: *The Naval History of Great Britain* by William James (1822) and Admiral Mahan's *Influence of Sea Power upon the French Revolution and Empire*.

For original research for this book, I consulted the logs and journals of the ship preserved in the Maritime Museum and the Public Record Office. Also in the Maritime Museum are the Keith Papers, Flinder's Journal, Collingwood Letters and a collection of papers on the battle of the Nile. I also made use of certain dispatches of Admiral Gardner while Commander-in-Chief Channel Fleet in 1808–9, which I have in my possession.

For the illustrations reproduced, I am in the main indebted to the staff of the Print Room of the Maritime Museum; and for the photographs of the *Bellerophon* relics at the Victory Museum, Portsmouth, I am grateful for the co-operation of the Curator, Captain Jackson.

I am indebted to Rear-Admiral Taylor and the Society for Nautical Research for the plan of Trafalgar. The plan of the Nile is reproduced from the *Life of Nelson* by Clarke and M'Arthur (1809).

For help in the preparation of this work, I acknowledge the help and co-operation of the staffs of the Maritime Museum and Public Record Office. For material reproduced from the Maritime Museum I am indebted for the permission of the Trustees. Material used from the records of the Public Record Office appear by permission of the Controller of Her Majesty's Stationery Office.* I must also express my gratitude to Mr Oliver Warner for his guidance in choice of subject, for agreeing to read the manuscript when completed, and for the suggestions which he made. I am also grateful to Professor Christopher Lloyd for writing the Preface.

Finally I must thank Mrs Rosemary Wilson for her work in retyping the manuscript in its final form, and my publishers John Baker Ltd for their co-operation while the book was being made ready for press. To all other persons who have helped in any way whatever, I express my sincere thanks.

C. A. PENGELLY

Weybridge
24th March, 1965

* See List of Sources, page 291.

1

Construction

H.M.S. *BELLEROPHON*, the 'Billy Ruffian' as she was known to the 'tars' of the period, was one of the most outstanding ships of the Revolutionary and Napoleonic Wars. She fought in three of the great sea battles and greatly distinguished herself in all of them: first under the flag of Lord Howe at the 'Glorious First of June' in 1794, later under the flag of Lord Nelson at the battles of the Nile and Trafalgar. Her record in these battles has largely been forgotten, and she is only remembered today as the ship to which Napoleon surrendered after the battle of Waterloo in 1815.

Before recounting her story, it might be well to give a brief description of the construction of a wooden line-of-battle ship. The methods described in this chapter are standard for all wooden ships and can therefore serve as a general guide.

The *Bellerophon* was a 74-gun ship, and for the construction of a ship of that size the following materials were needed. First of all, 2,000 oaks, each at least one hundred years of age. The Admiralty specification for the construction of ships often stipulated 'good Sussex oak' as this was considered to be the toughest obtainable. By this time English oak was growing scarce, and timber and other materials had to be imported from the Continent. The shortage was due to the careless use of the timber reserves of the country by the Navy under the Commonwealth, Restoration, and in the early eighteenth century. During this period there was such an increase in construction that our forests became seriously depleted. By the time of the war of 1739–48 and the Seven Years' War, the danger had been recognized and steps were taken to remedy the situation. By 1783, when the *Bellerophon* was begun, timber was once again in short supply because of the huge building programme necessitated by the American War.

Besides oak, one hundred tons of wrought iron were needed for all the various metal fittings in the ship, and thirty tons of copper nails and bolts for the joining of the wood.

The approximate time for the construction of a '74' was two and a half years.

The *Bellerophon* was built to the design of Sir Thomas Slade who was also responsible for H.M.S. *Victory*. Sir Thomas Slade had died in 1772, and the design which was handed to the shipwrights was dated 1759 and was the original design for the first '74s' introduced into the Royal Navy. This had been such a success that when such ships were wanted in a time of great emergency during the American War, the Admiralty decided to use it again.

The contract for the construction of the *Bellerophon* was given to the firm of Messrs Graves & Nicholson, who had their yards on the River Medway near Chatham. This firm had had several previous contracts from the Navy and was well equipped to carry out the construction of a ship of the line.

The art of the construction of large wooden sailing ships is now very largely lost to the world. Most of the material for this chapter comes from the excellent book by Nepean Longridge, *The Anatomy of Nelson's Ships*, which is a great mine of information for the enthusiast.

The first stage in the construction of any ship is to lay the keel, and in wooden ships the keel was composed of English elm, a wood capable of standing long periods of immersion in salt water, and obtainable in good lengths. The keel of the *Bellerophon* was 138 feet and consequently had to be made up of several pieces joined together. The joints used were called 'scarphs', and were often as much as 5 feet in length. After being cut to shape, the joints were bolted together with copper bolts which were found to have a greater resistance to corrosion than iron. At its deepest part the keel could be as much as 21 inches, and the width (amidships) also 21 inches. At a later stage of construction a false keel was added to the proper keel. The purpose of this was to prevent 'hogging', or the arching upwards of the central portion of the keel under the strain which was imposed on it by the rest of the ship. It also constituted a section which would become detached easily if the vessel ever went aground, and helped to prevent the ship 'sagging' to leeward when under way against the wind. The term 'sagging' meant the amount of leeway or sideways movement made by the ship when she was proceeding against the wind.

The first timber to be fitted to the keel was the sternpost, made of a single log of first-class oak, just under 30 feet long, 2 foot 2 inches square at the upper end, and tapering to 1 foot 4 inches at the keel. It was joined to the keel by a mortise and tenon and set with a pronounced rake aft. A groove, called the 'rabbet', was cut out of the sternpost to take the planking of the ship when it was eventually added. An innerpost was 'fayed' to the foreside of the sternpost. To 'fay' two pieces of wood means to join them so that the fayed or joined surfaces are completely in contact. Copper bolts were used to hold the innerpost to the sternpost.

The next timber to be fitted to the keel was the 'deadwood'. This went on top of the keel and was made of oak. Its purpose was to enable the side frames or 'square' frames to be joined to the keel. It was composed of several pieces of oak scarphed together and held by copper bolts.

Following the deadwood, the stempost was fixed to the keel. This, as its name suggests, was fitted at the bows of the ship. It was made of several pieces of oak scarphed together and joined to the keel with a forward rake. The joint of the keel and the stempost was called the 'boxing', and another timber, the 'apron', was laid over it for extra strength. Fixed to the other side of the stempost was the 'stemson', also made of oak. At this stage of construction, with the stem and sternposts fixed to the keel, the whole assembly was carefully lined up and plumbed for accuracy. Then the whole was 'shored' in position so that it could not move.

The next stage was the construction of the 'knee of the head' which determined the shape of the bows. In a ship of the eighteenth and early nineteenth centuries this was usually bluff, rather after the style of the Dutch galliot. A look at H.M.S. *Victory* in Portsmouth dockyard will give one an idea of the shape of the ships of the period.

Following the construction of the 'knee of the head', a 'beakhead' was built. This was composed of about six pieces of timber assembled by bolting and scarphing. It is the beakhead which gives the bows of the line-of-battle ship the 'graceful serpentine appearance' so pronounced in H.M.S. *Victory*. The parts comprising the beakhead were as follows: (i) the gammoning knee and extension piece, (ii) the gammon piece, (iii) the chock piece, (iv) the lacing, (v) the main piece, and (vi) the figurehead. The whole assembly was fixed to the stempost and the 'gripe', which was an upwards extension of the keel. The main piece had two holes drilled in it to take the 'bobstays'; above the main piece was fitted the gammon piece. This had two slots cut in it to take the gammoning rope which lashed down the bowsprit. In the angle between the stem and the gammon piece was set the gammoning knee, which had a large hole drilled in it to take the mainstay collar. The beakhead on the line-of-battle ship of the late eighteenth and early nineteenth centuries was a relic of the Middle Ages when a similar device was used for ramming enemy ships. The only practical use to which it was put during the period with which we are concerned was to hold the bowsprit in place, which in turn held the entire pull of the foremast. To prevent the bowsprit moving sideways, two stout timbers called the 'knightheads' were set one on each side of the stem.

While this construction was taking place in the bows, work was also continuing at the stern. This involved the fixing of the 'wing transom', one of the most important timbers in the rear of the ship. The wing transom formed a cross with the sternpost, and was made from a single log of oak. It was situated about 3 feet from the top of the sternpost and fixed to it by means of a shallow recess cut in the centre of its face and bolted to the sternpost. It was further braced by the addition of two 'knees', bolted to both the transom and the side frames.

The basic skeleton of the ship was now complete. With the keel laid, stern and stemposts fixed to it and the beakheads and wing transom fitted to the stem sternposts, the next step was the 'framing' of the ship. This determined the shape of the sides of the ship, which in a warship were more bulbous towards the waterline.

The frames themselves were up to 50 feet high and were made of several pieces of oak. For maximum strength, the grain in these had to run as far as possible in the same direction as the curve of the frame. The actual building of the frames was a complicated process and took a considerable time. First of all a rough drawing was made on the floor of the workshop or yard and this was altered and redrawn until it met with the shipwright's satisfaction. A mould was then made to the final shape from thin pieces of planking, and all necessary markings for deck levels made on it. A piece of timber was then taken and shaped to fit the first section of the mould, and the process was repeated until the whole frame had been completely moulded out of timber. The joining of the pieces was done as usual by scarphs and copper bolts. The process would be repeated until enough timbers had been shaped to complete all the side frames of the ship.

The erection of the frames was a difficult process, for until they were bolted and braced in position they were liable to distortion. This made them hard to handle and great care was taken to get the frames erected as true as possible. To facilitate erection they were braced together by 'crosspales' before being fixed to the keel.

The frames which were fixed at right angles to the keel were called 'square' frames. It will be appreciated that as all ships taper towards the bows and stern, not all frames could be fitted at right angles, therefore the fore and aft frames had to be fitted to the keel at such an angle that a flat surface was presented for the planking. These frames were called 'cant' frames to distinguish them from the 'square' frames. Once all the square frames were in position, the crosspales were removed and further bracing was supplied by long stout pieces of timber called 'ribbands', fixed to the outer surface and removed when the inner planking was in position. There was always a space between the last of the cant frames and the stem and sternposts. This space had to be filled in, and for the purpose the shipwright used several pieces of upright timber. At the stern they were called 'filling' transoms and at the bows were set parallel with the knightheads. Finally, joining the cant frames were specially pre-shaped pieces of wood called 'hairpins' which, like the ribbands, were removed after the inner planking had been nailed in position.

The actual framing was now complete, but the shipwright had one more job to do which would ensure that the frames remained rigidly attached to the keel. He fixed what was called a 'keelson' along the top of the deadwood where the frames joined the keel. This keelson was composed of six pieces of elm and was bolted through at each point where a frame joined the keel. At either end of the keel it was connected to the stemson and sternson.

With the keelson in place and the frames rigid, the complete skeleton of the ship was now ready for planking.

The planking was always done in two layers, an inner and an outer layer. Of these the inner layer was always put in position first. All planking was done with oak, whereby we get the title of the song 'Hearts of Oak'! The planking was fixed in place by copper nails and bolts, and was from 3 inches thick at the top on the outer layer to about 6 inches at the bottom. The inner layer was of about the same thickness, so it will be seen that some warships had as much as one foot of solid oak as protection on their sides.

When the inner planking was in place, ventilation holes were cut in it to allow the air to circulate freely and counteract the effects of rot; and as a further strengthening measure an inner frame called a 'rider' was added. Rot, as will be appreciated, was the great enemy of all wooden ships, and it is testimony to the excellence of construction of the *Bellerophon* that she remained afloat for half a century, whereas most ships of the time were reckoned to have a life of only twenty to thirty years. There were of course exceptions, the *Royal William*, for example, had been launched in 1692 and was still afloat over a century later, although it was not operational.

The hull was now ready for the addition of the decks, which were supported by what were called 'deck clamps'. These were fixed to the inner frames a little below the actual deck level. Joining these deck clamps were the deck beams which ran across the ship. In a large ship such as the *Bellerophon* they were often composed of two or even three pieces of timber joined by a log scarph. The outer ends of the beams rested on the clamps and were later bolted in position. In addition there were usually two or more large stout pillars supporting the centre.

The decks of a ship of the line were called, working downwards, upper deck, middle deck, gun deck, and orlop deck. Above the upper deck were the forecastle (fo'c's'le) at the front and the quarter-deck at the stern. On the aft end of the quarter-deck was the poop deck.

Before the deck planking was added, the outer planking of the hull was nailed in position. In times of peace it was quite usual to leave a ship in this state for a couple of years to help season the timbers, but in time of war the ship would be rushed forward to the launch as fast as possible. By the time the *Bellerophon* reached this stage, war was over and there was no longer the urgent need for ships that there had been when she was laid down. Therefore she was left to season for a couple of years, and this was probably the reason for her remarkable longevity compared with many of her contemporaries.

If we assume that the ship was wanted straight away, the next stage after the planking of the outer hull would be the deck planking. This was a relatively simple process and requires little description. The deck planks were usually of white pine, which stood the ravages of the sea well and also gave a good polish on ceremonial occasions!

The lower hull was then plated with sheets of copper—a method first used on the frigate H.M.S. *Alarm* in 1761 on the orders of Admiral Lord Anson. The experiment proved successful and from then on increasing numbers of ships in the Navy were fitted with a copper bottom. By the time of the American War a good proportion of the ships of the Navy had been so treated, and it proved of great assistance in that struggle. Lord Rodney's famous victory over the Spaniards on the 16th-17th January 1780 had been gained mainly by the speed of his coppered ships, which far outmatched that of the Spaniards. In a stern chase such as Rodney's action, the value of coppered ships was inestimable. The hulls of wooden ships harboured all sorts of marine growths such as barnacles and seaweed, but it was found by experiment that these did not take to copper as kindly as to wood. First the sheets of copper were fixed on with iron nails, but it was realized that these soon corroded, and the switch was made to copper nails. The resistance of copper was such that often the wood would become rotten, but the ship would be kept afloat by the protective coating of copper sheets. Lord Collingwood had once reported that 'for the last six months we have been sailing with only a sheet of copper between us and eternity'!

With the completion of the deck planking and the coppering the hull was ready for launching, but before this happened there was one more piece to be added and this was the figurehead. For the *Bellerophon* the figurehead was carved by a Chatham firm which had been doing such work for the Admiralty for over a hundred years. This figurehead, 'a feminine looking head wearing a helmet with heavy white plumes', is still to be seen in the Victory Museum at Portsmouth. The figurehead of a ship had a special place in the hearts of the crew, and was always treated with the greatest care.

The hull is now ready for launching, and this was as much an occasion for ceremony then as it is now. It would be performed by some local dignitary, either the mayor of Chatham, the admiral's wife or one of the Lords of the Admiralty from London. Bands would be playing such tunes as 'Hearts of Oak' and 'Rule Britannia', and flags would be flying both on shore and on the hull as she slid into the water. Once the hull was afloat it would be warped alongside a sheerhulk and masts would be fitted, or if it was not needed immediately it would be laid up until required.

The *Bellerophon* was launched on the 6th October 1786, and the complete cost of construction would work out as £30,232 14s. 3d.

If a ship was going straight into commission it would be given the colour scheme of the period. For the early part of the Revolutionary War and before, this was plain varnish outside and red décor inside. The latter was to minimize the effect of blood stains. The colour scheme favoured by Lord Nelson was black with yellow stripes along the level of the gun decks, with black gun ports. The *Bellerophon* fought under this colour scheme at the battle of Trafalgar. The black and white chequer scheme was not introduced until the later stages of the war, and she would have been wearing this scheme when she received Napoleon on board off Rochefort in 1815.

Assuming that a '74' was wanted urgently by the Navy, the armament would be taken on board almost immediately after the launch. For all ships of that class this was comprised as follows:

(1) 28–32 pounders. Cost £50 each. Cast iron. 6-inch diameter, 10 lb. gunpowder. Range three miles. Situated on the lower deck and comprised the main armament. Weight 3½ tons. Crew fourteen men, but only seven when the ship was engaged on both sides.

(2) 28-18 pounders ('Long Eighteens'). 5-inch bore. Situated on the main deck.
(3) 18-9 pounders. 4-inch bore. Situated on the quarter-deck.
(4) 2-32 pounder carronades. Situated on the forecastle.
(5) 6-18 pounder carronades. Situated on the poop.

The carronades were only an auxiliary armament, and were not counted in the number of guns the ships carried. They were so named after the firm of John Carron who had invented them and cast them at his foundry in Stirlingshire. They were very effective at close range and their power was such that the French frigate *Hébé* when attacked by H.M.S. *Rainbow* which was fitted with carronades, hauled down her colours because she thought her opponent was a ship of the line! They were first introduced into the Navy in 1779, and probably reached their peak of perfection by the time of the battle of Trafalgar and in the frigate actions of the war of 1812–15.

The ammunition allowance for ships differed, depending on whether they were in the Channel or the Mediterranean Fleet. The allowance for the Channel Fleet was:

60 rounds to each 32-pounder.
70 rounds to all other guns, plus
10 rounds per gun of grape-shot and cannister.

The allowance for the Mediterranean Fleet was slightly larger. This comprised:

80 rounds to each 32-pounder.
100 rounds to all other guns, plus
12 rounds of grape and cannister per gun.

All shot was stowed in the shot locker in the hold.

A total of 300 90-lb. barrels of gunpowder was stowed in the powder magazine, situated below the water-line and in the centre of the ship. This was the most dangerous part of the ship, and no naked lights were allowed near. All people working in the magazine had to wear special felt shoes to lessen the risk of sparks. What could happen to a ship which caught fire was demonstrated by the destruction of *L'Orient* at the battle of the Nile, when the explosion was heard several miles away. A single broadside from the *Bellerophon* weighed 8 cwt., and the destructive effect of this on a wooden ship had to be seen to be believed.

We have now covered the complete construction and initial fitting out of a ship of the line. In the case of the *Bellerophon* the final points of interest are the dimensions of the ship, which surviving records show to have been as follows:

Length of gun deck—168 feet
Length of keel—138 feet
Breadth—46 feet, 10 inches
Depth (of hull)—19 feet, 9 inches
Tonnage—1,613 tons.

2

Life on board a Sailing Ship

IT IS useful before embarking on the history of any ship of
the days of sail to give first of all an idea of what life was like
aboard.

In the ships of the Royal Navy during the seventeenth,
eighteenth, and early nineteenth centuries, life was incredibly
hard. The rates of pay had remained unchanged since the
time of Charles II but the cost of living had risen many times
since then. Seamen would always prefer to serve aboard a
merchantman rather than a royal ship. The pay was higher,
the living conditions better, and discipline easier.

First of all, what sort of men would be likely to be found
aboard one of His Majesty's ships during the period of the
Revolutionary and Napoleonic Wars? There would be three
types or classes. First the volunteers: some of these had been
in the Navy since they were boys and had stayed on because
they knew no other way of earning a living. Others had joined
in a fit of patriotic fervour, but had since repented of their
decision and wanted to get out again. They seldom had a
chance to do this because of the infrequency of calls at home
ports, and the close watch kept on all the crew by the officers
and petty officers. Others might have joined because the captain
of a certain ship had come from their district and they liked to
follow him. Sir Edward Pellew could always rely on having a
good number of Cornishmen in his crew; Lord Cochrane had
a large following because of his success with prize money.

The second group were the 'pressed' men—men taken by
the Navy from either merchant ships or the ports. Sometimes
a press-gang would rove far inland to try and complete the

complement of a ship which was due to sail. The best men of all were of course the prime seamen from the merchant and fishing fleets. Admirals and captains would wait until a merchant fleet anchored and then send across a boat of armed sailors under the command of a midshipman or a sub-lieutenant and demand their quota of the crews.

There is an interesting account of the pressing of a convoy in the Downs in the book *The Life and Adventures of John Nicol, Mariner*. Nicol was a seaman aboard the merchantman *Nottingham* which was returning from China in 1794. He had previously served in the Royal Navy during the American War, and consequently knew what to expect when the ship arrived in the Downs. During the voyage he had grown a beard and let himself get as dirty as possible so as to appear more unattractive to the Navy when they came aboard! In his book Nicol says of the incident: 'Nothing uncommon happened until we reached the Downs.' When the Navy came aboard, Nicol was ' . . . in the hold sorting amongst the water casks and escaped'. Unfortunately for Nicol one of those taken ' . . . had a sore leg. The boat brought him back and I had the bad luck to be taken and he was left.' After being taken off the *Nottingham*, Nicol was sent to H.M.S. *Venerable*, flagship of Admiral Duncan (later Lord Duncan and victor of the battle of Camperdown). From the *Venerable* he was transferred to the '74' H.M.S. *Edgar*, under Captain Sir Henry Knowles, where he was put to work among the gun crews. A short while afterwards, the *Edgar* was lying in the Leith Roads off Scotland, his home country. There an incident occurred which is worth describing as an illustration of what could happen in the Royal Navy. Nicol says: 'While in Leith Roads there was a mutiny in the *Defiance*, 74, because of the five-part watering of the grog. The *Edgar* was ordered alongside to fire if necessary, . . . but the crew of the *Defiance* returned to duty.' Nicol expressed himself thankful in his book that he did not have to fire on the *Defiance*, as he was not sure that he and his shipmates did not sympathize more with the crew of the *Defiance* than with the captain. According to Nicol, the usual watering of rum was only three-part, and this was all the more welcome as it was winter at the time and the weather very cold. In the tropics, Nicol says, the men would have been glad to have the five-part watered grog.

The third and last group to be found aboard a warship of the period would be the criminals, who had selected a life of hardship at sea rather than imprisonment or possible execution on land. A law of the time of Queen Elizabeth I laid down that 'rogues, vagabonds, and sturdy beggars shall be, and are hereby directed to be taken up, conducted, and conveyed unto H.M. Service at sea.' A man branded as a criminal in those days would not necessarily be in the same class nowadays. There were then over a hundred crimes for which one could be executed, among them the stealing of a pocket handkerchief; so it will be seen that it was not a flow of hardened criminals which the Navy had to deal with, but most probably a farm labourer who had been caught poaching because his family was hungry, or a man who had stolen a few coppers to buy some bread. Under the rigorous rule of the Navy and the self-imposed creed of the seamen, any criminal who felt like carrying on in his old ways was soon enlightened.

Of all these systems the press was the most iniquitous and the most feared. Only old people, gentlemen, and invalids were safe from its clutches. Once on board, the wretched fellows had little or no chance to escape. Very often certain inns or 'houses of ill repute' would co-operate with the Navy in getting their unfortunate customers pressed. Occasionally the victims would put up a fight against the press-gang and drive them off, but more likely they would be so drunk that they did not know what was happening until they woke up in the morning aboard a ship of war. According to the Act which permitted press-gangs, only seamen could be taken, but little attention was paid to this in the dark alleys of Portsmouth, Dover, and Wapping.

Eighteenth-century opinion regarded the press-gang as a necessary evil. In the event of war the first action of any British Government was to expand the establishment of the Fleet. Little thought was given to what effect such an expansion would have on the ordinary family man who was likely to be seized by the press-gang to turn the Government's figures into reality. Not only were British seamen pressed, but foreign seamen as well. Among the muster books of the Royal Navy one can find the names of seamen from America, France, Sweden, Russia, Spain, Italy and Denmark. It was the pressing of alleged British seamen from American ships which was one of the causes of the war of 1812–15.

On the eve of the Revolutionary War with France an Impress Service was founded, with the Royal Navy to take over the responsibility of pressing from individual captains, although many continued to exercise this right. In times of emergency certain towns offered bounties to those of their citizens who would enlist in the Navy. Most of the men who accepted this bounty were 'the very refuse and outcasts of society', ignorant of the naval life, and virtually useless for many weeks until properly trained.

Having been got aboard, what sort of life were the men likely to lead? It can only be described as hard, but life both afloat and ashore was hard for the common man in the eighteenth century. Afloat he was at least free of the petty restrictions which bound his existence when ashore. In the Navy he could work up to a position of rank and authority, and promotions from the lower deck to commissioned officer were not uncommon. The master of the *Queen Charlotte*, Lord Howe's flagship at the Glorious First of June, was later given a commission and rose very quickly to become an admiral.

The pay of the Royal Navy, as stated above, had remained stationary since the time of Charles II. The pay of the Army had risen two or three times since then, and even the pension of a Chelsea Pensioner was larger than that of a Greenwich Pensioner. Lord Duncan considered the question of pay to be the seamen's most valid cause for complaint. The mutinies of 1797 substantially improved the conditions of the men of the Royal Navy, and the pay then was 22s. 6d. a month for landsmen and 25s. 6d. a month for ordinary seamen. This was the rate laid down by the Government and the Admiralty, though it was hardly ever paid in money, but in tickets. These tickets were difficult to cash, and many seamen never managed to obtain more than three-quarters of their face value. It was for this reason that a captain who had a good reputation for taking prizes would always find a ready following among seamen and landsmen. A prize taken meant prize money, and this was shared out amongst the successful ship or ships, starting from the admiral down to the lowest of the seamen. The share of the admiral might be over £100,000, in which case each seaman would get something in the region of £2 or

£3. After the taking of Havana in 1762, the share of the admiral was £122,700 and the share of each seaman was £3. 14s. 10d. Many officers became almost millionaires in their time at sea, an example being Lord Keith who served in the Mediterranean at the turn of the century. The seaman would of course soon spend his share, but a few careful souls did manage to accumulate a fair amount of money during a cruise. Some left the ship at the end of a cruise or a war with as much as £500 which could set them up for life, provided they were not pressed into the Navy again.

The duty roster of a ship of the line was made out by either the captain or the first lieutenant. This roster split the whole crew into five groups. First of all, the fo'c's'le or sheet-anchor men: these were the oldest, most trustworthy, and most experienced seamen on the ship. As their name suggests, they were stationed on the forecastle or fo'c's'le, and were responsible for the working of the anchors, bowsprit, and fore-yards.

The next group to be selected by the captain were the topmen. These were the more young and active members of the crew who had to work the sails scores of feet above the deck. There is still in existence in the National Maritime Museum at Greenwich the Journal of Lieutenant Mathew Flinders of H.M.S. *Bellerophon*, which has several entries of interest with regard to the running of the ship. The entry for Saturday 25th January 1794 reads:

Handed the Topsails, in doing which David Dugal, Captain of the Maintop was unfortunately thrown off the yard and overboard and drowned.

It will be seen by this that the job of the topmen required no little skill and daring. Any captain would make his selection of topmen carefully, for a ship's smartness could be gauged in the eyes of onlookers by the speed with which she worked her sails. If a landsman was chosen for this work, special training had to be given. In a booklet of additional rules for H.M.S. *London*, Rule 3 states:

It is expected that the Lts. and Midshipmen make themselves acquainted with the character and abilities of the people of their Division and consider them immediately under their charge ... At all convenient opportunities they are to exercise ... the Ordinary Seamen and Landsmen at Reefing and handing sails and going aloft, until they become expert and active in every part of this duty.

The next group of men selected by the captain were the afterguard, who were considered inferior beings by the topmen and sheet-anchor men! These men, the less experienced seamen and landsmen on the ship, were responsible for the working of the braces and lower mainsails. They were also responsible for the cleaning of the after part of the ship and working the guns as well as the sails when the ship was in action.

The largest group was called the 'waisters' because they worked in the waist or midship section, situated midway between the fo'c's'le and the quarter-deck. This group was composed of the more common landsmen and the more 'unenlightened' of the seamen. They were responsible for the working of the fore and main sheets and for the cleanliness of the waist. Because they were the odd-job men of the ship they also took on the unskilled tasks such as looking after the ship's pig or other livestock.

The fifth and last group were the idlers. These were the men who did not work a shift system, i.e. working all day and standing a watch at night. They worked during the day but did not have a watch at night. Among their ranks were to be found the ship's barber, butcher, painter, cooper, loblolly boys (who assisted the surgeon), and the captain-of-the-head. The latter was responsible for maintaining the cleanliness of the ship's crude lavatory.

Each man when off duty rested below in his hammock. When he came aboard he was issued with two hammocks, one to use and one as a spare. He was allowed 14 inches to sling it in, but the actual space available was more than this as by the watch and watch system every alternate hammock would be empty. The hammocks were slung crosswise on the ship and were attached to the deck beams.

For meals the crew was split into messes of up to eight persons. Each mess had its own table which when not in use was slung between the deck beams over the guns. A 'cook' was elected by each mess, whose job it was to collect the food from the purser and then take it to the ship's cook for preparation. The food was plentiful, but its quality was necessarily poor because of the length of time it had to be kept. Fresh meat was eaten as long as the ship's animals lasted, but this was usually a short time, and after that recourse was had to salt meat, either beef or pork. This had usually been in the cask a long time, and was covered with gleaming salt crystals and almost inedible. It was discovered that this meat could be used for carving small articles, and would take a good polish, like fine-grain wood! The salt meat was not only served to the men but also to the officers and midshipmen when fresh meat was no longer available. A ship on blockade duty would have to go off at regular intervals for provisioning. Several entries in Flinders's Journal, when the war at sea was less severe than later on, tell of frequent provisioning. The entry for Thursday 10th April 1794 reads: 'A.M. Rec'd a supply of provisions to complete four months'. A ship could either return to port to revictual or use the services of a victualling ship. Under the lax regime of Howe and Bridport in the Channel, the squadrons blockading Brest and Rochefort would often be in Torbay sheltering from a gale or revictualling. With the stricter rule of Jervis and Cornwallis, the fleets would only quit their stations in face of the fiercest gales and consequently more use was made of the victualling ships.

One of the main complaints of the men as regards provisions was about the quality of the water. This was stored in wooden casks and, as was inevitable on a long cruise, it would turn sour. It sometimes became so foul that the men refused to drink it and preferred beer instead. When the beer ran out, as it would soon do with an allowance of a gallon a day for each man, the sailors fell back on either rum, brandy, or wine. The regulations allowed for a pint of wine a day or half a pint of rum or brandy. Rum was preferred to brandy or wine, and was popularly known in the Navy as 'grog'. This was because Admiral Vernon had ordered the watering of the rum ration to improve the health of his men. The Navy was understandably rather annoyed, and transferred Vernon's nickname, 'Old Grog', from the admiral to the drink! If wine had to be drunk, white was preferred to red (Black Strap) and the favourite white wine was the Spanish Mistela, anglicized by the 'tars' as Miss Taylor!

The other pillar of the naval diet was the ship's biscuit. Like the water and the salted meat these were not exactly appetizing. They were usually very old and hard, and the home of whole families of weevils. Whereas one could see the living organisms in the water, one could not see them in the biscuits. The general rule was to tap them on the table before eating them so as to dislodge the weevils which were living inside. Many people preferred to consume them in the dark so as not to see what they were eating! Another method was to make 'Scotch coffee' with them. This was made by first burning the biscuits in the oven to kill all the weevils, then the biscuit was boiled in water and the resultant liquid sweetened with sugar. In his excellent book *England Expects*, Dudley Pope has quoted the weekly ration for a seaman as: 7 lb. of biscuits, 7 gal. of beer, 4 lb. of beef, 2 lb. of pork, 2 pints of peas, $1\frac{1}{2}$ pints of oatmeal, 6 oz. of sugar, 6 oz. of butter and 12 oz. of cheese. Added to this was an allowance of vinegar 'not to exceed half a pint to each man'.

The next most important question after food was health. With the overcrowding prevailing on board wooden ships this was often poor. Conditions had improved by the beginning of the Revolutionary period, but the mortality rate was still extremely high. The most important contributions towards improved hygiene on His Majesty's ships before the outbreak of the war were made by Lord Hawke, Lord Anson, Boscawen, Cook, and Howe. On his voyage round the world in 1772-5 Captain Cook lost only one man through sickness. Boscawen was a pioneer of artificial ventilation in ships, first in his own, and eventually throughout the whole Navy. In the Royal Navy of the eighteenth century, more men died of sickness than were killed in battle, an outstanding record. The main killers were scurvy, typhus, and 'Yellow Jack' which was particularly common on the West Indian station. Much of the sickness was due to the poor quality of the provisions supplied, and much to overcrowding. The cause of scurvy was known, and a remedy also—lime or other citrus juices—but this was often ignored by captains and physicians, and the disease was still a major threat right into the latter half of the eighteenth century.

The last aspect which concerned the men was discipline. In the Royal Navy of the period it was strict. A man could be flogged for many offences ranging from desertion to being last down from the maintop. One captain used to make a point of arbitrarily flogging the last man down to improve the speed of the crew. In this way the crews in some ships were flogged into a state of insubordination or mutiny, a situation which usually had a bloody ending. The Journal of Lieutenant Flinders has many entries on discipline, and some of them are worth quoting. The entry for Saturday 30th November 1793 reads: 'Punished Edward Goodenough and William Ridley (Seamen) for neglect of duty with 12 lashes each.' And on Wednesday 4th December 1793: 'Read Articles of War and punished John Chapman (Marine) for neglect of duty and John Bayley for theft. 12 lashes each.'

The regulations about theft were very strict on all Royal Navy ships, and Additional Rule 9 of H.M.S. *London* states that: 'any person finding money, clothes or other articles . . . to bring them immediately to the Quarter Deck, for if any such things should be found in their possession it will be considered to all intents and purposes as theft.'

Sometimes a seaman who was tried by court martial was lucky and got off. Such a case is recorded by Lieutenant Flinders on the 8th January 1794: 'John Charles (Seaman) belonging to this ship was tried today on board of the *Royal William* for desertion when we were in Torbay, but the charge not being clearly proved he was acquitted.'

Captains with a more religious turn of mind than others used to punish their men for swearing, and the captain of H.M.S. *London* must have been one of these. Additional Rule 7 reads: 'Cursing and swearing to be discouraged, and checks made at all times. But any man making use of that scandalous and infamous word Buggar will certainly be punished'! Additional Rule 14 of H.M.S. *London* concerns politeness to officers and says: 'The respect of touching or taking off the hat is to be paid to superiors . . . either on board or ashore.'

We have now covered very briefly the life of the men aboard a line-of-battle ship of the late eighteenth century, and we now touch even more briefly on the life of the officers.

The officer of the Royal Navy was its backbone. He was a skilled professional and knew every facet of his job. The officers were permanent while the crews changed almost every trip. There was not so much patronage in the Navy as there was in the Army and this was mainly due to Lord Anson. Many officers rose from the lower decks, and many others came from humble beginnings ashore. This was held against the Navy by many of the shore-going 'gentlemen' of the period because they said it brought into prominence people who had previously been of no consequence.

The professional naval officer started his naval career very young as a midshipman. He would probably join his first ship at the age of twelve, perhaps even younger. The midshipman was the final development of the old 'King's Letter Boys' who were started by Charles II. One of the last and most distinguished of the King's Letter Boys was Admiral Lord Rodney. The midshipman was trained at sea and obtained thereby a thorough grounding in his profession. By the time he was twenty-one he knew everything there was to know about the handling and fighting of a wooden line-of-battle ship. There were, of course, exceptions, including the famous Billy Culmer, the oldest midshipman in the service; he was still a midshipman when sixty years of age!

The standard of living of officers was often quite high, but they were as inured to 'salt beef and black strap' as the men. Preserved in the Maritime Museum is a menu for H.M.S. *Vernon* when she was serving in the West Indies in 1781 as the flagship of Admiral Digby. The menu for Sunday 18th August 1781 reads: 'Tarts, Butter, Purtato, French Beans, Whipt Cream, Fruit Fritters, Beackon, Apple Pye, Boiled Tart, Carrats and Turnips, Whipt Cream, Albacore, Spanish Fritters, Butter, Tarts, Boiled Beef and Roast Mutton.' This layout was to provide all the meals that day for the admiral, the captain, and all his officers, perhaps a total of a dozen persons.

The discipline for officers was also strict, though not to the same extent as for the men. An order for H.M.S. *Pegasus* for 1786–8 reads:

Too frequent accidents have occurred from Officers reading in Bed by Candle Light or Leaving Candles burning in their cabins which . . . has been productive of the most fatal consequences. The more effectually to prevent whereof it is my positive order that no officer or other person do read in bed by candle light.

The life just described produced the greatest fighting seamen which the world has ever known. They were taught all the rules of the sea at a very early age and they were complete masters of their calling. It was with this excellent combination of officers and men that the Royal Navy won its great victories during the Revolutionary and Napoleonic Wars. The seamanship of the British Fleet was on the whole superior to that of all its opponents throughout the period, and was a more important factor than the ships themselves. These were often of inferior design to their French, Spanish, or Dutch opponents, but the skill with which the crews handled them outweighed any advantage which the allied fleets might have had in speed.

The conditions described above were typical of all Royal Navy ships of the period. It was in such conditions that people like John Nicol lived, fought, and died in the great struggle that lay ahead. Over all lay a certain humility and belief in God and the rightness of their cause. Even if the belief was not deeply felt, it was professed, and religious services were held every Sunday on ships of war. The log book of the *Bellerophon* gives an example dated Sunday 8th December 1793, which shows how the Navy combined worship with duty.

Performed Divine Service. *Phoenix* made the signal to speak us, brought to. Two large ships to the S.E. standing towards us, cleared for action and made sail towards them . . . proved to be *Monarch*, Sir James Douglas and *Culloden*, Sir Thomas Rich.

Christmas too was celebrated as far as duty would allow: '. . . being Christmas Day, very little work was done. An allowance of grog was served to the ship's company'.

3

Skirmishes with the French

THE *Bellerophon* first entered the water on the 6th October 1786. By this time the American War was over and a period of austerity under the younger Pitt had begun. For this reason the *Bellerophon* was laid up 'In Ordinary', which is to say in modern terms, the 'Mothball' Fleet. She might have remained in this state had it not been for the crisis with Spain, called the Nootka Sound affair, which necessitated temporary strengthening of the Navy. She was recommissioned on the 19th July 1790, and the captain was to be Captain (later Admiral Sir) Thomas Pasley, a Scot born in Dumfriesshire. The log kept by the master of the *Bellerophon* for this date states: 'Capt. Pasley appointed to command the ship. The pendant was hoisted. Mr Malcolm 3rd Lieutenant came on board.'

The next four weeks were a period of feverish activity for the officers and men of the *Bellerophon*. All the work of getting a ship into commission had to be completed as quickly as possible. She was moored at the time at Chatham, quite near to her place of launch, and was one of a number of ships in the same condition and awaiting commissioning. Her own crew, still incomplete, were assisted by drafts of men from the depot ship at Chatham, the *Sandwich*, and work was carried out on the rigging, hull, trimming the ballast and receiving provisions and stores.

By the 16th August she was ready for the next stage and was moved to Blackstakes in the Thames. At Blackstakes the work went on as before: the ship was now nearing readiness and boats were sent ashore to press men to complete her complement. It was rare for any ship to sail with a complete crew, and the *Bellerophon* was far short of her complement of 600 men when she 'made sail to the eastward' on Monday 30th August 1790. The next day she arrived in the Downs, and joined a squadron under Admiral King which she found there. The following Sunday Admiral Elliott hoisted his flag aboard the *Bellerophon*, an event which is recorded in the master's log: 'At 3 Adml. Elliott hoisted his flag on board of this ship.' Work continued, with the receiving of provisions, cleaning the ship, trimming the ballast and working on the rigging. Captain Pasley took the opportunity when a convoy of West Indiamen arrived in the Downs to press some of their seamen to make up his complement.

On the 23rd September, she weighed anchor again, and by noon that day she was moored opposite the South Foreland, and later passed Dover on the way to join the rest of the fleet at Spithead. She was in St Helen's Road on Saturday 25th September, and the next day joined the Channel Fleet assembled at Spithead under Admiral Barrington.

Elliott was promoted to Vice-Admiral of the Blue on the 27th September, and the necessary change of pendant made on the *Bellerophon*. A change of command occurred on the 28th when Barrington struck his flag as Commander-in-Chief of the Channel Fleet. The *Bellerophon* lost Elliott when he transferred his flag to the *Barfleur* of 98 guns on the 7th October. She was evidently still short of her complement, for the entry in the log for Saturday 23rd October reads: 'Rec'd. 73 men from the 12th & 31st Regiments.' These men were to serve on board as Marines. The following day she 'rec'd. 48 men from the *Culloden*', and by this time her complement must have been nearly complete.

At last a move was made, and on the 20th November the *Bellerophon*, in company with five other ships of the line, made sail from Spithead. The move was not against the Spanish, but back to the Nore where they anchored on the 21st and worked their way up to Sheerness. At Sheerness another period of waiting ensued, with the crew employed 'occasionally' about the ship. The only event of interest was the striking of the flag of Admiral Dalrymple as Commander-in-Chief at the Nore on the 9th December. On the 14th a party of thirty-five seamen under the command of a lieutenant and three midshipmen was sent to the *Boyne*, which was undermanned, to help her work her way to Plymouth. Strong gales blew up on the 15th and 16th December, but the ships anchored at Sheerness escaped any serious damage. The Spanish crisis was now over, but the *Bellerophon* was kept in commission though not on active service.

The difficulties of keeping a full crew when lying at anchor will be appreciated when the entry in the captain's log for the 27th December is read: 'At 9 came on board under charge of a guard, Charles Scott a Marine to be tried on board for desertion.' A later entry says that Scott was released from confinement on the 28th December, so possibly the case was never proved.

Still desperate for men, Pasley sent a lieutenant and two midshipmen to London to see what they could find to help the ship make up her complement. The men lent to the *Boyne* returned to the ship on the 18th January 1791, and a party of Marines which had been lent to the Botany Bay ships returned on the 28th March.

On the 20th April she made her way back to the Nore where she arrived on the 21st, sailing a week later for Spithead. The concentration at Spithead was due to fears of a war with Russia over her gains in her struggle with the Turks. It was one of the largest forces ever assembled there, totalling thirty-six ships of the line and several frigates. The nominal reason for the assembly was a review by George III in July, but the real reason was plain to the officers and men of the fleet. The *Bellerophon* station was in the rear division of the southern line under the command of Rear-Admiral Cosby who hoisted his flag in the *Impregnable*, a '98' on the 19th May. The other ships in this division were the *Ardent* '64', *Courageux* '74' and *Robust* '74'. The flagship of the whole fleet was the *Victory* which was in the centre division of the northern line. A royal visit was made to the Fleet on the 29th June, when the Duke of Gloucester visited some of the ships assembled and was received by twenty-one gun salutes.

A signal from the *Victory* to prepare to put to sea was received on board the *Bellerophon* on the 22nd August, and the following day she sailed in company with the *Formidable*, *Barfleur*, *Vengeance*, *Cyclops*, and *Hébé*, bound for the Nore.

The captain's log for the 23rd August 1791 reads: 'Served spirits to the ship's company, the beer being unfit to drink'.

This means that the beer must have been in a very unpalatable state for the Navy to class it as undrinkable!

At noon on the 25th the *Bellerophon* was anchored in Queen's Channel. She was accompanied by *Robust* and *Vengeance* and the frigates—the *Formidable* and *Barfleur* having parted company with them on the way. She moved to Blackstakes wharf on the 26th August, where she was joined by Admiral Dalrymple aboard the *Dictator* accompanied by the *Marlborough*, *Alfred*, *Assistance*, and *Roebuck*. Another move was made to Chatham on the 31st August accompanied this time by the *Dictator* and *Marlborough*. The trio arrived at the Royal Dockyards at Chatham on the 1st September and the dismantling of the ship was begun. As before she was to be laid up until required. She was finally paid off on the 9th September 1791, and the entry in the captain's log for this date reads: 'Commissioners came on board and paid off the ship'. The officers were either transferred to another ship, or if unlucky were put ashore on half-pay until required again. The men would probably be discharged, or perhaps a few volunteers would be transferred to other ships.

For the next eighteen months the *Bellerophon* remained at Chatham, but soon she was needed again. It was a war this time and not just a crisis. The opponent was France as so often before in the century, not this time a Bourboun France, but Republican. British opinion had been incensed by the execution of Louis XVI, and the Government was alarmed by the continual growth of the French power on the Continent. France declared war on Britain and Holland on the 1st February 1793, and the twenty-two year long struggle was about to commence.

The *Bellerophon* was recommissioned on the 16th March 1793. The captain was again Thomas Pasley who had asked the Admiralty for her command. Chatham was full that month of naval officers hurrying to their ships, glad of the chance of serving afloat again. Moored nearby was the *Agamemnon*, whose captain was a certain Horatio Nelson under whose command she was to win fame in the Mediterranean.

The first of the crew, a draft from the *Enterprise*, came on board on the 17th March and from that date the preparations went ahead at full speed. On the 29th March the masts were hauled on board and on the same day she went into dock for an inspection. The log says that the bottom was 'found in good order'. Thirty-three men from the *Sandwich* were received on board on the 2nd April. A further twenty-two arrived from Greenwich Hospital on the 12th April and another thirty from the *Sandwich* on the 21st April. The press-gang was sent ashore on the night of the 24th April, and the entry in the log regarding its findings states: 'Rec'd upwards of 40 men.' On the 26th April the ship was moved to Gillingham Reach with the aid of a pilot, and on the 27th she was at Blackstakes. Here she returned the men from the *Sandwich*. On the 30th April an officer and twenty-eight Marines were received aboard from the *Robust*. In the afternoon the lighters brought over the gunners' stores and fresh beef; the guns were hoisted on board from the 3rd until the 8th May and placed on their respective decks. By the 8th she was ready to sail, which she did that afternoon, arriving at the Nore on the 9th. Perhaps to show her appreciation of the help she had received in refitting she 'cheered the *Sandwich* in passing'. On the 1st June Admiral Bowyer transferred his flag from the *Brunswick* to the *Bellerophon*, the first of a line of admirals to use her services during the coming war.

The *Bellerophon* was still busy pressing men as fast as she could both on shore and afloat. Competition was keen amongst the ships at the Nore to get as many men as they possibly could.

Friday 14th June saw the *Bellerophon* make sail and get under way for Spithead. She anchored in the Downs for the night of the 14th, finding there two frigates. She arrived at Spithead next day and found the *Royal William, Boyne, Cumberland, Queen Charlotte, Royal George, Brunswick, Ganges, Montagu, Sceptre, Veteran,* and *Assistance* with several frigates. The 21st June saw the arrival at Spithead of the frigate *Le Nymph*, Captain E. Pellew, with the French frigate *Cleopâtre* which she had taken on the previous day after an action in the Channel. No doubt this raised the hopes of the crews of the Channel Fleet regarding prize money and a quick end to the war. The following day saw another French prize reach Spithead, a ship of twenty guns taken by the frigate *Phaeton*.

The fleet mustered at Spithead must have presented an outstanding sight to anyone viewing it from the shore. Lines of ships all as neat and tidy as the crews could make them, with the rigging and spars standing out against the summer sky. To see a fleet make sail was a sight not to be forgotten. Prince Metternich, when an exile in England in 1794, saw the Channel Fleet under Lord Howe escorting a convoy to sea in the May of that year, and was impressed by the discipline and training of the men. Large fleets were common enough to the people of Portsmouth, but even they would always stop to watch a ship or ships of war putting to sea.

The *Bellerophon* records in her log for the 24th June:

Arrived here the *Royal Sovereign*, Vice-Admiral Graves. At 8 a.m. Admiral Earl Howe's Flag was hoisted on board the *Queen Charlotte* and Vice-Admiral Sir Alexander Hood's on board of the *Royal George*.

Two days later Howe detached three of his ships, the *Majestic*, *Raisonnable*, and *Dromedary*, to escort an outward-bound convoy of ten or twelve East India ships. The frigate *Phoenix* entered harbour on the 30th June with a French prize she had taken while escorting a convoy of four East Indiamen bound for England.

The following day Howe received his orders from the Admiralty. The contents of these orders, briefly summarized, were to protect British trade from the attack of the French fleet or privateers, to attack the French fleet and merchant convoys, and some information about eight or nine ships of the line having sailed from Brest and attempting to join five more from Lorient or Rochefort. He was to prevent their return to Brest and also their junction with the Lorient or Rochefort squadron. For this purpose he had a fleet of, at any one time, twenty-three ships of the line and their attendant frigates. As always in a war, the force he had to hand was barely sufficient for the task he had been allotted.

The *Bellerophon* lost her role as admiral's flagship when Rear-Admiral Bowyer hauled down his flag in her on the 4th July and rehoisted it in the *Vanguard*, another '74' and later to be Nelson's flagship at the battle of the Nile.

Ten days later the long awaited signal was made from the flagship the *Queen Charlotte* and the fleet prepared to put to sea. The *Bellerophon* made her way into St Helen's Road to await a favourable wind for entering the Channel. She was still there when the rest of the fleet joined her. The entry for the 14th July, marked 'Moored in St Helen's Road at Single Anchor', says:

Admiral Earl Howe in the *Queen Charlotte* came from Spithead and anchored here accompanied by the *Royal Sovereign* (Vice-Admiral Graves), *Royal George* (Vice-Admiral Hood), *Brunswick, Edgar, Majestic, Phaeton, Latona, Niger, Venus, Lapwing,⸢Pegasus* and the *Incendiary* (Fireship).

A favourable wind was not obtained until the following day when Howe made sail with twenty-three of the line in two divisions under Hood and Graves. At long last the Channel Fleet was at sea to seek the enemy and hopes were entertained in the ships of a decisive victory over the French that year on sea and land, and back in port by Christmas. Howe knew of the serious shortage of food in France and that the Republican agents were buying up quantities of grain in America as fast as they could. He had been informed that a large convoy would be sailing from America to try to bring relief to the starving people of France. What he did not know was the date of sailing of this convoy.

Bad luck was to befall the *Bellerophon* on this her first cruise in the Channel Fleet. For the past few days Howe had been exercising his fleet by racing his ships one against the other, and the *Bellerophon* was proving herself to be the fastest. Frequent entries in her log for this period make such remarks as, 'Made sail and passed all the fleet', and she thus gained for herself the title of the 'flying' *Bellerophon*. All seemed to be going well for her, her crew was just getting into shape and this without extensive use of the lash, and she was fast becoming the most efficient ship in the fleet.

On Friday 19th July, while fifteen or sixteen leagues off Cape Cornwall, the fleet was hit by a sudden squall. The *Bellerophon* weathered it satisfactorily but it took some of the ships by surprise, including the *Majestic* which was in front of the *Bellerophon* in sailing order. In attempting to wear, the *Majestic* was 'taken aback' and bore down on the *Bellerophon*. Pasley was in his cabin at the time and he describes the incident thus:

At half past three I was called in a great hurry and told that the *Majestic* would be on board of us. I ran out and found it was only too true and past remedy. She came down on us in the act of wearing and ran over our bowsprit which she carried away with the head and stem. There being a good deal of sea the foretopmast soon followed, carrying away the main-topmast and mainyard with a dreadful crash. Not one life was lost nor man hurt. Thanks be to God!

The more official entry in the log for this date reads:

At 3/4 past three A.M. the wind shifted to the northward with a squall. Most of the fleet was taken aback, the *Majestic* being next to us in order of sailing came about and in wearing to regain her station ran on board of us on the Larboard Bow and carried away our bowsprit head, broke the stock of our Larboard anchor . . . soon after came alongside, our sails and rigging tangled with her Boom Irons. In a very short time we got the ships disentangled . . . owing to the forestay and part of the weather rigging being gone the foremast fell over the Larboard gangway and carried away the mainyard and maintopmast etc. with all the sails & rigging that were above the tops. Examined the well and found she made no water. Although several of the people were about the rigging & masts fortunately none of them were hurt. At this time the bowsprit was laying under the Lee Bow. Cut away all the rigging sails etc. and by five o'clock with the assistance of several boats we were clear of the wreck and pre-paring to get up Jury Masts. About 8 we were taken in tow by the *Ram-illies*. People employed fitting Jury Masts.

The speed with which the relatively new crew of the *Bellero-phon* had cleared the ship of wreckage was most impressive. Once the jury masts were erected she cast off the tow, and under the orders of Howe to rejoin as soon as possible she made her way to Torbay.

Once in dock the *Bellerophon* was inspected by the officials of the Plymouth dockyards. She was not found to be in a really serious state, and that morning she was warped alongside a sheerhulk to have her masts and yards fixed. While this was taking place she sent a party of seamen and marines to the *London* which was to take her place in the line. All repairs were completed by the 6th August, and after a final inspection by the dock officials she dropped down from the Hamoaze where she had been moored, to Plymouth Sound to await a favourable breeze for putting to sea. While there, she was joined by the frigate *Venus* also under orders to join Lord Howe's fleet. She sailed on the 12th August for Torbay where the Channel Fleet was sheltering. In Torbay she again took her place in the line and received back the seamen and Marines she had lent to the *London*.

While the *Bellerophon* had been in Plymouth under repair the fleet had sighted the French. The first sighting was off Belle Isle on the 31st July, the strength of the French being fifteen of the line and two frigates. The next day the French were sighted again, but Howe was unable to close the gap between them, and the following day they had entirely disappeared and could not be found by the roving frigates. Heavy weather came up, and after several days of this Howe was forced to bear up for Torbay to repair the damage inflicted by a week of gales. He dropped anchor on the 10th August, and on the 13th the *Bellerophon* once again joined the fleet.

While sheltering in Torbay, Howe received definite information that the French were due to sail a convoy from America and were to escort it with their Channel fleet under Villaret-Joyeuse. When the weather lifted slightly Howe left Torbay with the fleet and escorted a merchant convoy to port. Heavy weather again forced the ships to put back to Torbay on the 4th September, after only two weeks at sea. For just over three weeks they were stormbound in Torbay and unable to get to sea. While there, the *Bellerophon* had been honoured by Howe because of her fast sailing qualities, and he had made Pasley a commodore of a 'flying' squadron which sailed independently of the main fleet and reported any strange sails to the *Queen Charlotte*.

When the fleet sailed again it was unable to take up a position beyond the Lizard, although several attempts were made, and once again Howe signalled each ship to make its way back to Torbay independently. Here again the *Bellerophon* proved her excellent sailing qualities, for the entry in the log for the 30th September reads: '. . . set all sail, passed all the ships and about five was anchored here [Torbay] and all our sails handed [furled] before any of the rest got a berth'.

The fleet was moored in Torbay from the 30th September until the 24th October, and in this time the ships were engaged in replenishing their stores and provisions, and exercising their crews at the sails and the guns. According to the log of the *Bellerophon* the weather was mainly fine with moderate and fresh breezes, so it is plain that Howe had taken this opportunity of revictualling in the hope of a longer cruise in the future. At last all was complete and on the 22nd October the *Bellerophon* worked out of Torbay ready to catch the first fair wind. The order was passed from the flagship for every man to stay aboard his respective ship in readiness to get to sea as quickly as possible. The expected signal was made on the 24th October, a Thursday, and the fleet put to sea. By noon it was 'off the Berry Head 4 or 5 miles'. Besides the *Bellerophon* there were the *Queen Charlotte, Royal Sovereign, Royal George, Prince, London, Cumberland, Brunswick, Invincible, Tremendous, Russell, Majestic, Defence, Ramillies, Marlborough, Ganges, Suffolk, Bellona, Audacious, Montagu, Vanguard, Alfred, Edgar,* and various frigates—a total of twenty-three of the line.

The fleet was forced temporarily into Cheshant Bay on the 25th, but was soon at sea again and by noon was off Start Point. The *Bellerophon* was now detached from the fleet in company with the *Suffolk, Hébé, Latona,* and *Venus* as a flying squadron to cruise between Scilly and Land's End. After two days they rejoined the fleet to report to Howe, and Captain Pasley went aboard the *Queen Charlotte.* Howe was at that time moored in Torbay where he had been driven by bad weather. By three in the afternoon the *Bellerophon* was under way again with her squadron. To show that the squadron was in good spirits the *Suffolk* and *Venus* cheered the *Bellerophon,* and this was heartily returned! The following day the *Suffolk* gave the signal for a man overboard, a search was made by the boats of the squadron but no trace of the seaman could be found.

By the 30th October they were once again cruising between Scilly and Land's End, the position in the log being Scilly N.W. by S. 7 Leagues; it was raining and visibility was limited. A fog descended and the *Bellerophon* lost sight of the frigates to windward of her. To avoid the risk of a collision she made the fog signal whenever she wore or changed course, as the *Suffolk* was sailing quite close to her. By three o'clock the fog had lifted and all the squadron was in sight again, but the *Hébé* signalled that she was unable to keep company with the squadron because she was disabled, with her main and topgallant mast carried away. The *Latona* was ordered to go to her aid, but it was obvious that she needed the facilities of a port to make the repairs. She was sent into Plymouth with orders to rejoin the squadron as soon as the repairs had been completed. The squadron, thus deprived of one frigate, had correspondingly less chance of spotting the enemy if they should be at sea, especially as the weather was beginning to turn foggy again and visibility was shortening all the time.

By the morning of the 31st October the weather had cleared and at about ten o'clock the *Latona* made the signal for a strange sail in sight. Pasley gave chase to the sail to see whether she was friend or foe. After a short chase she was identified as a friend although the log of the *Bellerophon* does not say what sort of ship it was. Soon after, the *Latona* sighted Land's End and the squadron set course for the Scillies. Another sail was sighted on the 1st November and the *Latona* was ordered to investigate, and later the *Venus* went to help her. The 'chase' was to windward and, according to the log, had all her sails set. The *Latona* signalled that it was a friend and she was recalled. After dark, the squadron sailed on a course for the Scillies, which were sighted next day by the *Latona* and later by the officers on the deck of the *Bellerophon*.

The following day being a Sunday, Divine Service was performed in the morning, but the work of the squadron and especially of the outlying frigates went on. The log of the *Bellerophon* reports: 'The *Venus* spoke a Brig to the Eastward and *Latona* a Brig to the Northward by signal.' As no further mention is made of the brigs in the log it is reasonable to suppose that they were British, possibly put into service against the swarms of French privateers which were preying on the merchant shipping in the Channel.

A high wind on the 4th carried the shore of the mainsail on the *Bellerophon* away, but a new one was fitted and the sail was set again in a very short time. Visibility was poor again. A signal to wear the squadron in sight of Land's End was not answered and it was repeated with a gun, whereupon it was answered by both the *Suffolk* and *Latona*. It seemed to be a day of misfortune for just after seven the *Suffolk* carried away her main topsail yard, and was ordered to proceed to the nearest port for repairs. The squadron was now down to *Bellerophon*, *Latona*, and *Venus* as the *Hébé* had still not rejoined from Plymouth. An American merchantman was sighted to the NE. and the *Bellerophon* spoke her by signal to inquire if she had seen the French. No information was received of any value and the squadron proceeded on its way. The entry for the 7th November in the log says: 'At 8 saw a fleet to windward, which proved to be the Channel Fleet.'

After rejoining, the first thing Captain Pasley did was to go on board the *Queen Charlotte* to report to Howe on the success of his cruise. Another fleet was sighted to the eastward the next day, but this too proved to be friendly. The fleet had formed close order of sailing upon the sighting and Howe signalled that they were to alter course by his example. Another sighting was made on the 9th, but when the *Phaeton* was sent to investigate it proved to be the same fleet as on the previous day, and the Channel Fleet continued on its course.

No sails at all were seen on the 10th, a day of very hard gales and rains, nor for the next two days. The 13th saw an improvement in the weather, and just before midday a line-of-battle ship was sighted to the eastward. The frigate sent to investigate again reported a friend, though the log of the *Bellerophon* makes no note of the nationality of the ship. It could, however, have been the *Alfred* which joined the fleet next day on returning from Plymouth. That day also the frigate *Phaeton* sailed off to Falmouth, and the following day the *Suffolk* left the fleet, and fog and mist once again descended. Some time during the day the foretopmast staysail was split and the *Bellerophon* had to strike her topmast. Mist, fog, and rain continued to surround the fleet and no ships were sighted during the next two days.

The French were in fact at sea. The French commander, Villaret-Joyeuse, had heard of an ammunition convoy which was reported to be sailing soon to the Mediterranean. He obtained his information from the British press, as Napoleon was to do after him, as at that time no thought was given to keeping the dates of the sailings of convoys secret. To intercept this he detached a part of his fleet under Rear-Admiral Vanstabel, who sailed from Brest in the middle of November. Vanstabel never sighted the convoy, but he did sight Howe whose fleet he mistook for it. He began to close, but as soon as he realized his mistake he headed for Brest as he had only ten sail of the line with him and Howe had twenty-three.

Vanstabel and his squadron had been sighted from the fleet on the morning of the 18th. The log of the *Bellerophon* reports the occurence thus:

... the signal was made for a strange fleet to windward. Saw 9 or 10 sail standing towards us. The Admiral made the *Russell*, *Audacious* and *Defence* signals to chase. Soon after our signal was made, by this time the fleet had brought too hull down to windward seemingly in some confusion. The *Ganges* being near to us astern her signal was made to chase. About 9 the Admiral made the signal that the strange fleet was an enemy and for the sternmost ships to make more sail. Split our Jib, unbent and bent another, the *Russell* seemed to have sprung her foremast. The signal was made for the frigates to keep sight of the enemy and lead the fleet. At 11 saw the *Defence* with her fore and main topmast carried away. At half past 9 (the next day) the signal was made to engage the enemy as we arrived up with them.

It will be seen that a certain ill luck seemed to be dogging the fleet, with the *Bellerophon*, *Russell*, and *Defence* all suffering mishaps within a short space of time. Soon after Howe had given the signal to engage as the ships came up with the enemy, darkness fell and the chase had to continue under conditions of sheer guesswork. During the night a ship crossed the bows of the *Bellerophon*, but Pasley did not give the order to fire as it could have been another of Howe's ships. The French were resighted next morning steering a course which would bring them fairly close to Howe. As it was only 2 a.m. a signal flag would not be visible and the *Bellerophon* hoisted a signal lantern to her main topmast head. This was seen by the *Caesar* but was not repeated. The reason for this, it would seem, was that the captain of the *Caesar* was in a bad temper that morning and when his first lieutenant asked if they should repeat the signal he replied: 'Dammit Sir! I am not a repeating frigate!' The signal was also seen from the deck of the *Queen Charlotte* but the flag captain, Sir Roger Curtis, would not act on it as he could not see it himself, and he did not want to awaken Howe who was sleeping in his cabin. Consequently, as the *Caesar* did not repeat it and he himself could not see it, the fleet continued on course and no interception was made. The situation seems very similar to that which prevailed at the battle of Jutland 120 years later. By daylight the French had crossed Howe's front and were once again fairly distant. The *Defence* was given orders to proceed to the nearest port for repairs and to rejoin the fleet as soon as possible.

The enemy was now well to windward, and appeared to have the legs of the British ships, for even the *Bellerophon* could not gain on them. The only ship able to do so was the frigate *Latona* which had worked to the rear of the French flying squadron. The French were no longer in full strength and the squadron only consisted of four of the line, two frigates, and one brig. Captain Thornborough of the *Latona* worked up near enough to the enemy to open fire and he let the rearmost Frenchman have his broadside. The French did not return the fire, but according to reports from prisoners captured later the broadside had caused a few casualties and some damage to the rigging. The log of the *Bellerophon* recorded the events of the action of the *Latona* in the briefest terms: '. . . this brought the *Latona* near the rear of the enemy at which she fired several shot which was hardly returned'. When Thornborough had tacked his ship and was ready to fire again he did receive some return fire from the French. The log of the *Bellerophon* says: 'she again tacked and fired which was returned by several of their rearmost ships.'

By dusk the enemy was at a distance of five or six miles, and the British fleet was now well spread out so that the *Bellerophon*, the ship of the line nearest to the enemy, did not feel like engaging the four Frenchmen unsupported. The log of the master makes it clear that the rest of the British fleet was well strung out to leeward of the *Bellerophon* at a distance of five to seven miles, and the French were on the larboard tack bearing SSE. to SSW. and slowly gaining on the British all the time. The pursuit continued in increasingly stormy weather with frequent showers of rain reducing visibility to a bare minimum. At nine the French were sighted again during a break in the rain, and the log says: 'Saw the enemy on the weather bow seemingly within hail of each other. Soon after saw one of them bear away large.'

The log of the captain of the *Bellerophon* at this stage records that: 'The enemy seemed to draw away from us by going free.' By 'going free' is meant running before the wind. Nelson in one of his early commands was the captain of a captured French merchantman which had been converted into a frigate, H.M.S. *Albemarle*, and he found her a very bad sailor on all points except dead before the wind! He said that her previous owner must only have trained her to run away. The fact as far as the chase of the French on the 18th–20th November 1793 is concerned is that the French were of a much better design than their British opponents, and were superior to the British in nearly all points of sailing. It was only after the French had been blockaded by the British for long periods in port that they lost their skill in seamanship which enabled the inferior British ships to catch them and engage them.

The *Bellerophon*, in a last attempt to close the gap, set the topgallant sails, but the weather was so rough that they had to be taken in again for fear of breaking the topmasts. The attempt was made several times but each time they had to be taken in because of the strength of the wind. By midday the speed of the *Bellerophon* and the haze which now hung over the sea combined to make her lose sight of the rest of the British following up astern. The weather cleared sufficiently round about two o'clock for the French to be sighted:

About 2 very heavy squalls with rain . . . when it cleared up a little saw two or three of the enemy ahead, the others on the lee bow, bore away between them and those on the larboard bow, seemed to steer WSW.

This would seem to mean that the main body of the enemy had been sighted once again and both were running for Brest. A touch of comedy was brought into the situation by

. . . the *Latona* and *Phoenix* who seemed to be suspicious of each other and on discovering that they were friends they both bore after one of the enemy ships which bore away from us about S. by W. nearly hull down and seemed to be steering WSW. to join two or three of the enemy we saw now and then to the westward of us between squalls.

The *Latona* signalled to the *Bellerophon* that the French were now definitely superior to the pursuers, and the *Bellerophon* flew the signal for the recall of the *Latona* and the *Phoenix*. A little later three more sails were sighted to the eastward and the *Phoenix* was ordered to chase, but

She not understanding the signal, made the signal to speak us when she came within hail the Commodore desired Sir Richard Strachan to make sail towards the ships to the eastward and if he found them to be friends to make the signal for an enemy with the point of bearing.

Also the *Bellerophon* hailed the *Latona*, 'who as well as us saw four large ships a little distance from us'.

The next day, the 20th November, saw the *Latona* and another frigate the *Phaeton* rejoin the *Bellerophon*, but they were soon off again to investigate twelve sail sighted to the eastwards. These proved to be merchants bound for England,

and they were warned of the presence of the enemy. Inquiries were made of several neutral ships as to the direction of the enemy, but these could not or would not help. While trying to board one of these ships, a Swede, the pinnace was stove in as she was being hoisted out and was nearly lost. A sail sighted next day proved to be the *Vanguard* which had had her main topmast carried away during Tuesday's pursuit and had become separated from the rest of the fleet. The *Vanguard* joined the *Bellerophon* and her frigates for mutual protection. The Mediterranean convoy was sighted under the escort of four-men-of-war, and the squadron hove to to speak with them. They had seen no sign of the French fleet and the squadron carried on its way with its outlying frigates peering for any sight of the enemy. On the 26th November a Dutch convoy was sighted but they too had seen no sign of the French.

A sail was sighted on the 27th November:

Made the general signal to chase, about 10 the *Phoenix* and *Latona* fired a few shot upon which she hoisted French Colours discharged her guns and struck. She proved to be the *Blonde* Corvette of 28 guns and 190 men, brought to and exchanged the Prisoners.

The Frenchman was probably one of the privateers which preyed upon the allied shipping passing up and down the Channel. The *Bellerophon* proceeded in company with her prize and on the 29th was joined by the *Gibraltar* which had also become separated from the fleet. Another line of sails sighted proved to be a fleet of transports bound for the West Indies escorted by Sir John Jervis in the *Boyne* and two other men-of-war. Pasley went aboard the *Boyne* for a discussion, and soon after the signal was made from the *Boyne* for the *Vanguard* to proceed to the nearest port for repairs. Pasley returned to the *Bellerophon* with orders from Jervis to cruise between the Lizard and the Scillies to watch the route to Ireland. On the 4th the *Phoenix* left for Falmouth for provisioning and was to rejoin as soon as possible. The *Latona* sailed for Falmouth on the morning of the 6th and the *Phoenix* rejoined the squadron that evening. News of Howe's fleet came from the *Lord Augustus Fitzroy* which had been with the fleet a few days previously, and on that information Pasley decided to make for Torbay. The *Phoenix* signalled that two large sail were approaching to the SE. and the *Bellerophon* cleared for action. They proved in fact to be the *Monarch* and *Culloden*, which joined the *Bellerophon*. Pasley hauled down his broad pendant and went on board the *Monarch*.

When the squadron reached Torbay they found the rest of the fleet under Howe already moored there. Howe decided to split up his fleet for refitting, and eight of the line and three frigates went to Plymouth and ten of the line and two frigates to Portsmouth. The *Bellerophon* was in the latter group and sailed for Spithead on the 13th December. She remained in Spithead provisioning and refitting for the rest of the month.

The year had been one of high hopes for the Channel Fleet, but there had only been a stern chase and no general action as had been hoped at the beginning. The most satisfactory achievement as far as the *Bellerophon* was concerned was the standing she had gained with the fleet as a fast sailer and an efficient ship. She had had no chance of glory but had done some useful work in her role as head of a flying squadron. The next year would see the courage and efficiency of the men of the *Bellerophon* tested to the full, and they were not to be found wanting in either commodity.

4

1794-1796

The Glorious First of June

WE left the *Bellerophon* at the end of 1793 refitting at Portsmouth after the operations in the Channel that year. Pasley had gone on leave during December and had been made a rear-admiral. The new captain of the *Bellerophon* was to be Captain William Hope. Pasley was still reappointed to the ship as rear-admiral.

Pasley and Hope did not report on board the *Bellerophon* until the 16th January, and that day she dropped down to St Helen's Road where she joined the *Culloden* and *Hannibal* while waiting to get out into the Channel. Pasley had hoisted his broad pendant as commodore and assumed command of the ships in St Helen's Road. These were joined the next day by the *Hector, Defence, Latona, Phaeton, Hébé,* and *Circe.* The *Culloden* and *Hannibal* sailed for Torbay soon after, and Pasley's squadron consisted of the last-named ships only. On the 17th January, Prince Augustus joined the fleet for a cruise in the Channel and was saluted by twenty-one guns from the *Bellerophon.* The squadron sailed at six that evening, and on their way down Channel sighted the squadron commanded by Captain Bazeley of the *Alfred* who was looking for French frigates which had been very active in operations against English commerce recently. By noon of the 19th they were off the Start Point 'NW. 5 or 6 Leagues' and had seen no sign of the French fleet or commerce raiders. Just after noon on the 20th four sails were sighted from the *Defence* to the eastward, but they were lost sight of during the ensuing night. On the 21st three more sails were sighted, but this proved to be the squadron with Prince Augustus on board which was cruising in the Channel. A merchantman bound for London from St Vincent was boarded on the 22nd, but could provide no useful information for Pasley.

By the 23rd the Lizard was in sight and the weather was becoming rougher. There were slight gales from the west and intermittent patches of fog and rain. As soon as the Lizard had been sighted the squadron wore round and headed back up the Channel. During strong gales on the 25th the *Phaeton* and *Circe* parted company from the squadron, but by two o'clock on the morning of the 26th the gales had eased and the squadron was able to reform. Pasley decided to run before the wind for Torbay in order to ride out the gales in comfort, anchoring in Torbay on the 29th January but sailing almost immediately on the 30th. The gales once again proved too rough for the squadron to stay out, and on the 31st they again headed for Torbay where they anchored on the 1st February. This time, however, they were at anchor only for a few hours, and that afternoon they sailed again with the *Hébé*, sent ahead by Pasley to reconnoitre. The squadron passed the Portland Bill at eleven that night. The destination was now Spithead and they reached this on the 3rd after twenty-four hours of strong gales and driving rain. They anchored in St Helen's Road in the morning and went up to Spithead in the afternoon where they found Lord Howe with the Channel Fleet totalling twenty-nine sail of the line. Pasley's broad pendant was hauled down and he came under the command of the admiral. A ship of the Spanish navy visited Spithead on the 6th and saluted the admiral as it came to anchor. The log of the *Bellerophon* gives it as a 74 but does not tell us its name.

For the 26th February the Journal of Mathew Flinders records a 'flogging round the fleet'. This is to say that the victim was taken to each ship of the fleet in a boat and received a certain number of lashes at each:

... signal was made on the *Royal William* to put the sentence of Court Martial into execution viz. John Marlowe belonging to the *Bellerophon* to receive 200 lashes, Samuel Moulis belonging to H.M. Ship *Marlborough* to receive 100 lashes, and George White also of the *Marlborough* to receive 100 lashes. Read the Articles of War and punished John Marlowe with 40 lashes and Samuel Moulis and George White with 25 lashes each as part of their punishment for Desertion.

From the *Bellerophon* the men were taken round to the *Orion*, *Tremendous*, *Sampson*, and *Marlborough* in turn until: 'About noon the signal was hauled down after the men had rec'd their punishment'. The unfortunate victim of a flogging round the fleet was unlikely to survive 200 lashes, and even if he did he was broken in spirit if not in body for ever.

The same day, while getting under way from Spithead, the *Defence* collided with the *Culloden* and carried away the latter's fore and main yards. No serious damage was done to the *Defence* and her departure was not unduly delayed.

On the 11th March, Admiral Bowyer sailed in the *Barfleur* with a squadron comprising the *Glory*, *Brunswick*, *Alfred*, *Ramillies*, *Tremendous*, *Majestic*, *Venus*, and *Pegasus* for a cruise in the Channel. Orders were received on the *Bellerophon* to put to sea on the 20th March, but no sooner had they unmoored the ship than the orders were contradicted. In the log of the *Bellerophon* no reason was given for the change. Lord Howe rehoisted his flag in the *Queen Charlotte* on the 21st March, and Pasley went on board to receive instructions. Howe ordered the *Bellerophon* to sea immediately and she sailed that day.

A few hours out from Spithead the *Bellerophon* sent a boarding party to a Torbay fishing boat for information. No sign of the French was evident. The next day three sails were sighted to the westward and the *Bellerophon* made the private signal to them which they answered; they were in fact the *Latona*, *Phaeton*, and *Hébé*. Pasley made the signal to speak to them and the frigates brought too. The captain of the *Phaeton*, Sir Andrew Douglas, came on board the *Bellerophon*, stayed a few minutes and then went back to his ship. The next day another strange sail was sighted and chased. When challenged she hoisted American colours, and said she was bound for London. Continuing down the Channel the *Bellerophon* sighted the Needles on the 27th March and on the 28th she anchored off Dunnose. From Dunnose she made her way to Spithead and Pasley went on board the *Queen Charlotte* with the report of his cruise. He returned a few hours later with orders to put to sea again for a reconnaissance of the French coast. A pilot joined the ship for the purpose of navigating the more difficult stretches of the coast. She sailed in company with the *Alexander* and *Orion*, while the *Russell* was under orders to join as soon as her refit was complete.

By the 30th the squadron was off Cape Barfleur and had passed Sir Andrew Douglas's squadron early that morning. One of his ships, the *Niger*, was detached to tell Admiral McBride, who was also in the area, of the presence of Pasley's squadron. While cruising off Cape Barfleur they saw several small French merchant vessels rounding the Cape close inshore, but they made no attempt to attack them. By the 31st they were off the Gasketts, where the *Niger* rejoined with a message from Admiral McBride that he would rendezvous with them off the Gasketts that afternoon. Later the *Niger* was damaged in a gale and after signalling her inability to keep company bore away for the nearest port. On the 1st April the frigates *Crescent* and *Druid* were sighted in the distance approaching the squadron. Three French pilots were taken on board the *Bellerophon* from the *Crescent* next day and distributed round the squadron. The weather was now getting rougher and in a gale on the 3rd April the main topmast was sprung. Pasley decided to head for Torbay for repairs and signalled this information to the squadron. He ordered them to carry on independently and to make their way to Spithead to report to Howe. The *Bellerophon* anchored in Torbay on the 4th April and for the next forty-eight hours the crew were engaged in repairs to rigging and masts caused by the gale. The ship was ready for sea by the 6th, but foul winds delayed her sailing for Spithead until 3 a.m. the next day.

For two weeks the *Bellerophon* lay with the fleet in Spithead, while work continued getting the ships ready for the spring operations in the Channel which would start with the escorting of three large convoys. Howe made the signal for the van and rear divisions to prepare for sea on the 21st April, and the *Bellerophon* worked her way out into the St Helen's Road on the 22nd in company with the *Royal Sovereign*, the flagship of Sir Alexander Hood. The remainder of the van and rear divisions arrived on the 23rd and Howe arrived with the rest of the fleet on the 25th.

For a week the fleet waited while the convoys were assembled, but at last all was ready. On the 2nd May Howe gave the signal to weigh anchor and put to sea. At the signal from the admiral all the ships loosed their sails and moved slowly out into the Channel. It was this sight which Prince Metternich, watching from a hill, described as the most beautiful he had ever seen. Those going to the East Indies went to the east of the Isle of Wight, and those going to the West Indies went to the west of the island.   Both groups were under escort of men-of-war and would meet on the far side of the island. The total numbers involved were 109 merchant ships, thirty-four ships of the line and fifteen frigates and other small vessels. By noon on the 3rd the fleets had joined and proceeded to The Lizard in company, when the merchant ships going SW. turned away under escort of eight ships of the line. The rest of the fleet turned to the south to reconnoitre Brest. On the 5th May Howe was off Ushant and he detached the *Orion, Latona,* and *Phaeton* to look into Brest. The *Bellerophon, Russell, Marlborough,* and *Thunderer* were ordered to keep to windward of the fleet to watch for any ships running for the cover of Brest.

On the 6th May the detachment which had been sent to look into Brest returned to report that one of the line, two frigates, and two brigs were at anchor in Camaret Bay, and twenty-two of the line in Goulet with 'a considerable number of smaller vessels'. Howe had known before he sailed that the long-awaited grain convoy was due to sail from America at any time, and might indeed even be at sea already. He knew that the convoy was vital to the survival of Revolutionary France and the Directory would risk all their fleet to get it safely to port. For this reason he had kept his fleet cruising off Ushant as a suitable position in which to intercept any incoming convoy and outgoing fleet.

Heavy weather on the 7th May caused the *Bellerophon* to spring her topmast again, but it was soon taken down and replaced. Thick fog descended on the fleet later that day restricting visibility to a few yards. The fog cleared on the 8th and Howe decided to try farther out in the Channel for a contact with the French. Two ships were sighted on the 10th and the *Thunderer* and *Russell* gave chase. The two British 74s hoisted French colours, whereupon the chase hoisted inverted Union Jacks which proved them to be British merchant ships taken by the enemy. The British ships soon overtook them and they were retaken and dispatched to Torbay with the French prize crews as prisoners on board. They had been taken a few days earlier by two French frigates but had seen no sign of any other French ships at all. The weather was now becoming hazy but the sea was calm and the fleet proceeded under easy sail.

A French brig was sighted, chased and captured by the frigate *Southampton* on the 13th, and she was sent back to Torbay with the two merchantmen recaptured earlier under the escort of a cutter on the 15th. Thick fog descended again at noon on the 15th and the ships proceeded with fog signals sounding. Over a week had passed since Howe had last looked into Brest and he decided to retrace his steps to see whether the French fleet were still there. He was too late, however, for on the night of the 17th, in a very thick fog, the French Admiral Villaret-Joyeuse had sailed with twenty-five of the line. He had actually passed close to Howe in the fog but this was unknown to either admiral at the time. Outside Brest the French admiral was joined by one more sail of the line and then headed out into the Atlantic to meet the convoy on which the fate of France, the war, and himself depended. He had on board his flagship the *Montagne* the Revolutionary commissar Jean Bon St André, sent by his government to give encouragement to the fleet. He was much detested by all the officers of the navy and soon proved to be more of a nuisance than encouragement! It was a sign of the state of things which had come about in the French navy under the rule of the Directory that politicians were allowed aboard men-of-war on a mission of vital importance.

Meanwhile Howe had reached Brest on the 19th and had found the French fleet gone. He was temporarily at a loss. His indecision was resolved by the news from an American brig that the French had sailed on the 17th, heading westward and in full strength. Also on the 19th the *Bellerophon*'s squadron hailed the *Santa Margarita*, which was carrying dispatches to London concerning the capture of Guadeloupe by Sir John Jervis. The *Russell* was dispatched to the fleet to carry this news to Howe.

On the 21st the British sighted a convoy of fifteen or sixteen brigs which proved to be French. They gave chase and sank or burnt nine of them, the rest managing to escape to Brest.

Knowing the French to be at sea, Howe was worried over the safety of Rear-Admiral Montagu who was cruising off Cape Finisterre with six of the line. For this reason, as soon as he had definite news of the French, he headed SW. towards Cape Finisterre. All sail was put on to get to Montagu before the French could meet him and destroy his tiny force.

The *Southampton* captured and destroyed another French brig on the 23rd, and also what Mathew Flinders calls in his Journal 'a fine little ship called the *Albion* of Bermuda set on fire by the *Glory*'. More news of the French was obtained from a Dutch vessel which had been taken by the French but was recaptured by the British. Information received from her prize crew and the original Dutch crew showed that Montagu was in no danger and that the French were last seen about seventy miles off to the windward. The final capture of the day was a French cutter which was brought into the fleet by the frigates and destroyed. The reason why Howe was destroying his prizes was because he had no men to spare for prize crews as his ships were undermanned, and there was a possibility of a battle with the French in the near future.

Various sightings of friendly sails were made on the 24th, but Howe now had only one course in mind—the interception of the French fleet. He was steering NW. under all the sail that he could carry. On the 25th the *Bellerophon* saw a French 74 with a prize in tow and gave chase. She was supported by the *Russell* and *Thunderer*. The Frenchman cast off the prize and made her escape, but she was identified by the crew of the merchantman as the *Audacieux* of the Rochefort squadron. After the chase the *Bellerophon*'s squadron was ordered by Howe to rejoin the fleet, and only the frigates remained away from the main body for scouting purposes. On the 26th, Howe tacked the whole fleet to the eastward at 6 a.m. and later changed course to NNW. The fleet proceeded in high hopes of a battle very soon and were confident of the outcome. The weather on the 27th was fine and visibility good. Howe altered the course of the fleet again, this time to SE. by S. At last on the 28th May the French fleet was sighted.

THE 'GLORIOUS FIRST OF JUNE', 28th MAY TO 1st JUNE 1794

The French were sighted in a long line to windward of the British fleet. At first Villaret-Joyeuse stood towards the British, thinking them inferior in numbers to himself. When he saw they were equal in numbers he decided to turn back and to lead them away from the probable course of the grain convoy. The log of the *Bellerophon*, recording the sighting on the morning of the 28th May, reports: ' . . . we counted 33 sail of which 24 or 25 appeared to be of the line and all standing down towards us. Our signal was made to reconnoitre the enemy as we were now certain they were'. The French were sailing in line ahead before the wind, and the British in order of sailing on a converging course. On the signal from Howe, the *Bellerophon* and her squadron began to put on more sail to gain on the French fleet. The *Bellerophon* was the fastest ship of her squadron and soon was leading the chase. The captain of the *Russell* was also making a great effort to close with the French, and it was his ship which fired the first shots in the five-day battle which was to become known as the 'Glorious First of June'. It took all morning and half the afternoon for the British squadron to approach the French near enough to open fire, but at last at 3 p.m. the *Russell* was in range. The log of the *Bellerophon* continues thus:

. . . Repeated the general signal for chase and battle. About 3 the *Russell* . . . began to fire on the enemy's rear as they were hauling on the starboard tack . . . We tacked before the rear ship on [our] beam which enabled us to bring them to action a considerable time before the other ships could get up to our assistance.

The ship engaged by the *Bellerophon* was the three-decker *Révolutionnaire* of 120 guns. While the *Russell* was engaging at relatively long range, Pasley on the *Bellerophon* had ordered Captain Hope to close with the rearmost ship of the enemy's line. For just over an hour the *Bellerophon* engaged her giant opponent, and did much damage to the Frenchman's sails and rigging. Howe, seeing the *Bellerophon* engaged with a three-decker, ordered the *Russell* and the *Marlborough* to go to her assistance. These two ships eventually joined the unequal combat, and the three 74s succeeded in reducing the three-decker to such a state that she took no further part in the campaign. Another British ship to be hotly engaged that day was the *Audacious* which was also badly damaged and took no further part in the fighting. The *Bellerophon* had received serious damage in the rigging, but by some miracle no one on board was killed. The rest of the fleet had come up with the action just before dark, and the *Leviathan* and *Thunderer* had also given their broadsides to the battered *Révolutionnaire*. The *Bellerophon* withdrew to repair her damage and the log states the position:

By this time having received sundry shot in different places, the main top was disabled and most likely to fall over the side, made the signal of inability

During this period the *Audacious* was seen alongside the *Révolutionnaire* and it was thought that the French ship had struck. It was observed that:

The rear ship of the enemy had lost her mizen mast, and bore up as we supposed with intention to strike us, but was intercepted by one of our ships who soon after silenced her fire and ran down to leeward of her.

The *Révolutionnaire* had in fact not struck, but, like the *Audacious*, was withdrawing from the battle badly damaged. She made her way back to France with no interference from the *Audacious* or anybody else. It was a matter of annoyance afterwards to Pasley and Hope and the officers of the *Bellerophon* that, after all their efforts during the day, a chance had been lost of taking the Frenchman when she appeared to be beaten to a standstill. It was thought she had been taken and it was only later that they were disillusioned.

After completing her repairs the *Bellerophon* rejoined the fleet and bore up in Howe's wake.

The most satisfactory aspect of the day's events had been the conduct of the *Bellerophon*, which was much admired and appreciated by Howe. The admiral had cause for satisfaction over the fact that he had reduced the strength of the enemy fleet by a first-rate of 120 guns, and closed the distance between them. He was still to the leeward of the French but he hoped to break through their line to the windward next day and gain the weather gauge. This would enable him to attack when and where he wanted. In the evening, with the French at a distance of five miles to windward, he made the signal to form line of battle and to keep it during the night. The only thing which marred the day from Howe's point of view was that the ships of the *Bellerophon*'s squadron did not support her properly. He said in a letter after the battle that the *Thunderer* and *Marlborough* were 'firing at the enemy from a distance far too considerable', and he had had to make the signal for those ships to close. During the night the fleets were kept in contact and Villaret-Joyeuse was unable to shake off the tenacious Howe.

May the 29th dawned clear and fine with the French still to windward of Howe. His object was to gain the weather gauge, and to do this he had to break through the French line. He ordered the fleet to take station as convenient, and as the *Bellerophon* was sailing near Howe she automatically dropped in astern of the *Queen Charlotte*. It was seen from the British fleet that the French were still in the same strength as the day before, as another ship of the line had joined Villaret-Joyeuse during the night. About 8 a.m. Howe ordered the fleet to tack in succession. By doing this he hoped to isolate three or four ships of the enemy's rear, which would mean that Villaret-Joyeuse would either have to tack his own fleet to bring help to his rear or leave them to their fate. The first course would bring on a general engagement, which was what Howe wanted; the second would mean that the strength of the French fleet would be further reduced, and that Howe would be left with the weather gauge, which was what he was hoping to obtain. The latter course was impracticable to an admiral of Revolutionary France. He could not leave over 2,000 sailors of the Republic to fight it out alone against the British fleet, even if by helping them he might lose his whole fleet and jeopardize the safe arrival of the grain convoy.

Howe hoisted signal No. 34 on board his flagship. This meant: 'Admiral intends to pass through the enemy's line to obtain weather gauge'; and soon after, No. 28: 'Ships are at liberty to fire on the enemy though not to bring them to general action'. Long-range cannonading began between the two fleets soon after 8 a.m.

The first British ships engaged were the two leading ones, the *Caesar* of 80 guns and the *Queen* of 90 guns. All morning Howe manoeuvred his fleet to close the distance between himself and the French, and by noon he had managed to reduce it to about three miles. Having obtained a favourable position, he ordered the van to tack and break through the enemy's line. No reply was received from the leading ship of his line, the *Caesar*, and the signal was flown again with the *Caesar*'s distinguishing pendants. Still no reply was made.

Howe was angry that the action of one ship was letting slip all the good work of the morning and the advantages he had obtained by his manoeuvres. At last the *Caesar* flew a signal of 'inability to comply' with the admiral's instructions, and instead of turning towards the French she turned away from them. This act threw the whole British fleet into confusion; only four of the leading ships, the *Queen, Orion, Invincible,* and *Valiant* followed the signal and tacked in accordance with Howe's instructions. Of these only the *Queen* was engaged at all closely with the enemy. Being unsupported she was unable to break through the enemy's line and she had to sail down the line looking for a place to break in and receiving all the broadsides of the French van.

Howe saw that unless something was done quickly all the manoeuvring of the morning would be in vain, and that the French would soon not only tack to save their own rear but also keep the weather gauge. He saw that some of his captains needed the 'force of his example', and decided to tack the *Queen Charlotte* before it came to her turn to tack in succession. He ordered Bowen, the master of the *Queen Charlotte*, to put over the helm of the ship and go through the enemy line. By doing this he hoped that the ships astern of the *Queen Charlotte* would be fired by his example and also break through the line. He was in fact followed by only two of the rear ships, the *Bellerophon* and the *Leviathan* captained by Lord Hugh Seymour. Howe broke through four ships from the end, but the *Bellerophon* and *Leviathan* following were unable to find an opening in the same spot because of the speed with which the French had closed their line. The two British ships sailed down the the French line and eventually broke through two ships from the end. As the *Bellerophon*'s log puts it:

The Admiral finding that our leading ships was passing to leeward of their line tacked in the midst of a very heavy fire and cannonade and cut through between the 4th and 5th ships in their rear. We followed and passed between the 2nd and 3rd ships.

An officer who was on the deck of the *Bellerophon* at the time states in his eye-witness report written after the battle:

. . . She could not penetrate the French line until she came to the second ship astern of the space through which Lord Howe had passed. Then brushing through she passed so close to one opponent as almost to touch and totally unrig her, bringing down her topmasts and lower yards with a starboard broadside, and raking the one to leeward at the same time.

Mathew Flinders, who was on the quarter-deck of the *Bellerophon* when she broke through the line, noticed that the quarter-deck guns had been left unmanned. The crews had been called away to man the braces and yards to tack the ship. He seized this opportunity of doing a spot of damage to the French, and getting a lighted match he went along the deck, firing as many of the guns as would bear. He was seen by Admiral Pasley who asked him what he meant by firing the guns without orders, and Flinders replied rather disarmingly that he had only wanted to have a 'bang at the French'. Pasley was so struck by the boy's initiative and spirit that he only gave him a mild reproof.

As in all actions of the day, the smoke of battle led to much confusion as to the relative positions of enemy and friend. They could never be sure whom they were firing at or who was firing at them; '. . . in the heat of the action it was difficult to know who was French or who was English. We was all firing through one another', as the log of the *Bellerophon* describes the battle.

The French had been taken by surprise and Villaret-Joyeuse faced the loss of four of his rear ships unless he could tack his van and bring it to the aid of his battered rear. Despite the fact that he had now broken the enemy's line, the situation was still not satisfactory for Howe. His van was too far away to support him properly, and followed the lead of the *Caesar* in tacking in the rear of the French line.

Howe in the midst of the fighting was hard pressed, but in spite of this he had time to notice that the *Leviathan* too was hard pressed, and took the *Queen Charlotte* down to her rescue—an action which drew from her captain, Seymour, after the battle a warm letter of appreciation. The French had meanwhile tacked the van of their own fleet and were coming down to the help of the rear. This move placed the disabled *Queen* in danger. She had been drifting down the line looking for a place to break through and receiving the broadside of every French ship as she passed. Seeing the peril, Howe summoned up some of the less damaged ships of his fleet to her rescue. The ships were the *Barfleur*, flagship of

Admiral Gardner captained by Cuthbert Collingwood, *Impregnable*, *Royal Sovereign*, and *Glory*, all three-deckers. By this move the threat to the *Queen* was removed and the situation saved. Despite the heavy battering they had received, none of the ships of the French rear had surrendered; the one opposing the *Bellerophon* was mentioned in her log: 'Their rear ship received many broadsides, even from our own three-deckers but still kept her colours flying'. They were, however, unfit for further fighting and had to withdraw to the nearest port. This reduced French numbers to twenty-two and Howe still had twenty-five to oppose them. After the French van had succoured the rear, both fleets drew off to undergo repairs. On the whole it had been a satisfactory day for Howe and the British fleet. He had gained the weather gauge, and reduced the French numerical superiority even further, in fact to inferiority. On the other hand he now knew that not all of his captains would do their duty. Captain Molloy of the *Caesar* had carefully kept out of the heavy fighting, and several other of the van ships had been conspicuous by their absence.

During the night thick fog descended which boded no good for the next day. All through the night Howe clung to the French fleet, while Villaret-Joyeuse edged farther to leeward to draw Howe away from the path of the grain convoy. The whole of the 30th was foggy, and the French were only sighted twice from the decks and masthead of the *Bellerophon* before the mist closed in again. By an incredible piece of luck the French met up with the four ships of Admiral Neilly's squadron, and this brought their strength up to twenty-six of the line, which it had been when first sighted by Howe on the 28th. The fog continued throughout the morning of the 31st May and did not clear until midday, when the enemy were once again sighted from the British fleet.

With great moral strength Howe decided to postpone his attack until the morning of the 1st June as he considered the time in hand to be insufficient for the job to be done. When the possibility of a night action was mentioned to him he declined with the remark that he needed daylight to see what his captains were doing! He utilized the remaining daylight hours, therefore, to draw closer to the French fleet. The letter of Lord Howe after the battle summarizes the day:

... the fleet advanced to get up abreast of them. But before that could be effected, the day was too far advanced for bringing them to action. It was therefore judged expedient to keep the wind with frigates of observation to notify any change in the enemy's motions during the night.

The action of Howe in refusing battle on the 31st was regarded in the French fleet as indicative of the pusillanimity of the British, and they looked forward to the actual day of battle with confidence.

On the morning of the 1st June the *Bellerophon* was second in the British line behind the *Caesar*. When the enemy had been sighted once more Howe signalled the fleet to send the men to breakfast. When the French saw that Howe again did not bear down on them, they retained a poor opinion of British nerve. Sir Thomas Troubridge, who was on one of the French ships as a prisoner, told the captain that he had read the signal to send the men down to breakfast, but as soon as they had finished they would pay the French a visit and give them their bellyful! The next signal to go up from the *Queen Charlotte* was for all ships to close on the van. By about 8 a.m. the leading ships of the British line were nearly in range and Howe signalled for each ship to engage her opposite number in the enemy line.

Howe's plan was to break through the enemy's line again and to engage them from leeward so to prevent their retreat. The conventional idea of the time when engaging from windward was to sail on the same tack engaged in cannonading the enemy. By breaking the line he was breaking convention; the only victory gained by that method in recent years was Rodney's victory of the Saintes in 1782; that, in fact, was the only decisive victory gained in the last century apart from the 'chase' victories like those of Hawke and Boscawen. The French had adopted the tactics of firing at the masts and rigging of their opponents to render them immobile, so that they could then either escape themselves or destroy them as circumstances demanded. These tactics had been employed with great success in the American War and had given them mastery of the seas for a short period. Therefore when Howe flew his signal from the *Queen Charlotte* for every captain to engage his opposite number in the enemy's line he was dumbfounded and annoyed when the leading ship, the *Caesar*, kept straight on her course and hoisted the inability to comply signal. Both Pasley and Howe were flying the signal for the *Caesar* to engage closer, but no response came from on board. Captain Molloy later claimed that a piece of French shot had jammed his rudder and the ship was no longer under control. Several ships did however break the line, among them the second ship in the British line, the *Bellerophon*. Because of the defection of the leading ship, the *Bellerophon* had to withstand the fire of the two leading ships of the French line. Her log disposes of this rather unnerving experience in a few lines: 'Ran down and lay upon her [the 2nd French ship's] quarter within musket shot. In going down was received a very heavy fire from 3 or 4 of the enemy's ships.'

Not only was the *Bellerophon* receiving the fire of the leading French ship, but she was getting occasional shot from the *Caesar* which was engaging the French at long range. After being involved in this lone struggle for nearly two hours, a French shot, smashing through the sides, struck Admiral Pasley and took off his leg. The log of the *Bellerophon* states: 'At 50 minutes past 10 the Admiral unfortunately lost his leg.' Before being carried below Pasley is reported to have said to two seamen who commiserated with him on the loss of the leg: 'Thank you, but never mind my leg, take care of my flag!'

For over an hour after Pasley had been hit the *Bellerophon* continued firing, but by noon she had silenced the fire of the leading French ship, the *Éole* and was trying to come alongside her to force her to strike. In doing this her main topmast, which had been shot through, came down, and shortly after the fore topmast followed it.

A little before noon the van of the enemy began to bear up, [we] having their fire; our topmasts being both gone and most of our lower shrouds shot away we were unable to follow. Made the *Latona*'s signal to come to our assistance.

The damage left the *Bellerophon* practically stationary in the middle of the fight, but luckily her other opponent had also had enough and drifted away. This second ship to be silenced by the *Bellerophon* was the *Trajan*, a 74. As the vessel could no longer manoeuvre, the *Bellerophon*'s gunners could only fire at ships which came within their field of fire.

The *Queen Charlotte* was another ship which had been successful in breaking through the French line. She went through just astern of the French flagship *La Montagne* of 120 guns. As she passed under the stern of the ship she raked her, and her heavy guns did enormous damage in the crowded interior of the French flagship. When Howe had ordered Bowen, the Master of the Fleet, to take the *Queen Charlotte* through the line, he (Bowen) had questioned an order to starboard the helm as, if they did so, they would be on board the next ship in the French line, the *Jacobin*. 'What is that to you, sir?' asked Howe. A slightly disgruntled Bowen said in an undertone, 'Damn my eyes if I care, if *you* don't! I'll go near enough to singe some of our whiskers.' Howe heard him and remarked to his Chief of Staff and captain of the *Queen Charlotte*, Sir Roger Curtis, 'That's a fine fellow'. The *Queen Charlotte* engaged both the *Jacobin* and the *Montagne* for nearly two hours.

One of the most notable ship duels in the action was that between the *Brunswick* and the *Vengeur*. Both were 74s and both fought extremely gallantly. Another French ship, *Le Juste*, came into the fight also but she too was silenced, as eventually was the *Vengeur*. The action won a place in the French navy equivalent to the fight of Sir Richard Grenville in the Azores and the duel between the *Leander* and *Généreux* off Crete in 1798.

After nearly two hours of hard fighting both fleets drew off and it was seen that six French ships had struck and one, the *Vengeur*, was on the point of sinking. The remainder of the damaged and undamaged ships of the French fleet had formed a line to leeward. Another ship, the *Jacobin*, sank before she could be seized. The day obviously rested with Howe and the British fleet, but in the eyes of many officers of the fleet the victory was not complete. They thought that the less damaged ships should be sent after the French to take and destroy as many as possible. This was not the view of the Captain of the Fleet, Sir Roger Curtis, who persuaded the exhausted Howe to be content with securing the prizes and repairing the damage. The prizes taken by the British were *Le Juste* and *Sans Pareil* of 80 guns, and *L'America*, *L'Achille*, *Le Northumberland*, and *L'Impétueux*, each of 74 guns. Undoubtedly the tactical honours lay with Howe, but the victory could not be complete until the grain convoy also was captured or destroyed—and the chase and destruction of the beaten French fleet would be a great step towards this. Curtis, however, decided not to pursue, for safety's sake. In retrospect, the First of June was a tactical victory for Howe and the British fleet, but a strategic victory for Villaret-Joyeuse. Howe had taken six ships of the line and sunk one, but he had not dealt the French a crippling blow and the grain convoy was to escape. Villaret-Joyeuse had saved the convoy, his country, his head, his command, and the Revolution.

The ships which most distinguished themselves in the action were the *Queen Charlotte, Bellerophon, Defence, Brunswick, Leviathan,* and *Russell.* Two ships which came in for some criticism from the senior officers of the fleet were the *Caesar* and the *Tremendous.* Casualties in the *Bellerophon* were surprisingly light, only four killed and twenty-seven wounded. In his letter to Howe after the victory, Pasley expressed himself most strongly about the lack of support which the *Bellerophon* had received during the battle. He mentioned particularly the *Gibraltar* and the *Caesar,* and of the captain of the *Caesar* he said, 'I make no doubt but Captain Molloy will explain to you the reasons for his conduct'. In fact Molloy was to demand a court martial to clear his name of the charges made against him. It did not assemble until ten months later, and the verdict was that 'he be removed from the command of His Majesty's Ship *Caesar*', and he was not employed at sea again. Pasley was full of praise for the conduct of the officers and men of the *Bellerophon* and also for the support given to him by the *Russell* and *Leviathan.*

The night after the battle was spent in clearing the decks of wreckage and attending to the casualties. These would be taken down to the sick bay in the hold of the ship for the surgeon to deal with. Pasley himself was suffering much pain from the stump of his leg and was unable to take full command of the ship or his squadron. The conduct of affairs was left to Captain Hope who soon had the ship operating efficiently again.

The morning of the 2nd June dawned fine with a scene of damaged ships floating on a calm sea. All the badly shattered vessels were in the act of putting up jury masts or had already got them up. The signal was made that morning from one of the frigates for nine enemy ships to the NNE. Soon they were seen from the fleet, but they too were engaged in repairs and the two sides made no effort to interfere with each other. Howe was still exhausted after the battle as a man of sixty-eight would be, and Curtis had full command of the fleet. The *Bellerophon* had her jury masts set up by the 3rd and the sails set. The French prisoners from the prizes were taken on board the English ships.

Howe's dispatch was sent to England by the *Phaeton* on the 5th, and the rest of the fleet was proceeding slowly back to port with the prizes in tow. The position at noon that day was: 'Scilly East 113 leagues. Wind moderate. Sea calm.' On the 6th the wind dropped and the fleet was becalmed. The boats were got out to tow the ships, and by noon the position of the fleet was: 'Scilly East 109 leagues. Winds ENE.' The 7th saw the wind rising again and the fleet made good progress in the twenty-four hours from noon on the 6th to noon on the 7th when the position was: 'Scilly 87 leagues. Wind NW. Sea calm.' Howe signalled on the 8th for the fleet to close round the admiral for greater security in their present damaged condition. On the 9th five strange sails were sighted but nothing further came of the sighting and they soon disappeared. Further good progress was made during the next twenty-four hours and by noon on the 10th the position was: 'Scilly 7 leagues. Wind SW.' On the 11th several of the ships of the fleet, including the *Royal Sovereign*, parted company and made for Plymouth.

On Friday 13th June the *Bellerophon* dropped anchor at Spithead having received a signal from Howe to proceed to the nearest port. Accompanying here were the *Barfleur* and *Queen*. The three ships anchored in Spithead at 11.30 and Pasley was sent ashore. The *Bellerophon* was to be his last ship as he was not considered fit enough with only one leg to serve afloat again. With him would have to go Captain Hope as he was too junior in the captains' list to command a ship of the line by himself. The log dismisses Pasley's removal with only a few words: 'At $\frac{1}{2}$ past 11 anchored at Spithead in 9 fathoms. Sent the Admiral ashore.'

On the 14th the *Ramillies* arrived at Spithead towing one of the prizes, the French 74 *Le Juste*. The *Bellerophon* landed her prisoners on the 15th and they were marched away inland by the Army. The same day the prizes *L'Impétueux* and *L'America* went into harbour. As a last gesture of defiance the *Le Juste* grounded when she was being towed in. She grounded on the Spit and all the ships in the vicinity sent boats to tow her off.

Spithead now presented a glorious sight: the fleet was home, and to prove their mastery of the seas six French prizes lay at anchor in the harbour—the first tangible fruits of the war which the people of Portsmouth had seen. Howe had entered with his ships in reasonable condition, with most of the damage under repair or repaired, but the prizes were mainly still in their battered state, with casualties cluttering up the decks and great gashes torn in the sides by the shot of the British. An unusual feature of the battle was that gold coins were found stuck in the side of the *Leviathan* after she had been engaging a French 74! They had evidently been used as grapeshot!

As a mark of favour to the victors George III decided to pay a visit to Portsmouth to welcome Howe. It was a thing he had never done before and was never to do again, but then Howe was always his favourite admiral, and was referred to in his correspondence as the 'Earl Richard'. It was through the influence of George III that Howe had been appointed to command the Channel fleet at the outbreak of the war. The King arrived at Portsmouth on the 20th and took up residence at the commissioner's house in the dockyard.

On the 21st the *Bellerophon* sent another party of men to assist a prize into harbour, this time the *Sans Pareil* of 80 guns. On the 24th she was warped alongside the *Royal William* and her new masts were fitted.

The King visited Howe on board the *Queen Charlotte* on the 27th. He was accompanied by the Royal Family, while Howe had his own family with him on the ship. He was presented with a sword set with diamonds and a gold chain to carry a medal which was to be issued later. When the Naval General Service Medal was issued in 1848, one of the recipients for the 'Glorious First of June' was the son born to the wife of a seaman of the *Tremendous* called McKenzie. The baby was born on the actual day of the battle. After the visit to the flagship the King was rowed round the fleet, an occurrence which caused much annoyance among those officers who had not been presented and whose ships the King never visited.

On the 28th the three-decker *Prince of Wales* was launched at Portsmouth. This ship was not to have a distinguished career, and is chiefly known as the flagship of Sir Robert Calder in the indecisive battle of Finisterre in 1805.

After his visit to the fleet the King left Portsmouth on the 29th on the frigate *Aquilon* accompanied by the frigate *Southampton*. They were to take the King to Southampton and then to return to the fleet at Spithead. Among the honours announced on the 4th July was a baronetcy for Pasley. Howe was promised various honours but they never materialized, to the disappointment of his family and friends.

5

With Cornwallis and Bridport in the Channel

ON the 9th July the flags of Admirals Pasley, Hood, and Bowyer were struck and Hood and Bowyer went ashore. Pasley was of course already ashore. Sir Roger Curtis hoisted his flag as admiral on board the *Queen Charlotte* on the 15th July while Howe was on leave.

A squadron of eleven ships of the line arrived at Spithead on the 23rd July under the command of Rear-Admiral Caldwell, and on the 26th the *Royal Sovereign* arrived there from Plymouth after her repairs. The 30th saw another admiral hoist his flag, this time Admiral Elphinstone (later Lord Keith) on board the *Barfleur*.

Seven Portuguese men-of-war, comprising four 74s, one 64, and three frigates, joined the fleet for the next Channel cruise. Howe did resume command of the fleet on the 2nd August and once again made his flagship the *Queen Charlotte*. He was now feeling his age and begged to be relieved by the Admiralty, but a personal request from George III had made him decide to stay on for just a little longer.

The *Bellerophon* was still in the middle of her repairs for the log of the 2nd August shows that on that day the ship was heeled over to have her bottom scraped. This was necessary for the ship had been many months in the water and even on the copper plates the sea growths would be very considerable.

On the 7th August Admiral Cornwallis, known in the Navy as 'Billy go tight' because of his ruddy complexion, hoisted his flag on board the *Caesar*. The 10th saw Sir Alexander Hood rehoist his flag on the *Royal George*, and on the 17th Admiral

Gardner rehoisted his flag on the *Queen*. Howe made the signal to prepare for sea and the fleet moved to St Helen's Road on the 22nd August to await a fair wind. The ships made an effort to get to sea on the 29th but could get no farther than the Culver Cliffs before being forced back to Spithead by contrary winds. At last the wind was right and the whole fleet put to sea on the 3rd September; it comprised thirty sail of the line (English) and five Portuguese. The *Barfleur*, with Admiral Elphinstone on board, was left at Spithead after suffering some damage in a collision with the *Russell* while working out of harbour. By noon on the 4th September Portland Bill was in sight. A fierce gale blew up on the night of the 4th–5th September and gunfire was heard in the distance from the *Bellerophon*. The firing of cannon at regular intervals was the signal for a ship in distress. When day dawned the *Bellerophon*:

. . . discovered the *Melampus* with her foremast and bowsprit carried away and one [other ship] totally dismasted and another with her mizen mast gone. Both of which proved to be East India ships . . . the *Invincible* took the *Melampus* into Plymouth and the *Venerable* took the dismasted ship in tow.

Because of the damage inflicted by the gale, Howe thought it necessary to go to Torbay for repairs and to lie to until better weather came. Accordingly he signalled for the fleet to make for Torbay where it anchored next day. On the 7th at 6 a.m. the fleet left Torbay and formed into three lines of sailing. They cruised in the direction of Ushant, and on the 10th Howe detached the *Leviathan*, *Russell*, and *Phaeton* to look into Brest. There were more gales on the 11th during which the *Bellerophon* struck her topgallant masts. The gale proved too much for the Portuguese ships, one being seen from the *Bellerophon* with her bowsprit and foremast gone, and on the next morning Howe gave permission for all five to leave the fleet. Howe made for Torbay again and anchored there on the 22nd at 8 a.m. This time he was there for nearly two weeks, not being able to leave until the 1st October.

The *Bellerophon* had a busy time on the 4th October when she chased three different ships: '. . . fired 2 shot at a lugger who hoisted English colours . . . chased by signal a ship, she hoisted Swedish colours . . . fired 2 shot at another ship who hoisted American colours.'

The fleet put back to Torbay on the 7th October, and was there for two weeks until the 21st October. On the 22nd Howe split his fleet and sent the *Culloden*, *Venerable*, *Audacious*, *Robust*, *Impregnable*, *Glory*, and *Ruby* to Plymouth, and with the remainder he steered in the direction of Ushant. He was on his station off Ushant by the 28th October, and finding nothing he cut across Channel again to the Lizard. Gales blew up on the last days of the month and on the 1st November the fleet was back in Torbay. From Torbay Howe wrote to the Admiralty asking to be relieved of his command for health reasons. He said he had a recurrence of his 'old complaint' and wished to go to Bath to take the waters which he had previously found beneficial. The Admiralty replied sympathetically to his letter and agreed that he should be allowed to go to Bath as soon as he had returned from the 'present intended service'. Howe was disappointed but a sense of public duty kept him at his post, although he professed to his friends that he found it disagreeable.

On the evening of the 8th November a sail was sighted from the bay which turned out to be the *Canada*. She came into the bay and reported that she had been chased by five French ships of the line when cruising in the Channel in company with the *Alexander*. Guessing that the French fleet might be out, Howe put to sea at once and sped across the Channel for Ushant under all sail. He was unlucky, for fog prevailed from the 9th until the 14th with only occasional patches of brightness. Nevertheless Howe continued to cruise in and around the waters of Ushant hoping to find the French fleet or at least a portion of it. On the 21st he decided that nothing further was to be gained by staying in the area and signalled for the fleet to steer for Spithead. They made slow time across the Channel, and did not anchor in St Helen's Road until the 29th, then moved up to Spithead the next day.

On the 1st December Captain Hope was finally recalled from the *Bellerophon* and a new captain was appointed. According to the log noting his arrival on board: 'At noon came on board the Right Honourable James, Lord Cranstoun and superseded Captain Hope. Read his Lordship's Commission to the Ship's Company.' Lord Cranstoun was a famous officer and had seen service in the American War.

Like Cornwallis, who was also in the Channel fleet, he had commanded a ship of the line at the battle of the Saintes in 1782. He was known throughout the service for his 'Diligence, zeal, and activity'.

Howe was still hoping to be relieved, and in one of his letters to a friend he said: 'In the operations of next year I hope I shall have no concern.' Once again George III persuaded him to stay on a little longer, and he resigned himself to a service which he knew was altogether too arduous and rigorous for a man of his years and state of health.

A great event for the men of the *Bellerophon* was the arrival on board of the prize agent to distribute the prize money for *La Blonde* which had been taken during the Channel cruise of 1793; but as the *Blonde* was only a small ship none of the sums paid out could have been impressive.

It is a distressing fact that during the *Bellerophon*'s time in harbour at the end of 1794 there were recurrent floggings for insolence, neglect of duty, drunkenness, bringing liquor on board, and fighting. The very last entry for 1794 on the 31st December runs: 'Punished John McCawley with 24 lashes for drawing his bayonet at Mr Ramsey (Mate) when on shore duty.' It is probable that the men were war weary after nearly two years afloat and with very little to show for it; there was possibly also a larger proportion of ne'er do-wells among the crew than at the start of the war, who would be more likely to cause trouble. This must stand as an explanation of the mutinies which broke out in 1797 among the Channel and Nore Fleets which was ignored by people in authority. In fact in that very January there was a minor mutiny on board the *Culloden*, but this was speedily put down. The log of the *Bellerophon* records: '. . . At 10 sent 2 boats Manned and Armed with an officer in each on board H.M. Ship *Culloden* to attend the execution of the 5 men condemned for Mutiny.' The signs were there for those who could read them. If these things could happen under an admiral deservedly popular with the sailors, such as 'Black Dick', something must be seriously wrong with the 'wooden walls of old England.'

The year 1795 opened with the *Bellerophon* and the other ships at Spithead refitting and reprovisioning. The port once again provided a scene of activity as long boats plied between the warships at anchor and the shore. This was a long established service in the Navy and usually flowed pretty smoothly, but accidents could happen like the one recorded in the log for the 14th January when one of the ropes hoisting the beef on board the *Bellerophon* broke and 243 lb. of salt beef went to the bottom of the sea.

Howe returned from leave on the 16th January, hoisted his flag in the *Queen Charlotte*, and resumed command of the fleet. On the 18th Admiral Gardner hoisted his flag aboard the three-decker *Queen*. The signal was made from the flagship to put to sea, and at 10 a.m. on the 29th January the spectators on the shore were presented with the now familiar sight of the Channel Fleet sailing away. Howe made his way down the coast to Torbay where he anchored on the 2nd February. While moored in Torbay a violent gale blew up and the *Valiant* broke from her mooring and was driven out to sea. There was no panic among her crew and she returned safely to port the next day. The weather kept Howe in Torbay until the 14th February, but on that day the wind changed and moderated enough for him to take the fleet safely out.

Howe had decided on a cruise in the mouth of the Channel and he headed west. On the 17th the fleet passed Ushant and on the 18th Cape Finisterre was sighted. The course was altered on the 19th to southward and Cape Balem was passed by 'SE. $\frac{1}{4}$ E. 20 leagues' on the 20th. The frigate *Thalia* captured a French brig on the 21st and brought her into the fleet. Fresh gales on the 22nd caused the *Canada* to lose her main topmast and to bring to for repairs. The fleet had now altered course for the NE. and the position at noon on the 22nd was 47° 31′ N., 8° 30′ W. In view of the state of the weather Howe decided on the 22nd to sail for Spithead and the fleet anchored there on the 26th.

In the course of a rather lengthy stay at Spithead few things of interest happened. On the 8th March the *Prince of Wales*, the new three-decker launched in 1794, went out on her first commission. Accompanying her were the *Russell*, *Hector*, *Thunderer*, *Culloden*, *Marlborough*, and *Minotaur*—the *Prince of Wales* being a 98 and all the rest of the squadron 74s. Two captured French frigates were brought in by the frigates of Admiral Colpoy's squadron on the 16th, and another French prize was brought in by the *Niger* on the 19th April. The 24th April saw one of the most famous ships of the Navy with one of its most famous admirals ready to sail. It was the *Victory* with Admiral Lord Hood aboard, bound for the Mediterranean where he was Commander-in-Chief. He had been home to remonstrate with the Admiralty about the weakness of the fleet under his command. His mission had not been successful and he was preparing to sail back with Admiral Man and only a meagre reinforcement. He felt constrained to remonstrate once more with the Admiralty and his manner was even more blunt than before. Earl Spencer, the First Lord, on encountering this side of Hood's nature, ordered him to strike his flag and come on shore and the squadron sailed without him. Thus the fleet in the Mediterranean was deprived of possibly the greatest admiral of his day, and the feelings of the Mediterranean Fleet were expressed by the captain of the *Agamemnon*: 'Oh miserable Board of Admiralty. They have forced the first officer in the Service away from his command. His zeal, his activity for the honour and benefit of his King and Country are not abated. Upward of seventy, he possesses the mind of forty. . . .' The man who expressed these feelings was Captain Horatio Nelson, between whom and Lord Hood there existed the warmest feelings and confidence. Hood was never employed at sea again but lived to the ripe age of ninety-two, finally dying at Greenwich in 1816.

With the departure of the *Victory* to sea and the retirement of Lord Hood, Spithead resumed its normal activities—that is, until the 1st May when an event occurred which could have endangered the whole of the Channel Fleet. That day the *Boyne* caught fire while anchored in the harbour. Fire was the greatest danger of wooden ships for it could so easily get out of control and spread to the surrounding vessels; therefore when a fire was reported aboard the *Boyne* every ship in Spithead sent boats to help fight the blaze, the *Bellerophon* among them. Her crew were evacuated when it was seen that despite the combined efforts of the fleet the fire was increasing, and all ships to leeward of the burning ship got under way as quickly as possible to escape the blast when the fire reached the powder magazine. The fire on the *Boyne* burnt all through the night of the 1st-2nd May, but at around 1.30 a.m. she went adrift and grounded on the Spit. 'At $\frac{1}{2}$ past 1 the *Boyne* went adrift, at 4 took ground on the Spit sand, at $\frac{1}{2}$ past 5 blew up. All the ships came in and anchored again at Spithead.'

With the destruction of the *Boyne* the fleet resumed its comparatively calm existence while it waited to put to sea. On the 4th May the *Bellerophon* had its bottom scraped.

Even port life could be hazardous for the seamen of His Majesty's Navy. The entry for 16th May reads: 'At ½ past 10 Joseph Scott Seaman fell overboard and was drowned.' It was surprising that many officers of the Navy and an even greater number of the men could not swim. For a service which was to spend such a great amount of time at sea the proportion of swimmers to non-swimmers remained surprisingly high.

Action came at last for the *Bellerophon* on the 26th May when she was ordered to join a squadron under Admiral the Honourable William Cornwallis which was to watch the ports of the French coast during the coming operations in Quiberon Bay. The area assigned to the squadron was Lorient, Belleisle, and part of the Bay of Biscay. The squadron consisted of the following ships: *Royal Sovereign*, '100' (flagship); *Bellerophon*, *Mars*, *Triumph*, and *Brunswick*, all 74s; and the frigates *Phaeton* and *Pallas*, later joined by the *Kingfisher*. The actual plan of the Government concerning Quiberon was to land a force of Royalists on the coast armed with British weapons and supplied with British money. In May 1795 an army of invasion was formed in Hampshire and invitations were sent out to all the émigrés in Europe to join it. Rather unwisely, the Government even allowed a certain number of French prisoners to join the army on promising that they would support the Royalist cause. It did not supply any troops of its own, but it undertook to escort the expedition across the Channel to Quiberon Bay. The reason for choosing Quiberon Bay was the attachment of the Breton peasants in the area to the royal cause.

On the 17th June an advance guard of 4,000 men with arms for 20,000 more left Southampton and sailed for Quiberon Bay. Its escort was provided by a squadron under Sir John Borlase Warren, while the Channel Fleet under Lord Bridport (Sir Alexander Hood) made a sweep in the Channel. On the 20th they encountered the French fleet and took three prizes and chased the rest back to port. The landing itself was an initial success and they took the fort of Quiberon. The French acted promptly and sent General Hoche to put down the revolt in the west.

The Royalist leaders quarrelled among themselves and with the local patriots, and the result was disaster. On the 19th July the Republicans took the fort of Quiberon, some said by treachery, and destroyed or captured the entire Royalist force. Only the leader of the Royalists, the Comte de Puisaye, and a handful of followers escaped to the waiting British ships. The converted French prisoners soon showed their real colours. Out of this miserable story of bungling, treachery, procrastination, and sloth comes one of the most gallant naval actions of the entire war if not in the entire history of naval warfare.

The *Bellerophon*, in company with the other ships of the squadron, had sailed from Spithead on the 30th May. It is a mystery why Lord Bridport, who was now in command of the Channel Fleet, did not sail while the French fleet was known to be concentrated at Brest. As it was, he did not sail until ten days later and endangered Cornwallis's squadron. The French had an excellent intelligence operating in the ports of England and probably knew in advance of the sailing of Cornwallis's squadron, if not of the objective of the entire expedition.

On the 1st June, the anniversary of the great battle which had gained for the *Bellerophon* her reputation among the Fleet, she was at sea once more. On that day she sighted and hailed four of the frigates of the squadron of Sir John Borlase Warren, who had been allotted the job of escorting the transports of the forthcoming expedition. The squadron proceeded down Channel under light and fresh breezes, making in the direction of Ushant, and by noon on the 4th Ushant was sighted from the mastheads of the look-out frigates. A strange sail was seen on the 7th June and the squadron went after it with the *Phaeton* well out ahead. The *Phaeton* soon made the signal that the chase was an enemy and Cornwallis recalled the frigate to the squadron. The pursuit continued throughout the day and it was not until the next day that the British had got near enought to see that the chase was in fact a French squadron of three of the line, six frigates, a brig, and a cutter. With the distance between them closing fast, the admiral made the signal for the ships to engage as they came up with the enemy. Fortunately for the French the shoals of Belleisle were near at hand and to save themselves they ran in amongst them, a thing which Cornwallis could not do without a competent pilot on board. The log of the *Bellerophon* records:

. . . ¼ past 2 enemy got round inside of Belleisle and came to anchor. Saw 10 sail of pendants at anchor before they went in, at 20 minutes past 2 shortened sail and hauled the wind as per signal.

In his own dispatch describing the incident Cornwallis says:

As we came in with the land several large ships were seen under sail which proved to be a French squadron consisting of 3 line of Battle Ships, 6 Frigates, a Brig, Sloop and Cutter; some of them were at first standing off the shore but unfortunately the wind was fair for them to get into Belleisle Road where I saw several large ships at anchor. We had got very near the enemy's ships and I had hopes at first we should have got up with them before they could have reached their port, and I made the signal for the ships to form for their mutual support and engage the enemy as they came up. The *Phaeton* fired several shots which the Battle Ships returned from their sterns.

Having chased the French squadron into port, Cornwallis turned out to sea once more. Another set of sails sighted that afternoon proved to be two frigates escorting a convoy of twelve or fourteen sail of merchantmen. Cornwallis at once signalled the chase and steered to the south of Belleisle. This time he was more successful and eight of the convoy were taken, the rest saved themselves by running in among the shoals of Belleisle and making their way to port.

Two more prizes were brought in the next day by *Pallas* and *Kingfisher*, and the squadron's 'bag' was beginning to look quite respectable. So far the cruise had been a great success; ten prizes had been taken, a French squadron chased into port, and a convoy scattered. Heading north-west in the teeth of a gale, the prize being towed by the *Bellerophon* broke loose on the 10th in the early morning. It was fixed, but by 5.30 a.m. the tow had parted again and the sea was now running very high. The tow was not refixed until the 11th when Cornwallis decided to send the prizes back to England. He escorted them across the Channel and then returned to Ushant leaving the *Kingfisher* to accompany them their last few miles into port.

The weather was still very rough and the *Brunswick* was seen to be missing from the squadron on the 12th. Some fears were entertained for her safety as it was known that she did not sail as well as she should, but fortunately she rejoined the squadron on the following day. For the next three days the squadron cruised between Belleisle and Ushant but the seas

remained clear of enemy ships. It was not until the 16th that
the signal was made for a strange sail in sight and later for an
enemy fleet. The first sighting was made at 9 a.m. by the outlying frigate *Phaeton*.

... at 9 made the signal for a Fleet ESE at 25 minutes past 9 the *Phaeton*
made the signal for the fleet in sight to be an enemy and in superior force.

Cornwallis records the sighting as follows:

... on the 16th in the morning ... I sent the *Phaeton* and the *Bellerophon*
to follow and support her, both these ships having pilots on board. At
10 the *Phaeton* made me a signal for seeing a fleet ahead and afterwards
that they were of superior force.

A discrepancy will be noticed between the time stated in the
log of the *Bellerophon* and the time noted by Cornwallis in his
dispatch.

It was in fact the Brest fleet which had been sighted.
Villaret-Joyeuse had heard of the appearance of a British
squadron on the coast of France near Belleisle and was
alarmed at the damage they were doing to trade. He put to sea
with the whole of the Brest fleet to aid the ships moored at
Belleisle and to ease the danger of the British squadron to
local trade. He had found the Belleisle ships safe and was
returning to Brest with his force when he encountered
Cornwallis. Cornwallis had been half-way across the Channel
when Villaret-Joyeuse arrived at Brest and the two admirals
had missed each other, but now Cornwallis had returned to
the area and it was while he was sailing on his mission that he
encountered Villaret-Joyeuse.

The meeting was equally surprising to both admirals, as
each believed the other's force to be out of the area. As soon
as the frigate had reported the enemy to be in sight Cornwallis
signalled for their strength, thinking that they might be only a
small detachment of the French fleet which he could engage
and destroy. 'I enquired by signal their force; He [Captain
Stopford of the *Phaeton*] answered 13 sail of the line, 14
frigates and 2 Brigs and a cutter. In all 30 sail.'

Villaret-Joyeuse, on the sighting of the British squadron,
had ordered his fleet to split into two divisions. One to go to
the north and one to go to the southward to cut off the British.
This manoeuvre was seen from the deck of the *Bellerophon* and

duly reported to Cornwallis aboard the *Royal Sovereign*. Night fell on the two fleets and Cornwallis continued on his course. In his great cabin on the *Royal Sovereign* Cornwallis was doing some hard thinking. The enemy was obviously out in force, and that force was too great for his squadron to engage successfully. The only thing to do was to run before them and try to lead them on to the British fleet which was now at sea under Lord Bridport.

When the enemy was first sighted Cornwallis had been resting in his cabin suffering from an attack of gout, but as soon as the size of the force had been reported he came on deck and cheered the crew of the flagship with his remarks about not running away from any Frenchman! He also knew that two of the ships of his squadron were not good sailers, and these two, the *Bellerophon* and the *Brunswick*, could not be sacrificed to save the others. Both had been fast sailers during the operations of the previous year, but since then both had spent some time in the dockyards and had become sluggish— no doubt because the ballast had been wrongly trimmed. Whatever the cause, the fact now was that if it became a race for life against the French these two ships would be the first to drop behind. That was unacceptable to Cornwallis: they would all be saved or all go down together. During the night he called Cranstoun on board and asked him to lighten his ship as much as possible, and he did the same with the captain of the *Brunswick*. Both captains returned to their ships and put work in hand which could make all the difference between life and death for them in the operations of the following day. The log of the *Bellerophon* describes the events of the night and early morning as follows:

A.M. set all the carpenters to work, cut up the Launch and threw her overboard to clear Main Deck, cut 2 Bower anchors from the bows to lighten the ship. At daylight saw the French Fleet coming up very fast in 3 Divisions, the Weather Divisions nearly abreast consisting of 3 ships of the line and 5 frigates, Centre Division of 6 ships of the line and 4 frigates and Lee Division of 4 ships of the line, 5 frigates, 2 Brigs, and 2 Cutters. Cleared the ship for action. Started 16 tons of water in the Main Hold to lighten the ship, at 7 went to quarters, served Bread, Cheese and Wine to the Ship's Company at Quarters.

The *Bellerophon* and the rest of the squadron were now cleared and ready for action. It is remarkable that very high spirits prevailed in the ships at that moment, the crews cheering each other all along the line. Morale was high and the ships were in a state of preparedness: Cornwallis and his captains could do no more until they saw what the French moves were likely to be.

Cornwallis intended to let his two fastest ships remain astern of the *Royal Sovereign* while the two slowest went ahead. The two ships astern were the *Triumph* and *Mars* and the two ahead were the *Bellerophon* and the *Brunswick*. He had also sent the frigate *Phaeton* ahead to look for the Channel Fleet which should be in those waters, giving orders that if no fleet was sighted she was to signal a 'fake' sighting and make the appropriate move back towards the squadron as if leading in the British fleet. It will be seen later that these instructions of Cornwallis were paramount in saving his squadron.

The chase was now on in earnest and the French were slowly coming within range. Recounting the events of the morning so far he said in his dispatch to the Admiralty afterwards:

They were seen in the morning [of the 17th] before it was daylight upon both quarters of the squadron. I had called and sent to the ships in the evening when it was almost calm that I meant to lead during the night the better to accomplish any movement of tacking or altering the course (if a favourable opportunity should offer) without signal.

It was my intention to place the *Brunswick* and *Bellerophon* (the two worse sailing ships) ahead of me, but finding the *Brunswick* could not get ahead of me without stopping the whole I desired Lord Charles Fitzgerald to form astern. The *Bellerophon* (which ship also sailed very ill) got past me at last upon my yawing to fire at the enemy.

The *Bellerophon* had indeed passed but was having a hard job to stay there and was carrying every sail she could set to give her more speed.

The French had closed to within firing range of the *Mars*, the rear ship of Cornwallis's line, and just after 9 a.m. the firing commenced on both sides. The action was observed from the deck of the *Bellerophon*:

At 12 minutes past 9 the Enemy's van began firing on the *Mars* in the rear of our line which the *Mars* returned. At the same time the Admiral and the squadron hoisted their colours.

In his dispatch Cornwallis describes the opening of the action:

At nine in the morning one of the French line of Battle Ships began to fire upon the *Mars*. Their frigates were ranged up abreast of us to windward except one which kept to leeward and ran up upon the Larboard Quarter of the *Mars* then yawed and fired which was frequently repeated. This was the only frigate that attempted anything; the line of Battle Ships came up in succession, and a tearing fire with intervals was kept up the whole day.

While this was going on the *Bellerophon* was still gamely trying to pass the flagship and lead the squadron. She finally achieved this just before 9.30 when the *Royal Sovereign* yawed to fire at the enemy. As she struggled ahead the crew let Cornwallis know that they were not disheartened by the odds against them: 'Cheered the Admiral as we passed under his lee, 47 minutes past 11 The Admiral and Squadron began to fire stern chasers on the enemy.' Cornwallis noted the cheers and was 'pleased at the spirit manifested by all on board as she passed me'.

The action had become more heated by 11 a.m. with the three rear British ships engaging the French as they came up in succession. Although the *Bellerophon* was out of the firing she was not having an easy time trying to stay ahead of the line: 'Hove overboard to lighten the ship 32 Bags of Bread, 4 Casks of Beef, 4 Cannonades with carriages and different kinds of shot.' When a captain began to throw his armament overboard to lighten the ship it meant that he really was in a bad position; there was not much left once one had started to throw guns and ammunition away! This did, however, have the effect of lightening the ship considerably and she now managed to stay ahead of the line more easily. At the rear of the line the brunt of the fighting was borne by the *Mars* and the *Triumph* and a large amount of powder and shot was consumed aboard those ships during the course of the fight. The French were not pressing really hard, a fact which amazed many of the officers in the British ships. It was the opinion that a little more determination on the part of the French van could have cut off the rear ships of the British line, and this would have meant Cornwallis having to come to the rescue with the remainder of his ships and meeting his final defeat. Ahead of the fleet the *Phaeton* was scanning the horizon hopefully for a sign of the British fleet, but no sail marked the horizon. Her captain was in rather a quandary as to just when he should try the ruse which Cornwallis had explained to him.

The rear ships of the British line were giving as good as they got and were inflicting much damage on the two leading French ships.

At 1 the second ship in their van opened her fire on the rear of our Squadron. 30 minutes past 1 the enemy's Van ship lost her Main Topgallant masts by the fire from the *Mars*, she sheered off and went astern, her second astern coming up and opened a brisk fire on the *Mars* starboard quarter.

The *Mars* had been engaging the enemy for nearly four hours and was now seriously damaged and beginning to drop astern of the rest of the squadron. When they noticed this the French saw a chance to take her and redeem the day. Villaret-Joyeuse detached four of his line-of-battle ships to go after the *Mars* at about 4 p.m. when the position for the *Mars* was beginning to look a little grim. Cornwallis, watching from the quarter-deck of the *Royal Sovereign*, saw this movement and decided to take his flagship down to the aid of the crippled *Mars*.

In the evening they made a show of a more serious attack upon the *Mars* (which ship had gotten a little to leeward) and obliged me to bear up for Her support; this was their last effort, if anything they did can deserve that appellation.

Thus, in this matter of fact way, Cornwallis dismisses one of the crucial points of the action. Throughout his whole dispatch he gives the credit to his captains and takes none of it for himself.

The sight of the three-decked *Royal Sovereign* bearing down upon them relatively undamaged was too much for the French ships, for they ran back into line and the *Mars* was saved. In carrying out this manoeuvre Cornwallis hailed the *Brunswick* and *Bellerophon* to support him:

The Admiral hailed the *Bellerophon* and desired us to keep our station a little on his weather bow, the Admiral made the signal to the *Mars* to alter course to starboard. The Admiral at the same time bore round up gave the enemy his broadside and ran down to leeward with the van ships of our line to support the *Mars* and brought her in Closer Order in the Line of Battle. The enemy at the same time was bearing down with 4 heavy ships of their Van to cut off the *Mars* but by this evolution totally defeated their intentions.

The French, disheartened by their failure to capture the *Mars*, fell back a little, and ceased to press their attack at all. The French ships ceased to fire on the British about 7.15 p.m.; they had spotted the *Phaeton* on the horizon with signal flags flying, and although they could not read the signals they guessed what they meant—that the British fleet was at sea and was bearing down upon the scene of action. The *Phaeton* first of all signalled three ships in sight, then five, and then nine; finally she let go her topgallant sheets which was the recognized signal for a whole fleet in sight. At this the French began to retreat:

10 minutes past 7 the firing ceased, 23 minutes past 7 part of the enemy's fleet shortened sail and shortly afterwards the whole of the enemy's fleet tacked and stood to the eastward. At sun set the enemy's fleet hull down at the NE.

Lord Bridport had not arrived: it was only the captain of the *Phaeton* playing the card which Cornwallis had ordered as a last resort. The move had fooled Villaret-Joyeuse as Cornwallis had hoped it would and the squadron was safe, with the French making their way back to Brest as fast as they could.

The two days of the 16th and 17th June 1795 are notable in the Royal Navy for two reasons. First they are a supreme example of the right way to handle a fleet when facing overwhelming odds, and secondly they represent an action and an admiral almost unknown today. Cornwallis was the brother of the commander at Yorktown and rose to a high position in the Navy. He was responsible for the very efficient blockade of Brest in the Napoleonic War, but he never had another chance to engage the enemy's main fleet in action. He was a good example of the unlucky admiral whose associates had all the actions and he all the grinding work of the blockade.

Cornwallis was doubly lucky that the *Phaeton* signalled when she did, for just as the frigate gave the signal for a fleet in sight several small sails were sighted from the mastheads of the leading French ships, and this, together with the *Phaeton*'s signal, decided the enemy to break off the action. The sails sighted were in fact those of a merchant convoy bound for England. French officers were afterwards positive that it had been the sails of Lord Bridport's fleet that they had sighted.

The casualties in the British ships were surprisingly low.

In the *Mars*, the main ship engaged, there were only twelve men wounded and none killed. The damage in the *Triumph* was even less. The French had suffered little damage or casualties but their morale and confidence had deteriorated. They had failed to destroy a British squadron of vastly inferior force which had been in a bad position. The effect on the French navy must have been the same as that which the escape of Moore's army from Corunna fourteen years later was to have on the French army.

On the British side there was every reason to be jubilant and confident. Apart from the fact that an inferior force should never have been allowed to cruise in waters in which the French fleet was likely to be met, the Navy had come out of the whole situation remarkably well. For this the chief praise must go to Cornwallis, an admiral who has never had his proper worth appreciated. It always seemed his fate to meet the enemy while in inferior force and to have to extricate himself from tricky and dangerous situations while fighting rearguard actions. The efficiency of his blockade of Brest later in the Napoleonic War was marvellous. He refused honours offered him for his action of June 1795 as he felt that he had never earned them. It was his belief that, given a reasonable force, he could have defeated an enemy fleet, but for him the chance never came. His dispatch to the Secretary of the Admiralty is a model of generosity and humility. It contains these remarks on the *Bellerophon*, which ship took little part in the action:

The *Bellerophon* being nearly under the same circumstances [a slow sailer like the *Brunswick*, to which he had just referred] I was glad to keep her in some measure as a reserve; having reason at first to suppose there would be full occasion for the utmost exertions of us all, and being rather ahead of me was not able to fire much, I considered that ship as a treasure in store, having heard of Her former achievements and observing the spirit manifested by all on board when she passed me, joined to the activity and zeal shewn by Lord Cranstoun during the whole of the cruise.

This tribute to a ship which was virtually unemployed during that action, through no fault of the admiral or her captain, was extremely generous to say the very least.

Admiral Cornwallis and his captains were all thanked by both Houses of Parliament, Cornwallis refused a knighthood from George III because he thought the had not earned it. By special order of Cornwallis himself all the ordinary seamen of the fleet were created A.B.'s. Speaking of the spirit of his men after the battle he said:

> It was the greatest pleasure I ever received to see the spirit manifested by the men who instead of being castdown at seeing 30 sail of the enemy's ships attacking our little squadron, were in the highest spirits imaginable. I do not mean the *Royal Sovereign* alone; the same spirit was shown in all the ships as they came near me, and although circumstanced as we were, we had no great reason to complain of the conduct of the enemy, yet our men could not help repeatedly expressing their contempt of them. Could common prudence have allowed me to let loose their valour, I hardly know what might not have been accomplished by such men.

Cornwallis hoped that Bridport with the Channel Fleet might meet with the French while they were still at sea, and these hopes were realized. On the 23rd June Bridport with fourteen sail of the line encountered Villaret-Joyeuse and Admiral Bruix with twelve. The fleets met in the region of the Île de Groix, and Villaret-Joyeuse, seeing himself outnumbered, turned back for Brest. Bridport ordered a general chase, the ships to engage the enemy as they came up with them. After a short chase the fastest British ships were within firing range of the slower French ships. No amount of signals on the part of Villaret-Joyeuse could make the faster ships of his van tack and come to the aid of the rear. The British managed to take three ships, the last finally hauling down its flag when in sight of the haven of the Île de Groix. Bridport then decided to call off the chase and the rest of the French escaped into port.

It seems incredible when we think of the later victories of the war, culminating in Trafalgar, that an admiral with fourteen sail of the line, many of them unengaged, should let an opponent with only nine sail of the line calmly make his escape. It should be remembered that tradition was still a dominant factor in the naval fighting of the early Revolutionary War, and for 200 years it had been customary for admirals to secure their prizes at the end of the day. In the minds of men like Bridport it died hard; individually brave and fairly well liked in the Fleet, he was never a dashing admiral of the type of Nelson, Duncan, and Jervis. What contemporary public and service opinion thought of his action can be judged by the fact that he retained command of the Channel Fleet until 1799 when he retired. Only ten years later Sir Robert Calder was court martialled for nearly the same offence, i.e. failing to press his attack to the utmost, when he encountered the combined fleets of France and Spain as they were returning from the West Indies. At that engagement Calder was inferior in numbers to the allies and he was engaging in a fog. In Bridport's case he was engaging on a calm sea an enemy inferior in numbers and already running away. Ten years was to bring new standards to the Navy, and the tactics of men such as Nelson, Duncan, Jervis, and Saumarez were to revolutionize the war at sea.

After the battle, in accordance with his orders, Cornwallis decided to lead his squadron back to Cawsand Bay. Progress was rather slow across Channel and the ships did not anchor in the bay until the 25th June. On the 26th the shipwrights from Plymouth dockyard came on board the ships of the squadron to assess the damage and to refit the ships. On the same day the French prisoners taken from the captured merchantmen were landed in Plymouth and taken to the local jail. Those landed from the *Bellerophon* totalled only nine. While the ships were refitting they were also reprovisioning as it was Cornwallis's intention to sail again as soon as the state of his ships allowed. It was on the 5th July that the last ship was ready and Cornwallis gave the signal to put to sea.

The following day the squadron was joined at sea by His Majesty's brig *Orestes* with dispatches from the Admiralty including a letter from the Secretary of the Board of Admiralty, Evean Nepean, congratulating Cornwallis on his achievement of the 17th June. Ushant was sighted at noon of the 7th July, and shortly after the signal was made for strange sails in sight. Cornwallis flew the *Bellerophon*'s signal to investigate. The chase proved to be two French frigates and a convoy of small vessels working into Brest. After a short chase Cornwallis called off his ships and turned away. Another sighting was made on the 8th July, and this proved to be a French frigate sailing in the SE. Once again the signal was given to chase, but after a short while the wind dropped and boats had to be lowered from the ships to tow the frigates *Phaeton* and *Kingfisher* from under the lee of the land. In the afternoon the wind came again, the boats were taken up and the chase continued. The French frigate was holding her own and finally made her way between the Pont du Raz and the Pont de Saint. Seeing no chance of catching her before she reached Brest, Cornwallis called off his frigates and stood to the northward for the Île de Groix.

The signal was made for a fleet in sight early in the morning of the 9th July, and later for the Channel Fleet. Bridport was cruising in the region of the Île de Groix and Belleisle when he met Cornwallis. As soon as the Channel Fleet was in sight Cornwallis hove to and waited to join it.

Two British frigates were sent into the coastal waters around the Île de Groix to investigate and they were fired upon by the forts on the coast, but no apparent damage was done as far as could be seen from the deck of the *Bellerophon*. This was on the 10th July, and on the 11th heavy firing was heard in the morning in the direction of ENE. but nothing was sighted.

An open boat was sighted on the 14th July and on coming closer it was seen to contain seven men. They were Spaniards, the crew of a merchantman which had gone down in the entrance to the Channel a few days before. They were taken on board the *Bellerophon* and looked after. At this time Spain was no longer on the side of the allies of the First Coalition and was ostensibly neutral.

That same day another sail was sighted and chased, and this proved to be two British frigates escorting a convoy of transports containing French Royalists for the Quiberon Bay operation. After hailing the frigates Bridport stood to the southward and on the 19th July Belleisle was sighted. He then turned for the Île de Groix and cruised between there and Belleisle until the 12th September. During this period the operations at Quiberon were dragging on to their dismal failure with the embarkation of the remaining troops on board the British transports in the bay. The Government hopes of a rising in the west were dashed and they remained so for the rest of the war. Although there were further Royalist risings they were never viewed with anything but suspicion from then on, except of course by Dundas who was looking for opportunities to throw in Britain's slender army to topple the republicans.

On the 12th September Admiral Harvey joined the fleet with a squadron of ships of the line and a large number of transports. The transports went into the bay to evacuate the last remnant of the Royalist army, a task very skilfully accomplished by the Navy and entirely creditable to the people who directed it. The same day Bridport in the *Royal George* headed part of his fleet back to England. The ships which parted company were the *Royal George, Royal Sovereign, Queen, Sans Pareil* (a prize of the First of June taken into the Navy), *Invincible, Formidable, Valiant, Phaeton,* and *Pallas.* The *Bellerophon* herself parted company with the *Brunswick* on the 13th September and headed for England, sighting and boarding several vessels on the way, most of which were neutral and the majority American. She moored in Carrick Roads, Falmouth, on the 17th September in the late evening. At once she was engaged in the task of taking on stores of fresh beef and other necessaries and the water around her was crowded with heavily laden longboats and bumboats. She sailed from there with a fair wind on the 20th September and made her way eastwards up the Channel to Spithead where the rest of the fleet was anchored.

It was decided that the *Bellerophon* needed a complete refit and that she should be taken into the inner harbour. This was done on the 11th October when she was warped alongside a sheerhulk. Her masts and rigging were removed and this was followed by her shingle ballast. With all excess weight gone she was hauled into dock on the 27th October. Her crew were distributed about several vessels which were also refitting in the harbour, to help the regular crews in their work. The dockyard crews were soon at work on the *Bellerophon* and the ship was a scene of busy activity. All her masts and rigging had to be replaced and this was done by the 12th November, after which her ballast was put back and she was brought alongside the sheerhulk again for the final touches. A pilot was then put on board to guide her out of the inner harbour. The men of the *Bellerophon* suffered a rather personal loss when a 20-gallon puncheon of rum dropped from the slings as it was being hoisted on board and went to the bottom at Spithead!

The ship re-anchored in Spithead completely refitted and as good as new on the 26th November. Here she stayed until the 5th February 1796, and it will be seen that Bridport was pursuing the policy of Howe in keeping the majority of his big ships in port while he sent squadrons to cruise off the French coast. These squadrons were relieved after a certain period and returned to port. He hoped in this manner to preserve the health of his big ships and to be ready to put to sea as soon as one of his roving squadrons reported the French as at sea or likely to be at sea. The discipline in the Channel fleet was far easier than that of the Mediterranean fleet, and a later toast in the ships' wardrooms was: 'May the discipline of the Mediterranean fleet never be applied to the Channel fleet'. When Sir John Jervis took over a few years later, the officers of the fleet, who expected to be in port every winter so that they could visit their families, were rudely awakened!

The signal was given for the *Bellerophon* to go down to St Helen's Road on the 5th February which she did in company with the *Queen, Sans Pareil,* and *Aquilon*; joined later by the *Royal George, Triumph, Valiant, Commerce de Marseille* (a French 120-gun ship taken from Toulon by Lord Hood in 1793 when the port had surrendered to his fleet, she was so large that no dock at Portsmouth would take her), and *Colossus.*

The *Bellerophon* was sent from St Helen's Road on the 10th February in a squadron under the command of Admiral Gardner to escort a convoy. The escort was made up of seven ships of the line, one of 50 guns, and the convoy of seventy-four sail of merchantmen. Foul winds forced the convoy and escort to turn back to Spithead on the 12th February and they re-anchored on the 13th. The winds remained foul for the next ten days and the squadron and its charge were unable to sail until the 23rd February. During the time at Spithead a second convoy had been added to the first and the escort now had under its charge 140 sail of merchantmen. The Mediterranean convoy parted company from the rest on the 28th February, and the West Indian convoy left on the 1st March when in a position 160 leagues SW. of St Mary's Western Isle. With the convoy gone, Gardner headed his fleet to the region of Scilly preparatory to returning to Spithead. Scilly was passed on the 13th March, and the Lizard on the 19th with the wind blowing ESE.

The *Bellerophon* dropped anchor at Spithead on the 27th March. Her captain, Lord Cranstoun, had recently been suffering in health and had asked to be relieved of his command. On the 17th April Lord Cranstoun resigned and his place was taken by Captain John Loring who was to be acting captain until the Admiralty appointed their nominee.

Within a week of Loring's appointment the *Bellerophon* had been given another spell of convoy duty and she moved to St Helen's Road with the *Fame* to escort a convoy of ten sail to sea. Before the convoy and its escort could sail they were joined by the frigate *Druid*, and the three warships finally escorted the convoy to sea on the 26th April. The wind was fair and they made good time down the Channel, steering a south-westerly course to take the convoy past the hostile ports on the Bay of Biscay. On the 1st May the *Druid* and the convoy parted from the *Bellerophon* and her consort and the two warships turned away in the direction of Belleisle and the Île de Groix. After a short cruise in that area they reset their course for Spithead.

She was joined on the 24th by the ships of Admiral Colpoys's squadron, and the squadron, comprising seven of the line and two frigates, escorted a convoy of East Indiamen to sea on the 27th June. The wind was foul for a quick trip down the Channel, so the convoy was forced to anchor at Culver Cliffs that same day. The wind changed on the 28th and the convoy and its escort put to sea again on the morning breeze. Once they had passed Scilly the ships steered a SW. course for the region of Cape Finisterre, and on the 3rd July they were sixty-seven leagues SE. of that cape. The *Bellerophon* and *Alexander* parted company with the convoy and its escort on the 8th July and turned back for Scilly. With all sails set they soon passed Scilly and anchored in Torbay on the 19th July. After five days there they sailed again on the 24th July and made their way back across the Channel to Colpoys's squadron. They were forced to anchor in Cawsand Bay on the 25th August for nearly ten days, then finally joined the squadron, which was cruising off Ushant and Scilly. Admiral Colpoys now had a total of nine sail of the line under his command as well as frigates. A convoy had been sighted on the 16th August bound from the West Indies to London under the escort of the *Africa* of 64 guns, and Colpoys joined his force to this for a short time before turning away once more off Ushant. On the 23rd August a squadron of four frigates under the redoubtable Sir Edward Pellew was sighted and hailed. Pellew was to win fame later in the war for the action in which his frigates drove the French 74, the *Droits de l'Homme*, ashore a total wreck.

The new captain took over command of the *Bellerophon* on the 10th September, and his commission was read to the assembled ship's company while the *Bellerophon* was moored in Cawsand Bay. He was Captain Henry d'Esterre Darby, an Irishman and nephew of Admiral Darby, one of the commanders of the Channel fleet during the American War. His previous commands had all been frigates, and the *Bellerophon* was his first ship of the line. He came to her with a reputation as a disciplinarian, but he also had a reputation for fairness, and the number of floggings in the log noticeably decreases. On the 22nd September he came very near to never taking the *Bellerophon* to sea at all. He was invited to dine on the frigate *Amphion* with her captain Israel Pellew, the younger brother of the more famous Sir Edward Pellew, who had also invited Captain Swaffield. Captain Darby was rather late arriving, and Pellew and Swaffield decided to begin without him. Just as a servant was bringing in the first course there was a violent explosion. Both men were blown out of their chairs, Pellew scrambled to his feet and cried, 'The ship is blown up!' and rushed out to the quarter gallery. There a piece of falling wreckage struck him on the head and he was knocked senseless into the water. Another two lucky survivors were the Marine who was guarding the captain's door and who had just put his bayonet under his arm when the explosion occurred [he was found on the deck of the next ship with the bayonet still under his arm]; and the first lieutenant, who was blown straight through the stern windows into the sea. Swaffield and the servant were killed by the blast and were found later when the ship was raised.

What had happened was the forward magazine had blown up, killing over 300 people. The *Amphion* was split in half by the explosion and sank in a few minutes. Luckily Darby had not yet gone on board the frigate or he too might have been killed. An inquiry was held into the cause of the disaster, but Pellew was acquitted of any blame and was appointed to the command of another ship. His later career was only distinguished by his being captain of the *Conqueror* at the battle of Trafalgar and receiving the surrender of the French Commander-in-Chief, Admiral Villeneuve.

The *Bellerophon* left Cawsand Bay at 4.15 a.m. on the morning of the 17th October for Brest, and with a good wind Ushant was sighted by 8 p.m. that evening. She was part of a squadron under Admiral Colpoys whose duty it was to cruise in the vicinity of Brest to watch the port and to report the sailing of the French fleet there to Lord Bridport at Spithead. The squadron joined Sir Roger Curtis off Brest making a total of ten of the line, but Curtis left later the same day with seven of the line and two frigates, steering to the westward.

At this time the French were known to be preparing in Brest an expedition to sail for some unknown destination. Various guesses were made as to its possible goal, ranging from the Mediterranean to Portugal or Ireland. The main command had been given to the famous general Hoche, and the command of the sea forces to Villaret-Joyeuse. It was not a very happy union as Villaret-Joyeuse knew the condition of his ships and crews which General Hoche and the Directory in Paris did not.

The destination was Ireland which, as always, was in a very troubled state under the rule of Dublin Castle. The English had this one weak link in their armour of sea power, and the Directory meant to use it. Hoche had accepted the command with alacrity as it would give him a chance to outshine the rising star of the new general of the Republic in Italy, one Bonaparte. It was his idea to land 20,000 troops, which would give him numerical superiority without relying on the rising of the peasants which Irish agents had promised him. The English troops in Ireland were very few and of poor quality and certainly no match for the veterans of the French Army. To help overcome the British Navy he had sent for help to the North American squadron of Admiral Richery, the Toulon fleet, and the Spaniards. As it turned out, only one of these eventually arrived in Brest. The Spaniards never moved at all, the Toulon squadron arrived too late, and only two of Richery's ships were fit to make the trip to Ireland after their crossing of the Atlantic. The Toulon fleet was under Admiral Villeneuve who was later to command the combined fleet at Trafalgar.

Knowing the condition of his ships and crews, Villaret-Joyeuse was not very anxious for an operation which would almost certainly lead to a meeting with the British fleet. His idea, which was supported by the Minister of Marine in Paris, was to send some of his ships on a long cruise to the East Indian station. The long cruise, coupled with the good weather which might be reasonably expected, would give an opportunity of training his crews in the seamanship so essential for any schemes of the Directory for the invasion of England. The Minister in Paris was unable to stand up to the Directory, so he compromised that some of the fleet should go to the East Indies and the rest would go to Ireland. Villaret-Joyeuse was not satisfied, as he knew that the arrival of a superior French squadron in the East Indies would cause a panic in Britain, and therefore he did all that he could (under cover, as he could not act openly without losing his head) to delay the Irish expedition. Hoche was suspicious of his lukewarm attitude, and this, coupled with his personal dislike of Villaret-Joyeuse as a converted aristocrat, led him to force the admiral to resign his command of the Brest fleet. In his place was appointed Morard de Galles, an admiral more favourable to the Irish expedition but without Villaret-Joyeuse's ability. Hoche had a low opinion of the French Navy, which was to be shared by the succeeding generals of the Empire including Napoleon himself. Another who agreed with him was the Irish rebel Wolfe Tone, who was to sail with the expedition: in the pages of his private journal he is for ever damning and cursing the navy for their eternal delays.

The original date for the expedition to sail had been fixed for early autumn, but for various reasons, among them the non-arrival of the expected reinforcements, it was put back to the 1st November, and then finally to the middle of December. Admiral Richery's squadron did not reach Brest until the 11th December; out of the five ships which then arrived only two were found fit to make the crossing to Ireland and the expedition finally sailed on the 15th December.

Meanwhile the British squadron, including the *Bellerophon*, were cruising outside Brest. On the 20th December five ships were sighted which later proved to be five French Atlantic ships of the line bound for Brest. The signal was made for the *Bellerophon*, *Marlborough*, and *Impétueux* to chase. At this date these three ships were the only ships on station, as a storm in the middle of the month had blown Admiral Colpoys off station. He had chosen his cruising ground too far out and had in consequence been blown far out into the Atlantic.

During the storm the *Bellerophon, Marlborough*, and *Impétueux* had become separated from the main body. When the storm ceased they worked their way back to their station, expecting to find their squadron there, but no one was in sight. They also discovered that the Brest fleet had sailed and they had no idea in which direction. While the blockading squadron had been blown off station only three frigates had remained to watch the port. These were the squadron of Sir Edward Pellew, and Morard de Galles had driven them off so that the expedition could sail.

Pellew sent the *Phoebe* to report to Colpoys, who should have been in his position off Ushant, but when the *Phoebe* reached the rendezvous the squadron had gone, and the frigate did not find them until the 19th, nearly four days after the French had sailed. Meanwhile, with his other two frigates, the *Indefatigable* and *Révolutionnaire*, Pellew remained to watch the French expedition. He sent the *Révolutionnaire* to report to Bridport at Spithead and continued to shadow the French with his own frigate the *Indefatigable*.

At Spithead Bridport was having troubles of his own. He had half of his fleet at Spithead and half at St Helen's Roads. The wind was foul for getting out of St Helen's, but instead of signalling for all ships to go back to Spithead to sail from the other side of the Isle of Wight he sent the signal for the ships at Spithead to work down to join. It was a work of considerable difficulty, rather like struggling out of a narrow window when the door of the house was wide open! The attempt to get down to St Helen's was attended by disaster for the fleet: five of the three-decked ships collided or were otherwise damaged. The *Prince* had collided with the *Sans Pareil* and both had to be docked. The largest ship in the Navy, the *Ville de Paris* of 110 guns, had collided with the *Formidable* and both had to remain in port. Finally, to complete Bridport's cup of misery, the *Atlas* had run aground. The remainder, eight of the line, were, when all this was completed, still windbound at St Helen's.

Pellew was still watching the French fleet from a distance. Morard de Galles gave orders for the fleet to steer for the Passage du Raz so as to avoid meeting the British, whom he expected to be at sea off Brest. The Passage du Raz was a difficult stretch of water strewn with rocks and shoals, not to be attempted except under good conditions and with a pilot. The weather was blowing up rough and the French were not keeping good order owing to the poor quality of the officers and the inexperience of the men. Seeing this, Morard de Galles, who was on the frigate *Fraternité*, changed his mind, and seeing also that the British fleet was not in sight he cancelled his order to pass through the Passage du Raz. This cancellation was not seen or obeyed by all the ships because of the confusion due to the weather and the approach of darkness. Only six ships obeyed the signal, the rest held on their course for the Passage du Raz. Pellew seized his chance and stood in amongst the ships making for the passage, and followed them through the Iroise, firing coloured lights and signal guns. He was aided in his deception by the fact that the *Indefatigable* bore a considerable resemblance to a French frigate. The French ships were confused and any attempt on the part of de Galles to signal to his fleet only added to the confusion. As a result, the French 74 *Séduisant* ran on a rock and was wrecked.

With daylight Pellew withdrew and raced for Falmouth, hoping to find the fleet. The only ships he saw on his way across the Channel were the *Bellerophon* and her two companions, which had just been successful in diverting their chase from a course to Brest to the port of L'Orient. The ships they had been chasing were in fact the Toulon detachment under Villeneuve. Pellew continued on his way to Falmouth and the *Bellerophon* went on looking for Colpoys. In fact she came across the Channel fleet and joined it on the 22nd December.

After the confusion of the night of the 16th the French fleet could not reform and stood on for Ireland in three separate bodies each out of sight of the other. One of these sections under Admiral Bouvet was joined on the 19th December by a second, and it was decided to open the secret orders. These gave instructions to steer a little out into the Atlantic to avoid the British, and then to steer for Mizen Head where they might rendezvous with the rest of the expedition. With a force of thirty-five sail, fifteen of the line and twenty transports, this is what he did. Wolfe Tone was on one of the transports and he was very hopeful of making a landing in Bantry Bay. Unfortunately the wind changed while the armada was still outside the bay, and the secret orders had said that the fleet was to wait five days outside the bay for the missing section.

What was believed to be Mizen Head was sighted on the 21st, but it was in fact Dursey Island, which was on the western side of the bay while Mizen Head was on the eastern side. It would have been a comparatively simple task for the French to beat into the bay from the eastern side, but it was beyond their powers of seamanship to reach it from the west. Nevertheless Bouvet gave the order to try on the night of the 21st and the morning of the 22nd; but the task was hopeless with the ships continually crossing each other's paths and generally getting in each other's way. By nightfall on the 22nd only eight of the line and seven other vessels had got any nearer to the entrance to the bay. These had dropped anchor at Bear Island about twelve miles from the head of the bay. The remaining twenty ships were still under way and in hopeless confusion.

Gales prevented any further attempt on the 23rd, but on the 24th Bouvet decided to try to work his way in a little nearer with the force he had at his disposal, and to attempt a landing. The progress they made that day was less than before; Wolfe Tone said that the fleet had made hundreds of tacks but had not moved 100 yards in a straight line, and the ships were once again forced to anchor for the night. If the Channel fleet under Bridport had come along at this moment not one transport should have escaped and the expedition could have been entirely destroyed, but fortunately for Bouvet there was no sign of the British fleet. Another gale came up on the night of the 24th and continued throughout the day of the 25th, causing several ships to drag their anchors, including the flagship, and to be driven towards the shore. The admiral, seeing the danger, signalled the ships nearby to put to sea to save themselves, and by the next day only a few ships were left anywhere near the bay or Bear Island. At a council of war held on the 27th it was decided to abandon the attempt and to return to Brest. The few ships left near the bay hung on for a few more days, but in the end they too departed, with the exception of the *Droits de l'Homme*. Bouvet reached Brest on the 1st January 1797, and another section of his fleet reached port on the 12th. By the 14th January, thirty-five ships had returned to Brest, five ships had been lost by wreck, and six captured by the British cruisers. One was still outstanding, the *Droits de l'Homme* which had remained off the coast of

Ireland out of a sense of duty until the 5th January. On that day she had decided to return to Brest and set her course accordingly. Just over a week later, on the 13th January, she was found by Sir Edward Pellew in the *Indefatigable* accompanied by the *Amazon*. The sea was getting up and Pellew decided to engage, the frigates on each quarter of the battleship. Because the sea was so rough the French were unable to use their lower deck ports for fear of flooding the ship. Throughout the 13th Pellew kept up his fire on the big Frenchman, ably supported by the *Amazon*. On the morning of the 14th January land was sighted and it was discovered that all three ships were embayed in Audierne Bay with the rocks and breakers uncomfortably near. The *Indefatigable* managed to beat out of the bay, but the *Droits de l'Homme* ran aground and lay on her side on the bottom. The *Amazon* was not so favourably placed as the *Indefatigable* for beating out of the bay and she too ran aground, but, unlike the French ship which was overcrowded and undisciplined, her crew were saved although they were taken prisoner. The casualties in the *Droits de l'Homme* were 260 killed and wounded in action and 217 lost in the shipwreck, out of a total complement of about 1,300. This disaster made the name of Sir Edward Pellew even more familiar to the French than it already was.

Out at sea the *Bellerophon* had been cruising with the Channel Fleet, but seeing no sign of the French, Bridport had decided to return to port, which he did on the 2nd January anchoring at Spithead.

The three years described in this chapter had seen the *Bellerophon* employed in one fleet action and one chase, as well as upon the normal work of a ship of the Channel Fleet. Her commanders, Pasley, Hope, Cranstoun, Loring, and Darby, had conducted the ship in a distinguished manner and her reputation was high among the fleet where she was affectionately known as the 'Billy Ruff'n'. Soon she was to pass on to another theatre of war and even greater glory than she had won in the Channel.

6

The Battle of the Nile

WHILE the *Bellerophon* was moored in Cawsand Bay orders came for her to proceed to Ireland where a French landing was expected. As will have been seen in the previous chapter, the French attempt had already failed, and by the time the *Bellerophon* got to sea on 17th January most of the French were back in Brest. She finally cleared Cawsand Bay on the 18th and made sail to the west in company with the *Alfred* and *Edgar* (74s), *Santa Margarita* (frigate), and the cutter *Fox*. The weather for the first two days was very foggy with only occasional bright patches and soon fresh gales began to blow. Despite this the squadron made their way down channel and on the 3rd February were off Cork harbour asking for a pilot to lead them in. They moored there on the 4th and found already there the *Polyphemus* (64), flying the flag of Vice-Admiral Kingsmill, with several accompanying frigates.

With the news that the French alarm was definitely off, the squadron weighed and made sail again on the 14th February. As they were clearing the harbour a strange sail was sighted and the signal to chase was made. The pilot was hurriedly dropped and all sails were set. By the morning of the 15th it was established that the chase was a French privateer and that she appeared to be gaining on them in the light winds which then prevailed. When the wind worked up to gale force later the chase was abandoned, and the winds blew with such strength that the *Bellerophon* split her main topsail. Another was soon fitted and the squadron set course for Plymouth. Running before the wind they made good time to Plymouth and on the 17th February the squadron dropped anchor near Drake's Island.

On 2nd March, Lord Bridport took the Channel Fleet to sea for the spring cruise, but without the *Bellerophon*. Orders had come for her to join the Mediterranean fleet under Sir John Jervis. Owing to the French successes in Italy the Royal Navy had been withdrawn from the Mediterranean, and the entry of Spain into the war on the side of France had hastened that withdrawal. Apart from occasional British cruisers, the Mediterranean was now a French and Spanish 'lake'. To men of the calibre of Jervis the withdrawal was, to say the least, galling and he longed to get back and defeat the Spanish or French fleets. One of these ambitions had been realized on the 14th February, the day the *Bellerophon* was sailing from Cork, when Jervis with fifteen sail of the line met and defeated the Spanish fleet of twenty-eight sail of the line off Cape St Vincent—a victory which Britain badly needed in one of her numerous 'Darkest Hours', and one which first showed the talent of Nelson then a commodore.

Like Hood and Hotham before him, Jervis was always calling for more ships, and the group to which the *Bellerophon* belonged would be a very welcome reinforcement. It comprised, besides the *Bellerophon*, the *Theseus* (74) and the *Ville de Paris* (110), the largest ship ever built in Britain and named after the French flagship which had surrendered at the battle of the Saintes. In command of the three was Sir Robert Calder, a brave officer but one without the necessary moral courage and initiative for the new style of naval warfare.

The three ships moved down to St Helen's Road on the 18th March and left later that day in company with a convoy of East Indiamen under the escort of the *Raisonnable*. The next day the three battleships parted company with the convoy and made their way along the coast to Plymouth where they signalled the *Audacious* to come out and join them. Good time was made across the Bay of Biscay, and Cape Finisterre was sighted on the 24th March. Three days later the ships arrived at the mouth of the River Tagus where Jervis was sheltering with the fleet. Jervis was pleased to see them, doubly pleased because the *Ville de Paris* was to be his flagship in place of the *Victory* which had served as flagship of the fleet since the time of Lord Hood and was overdue for a refit.

The year 1797 is famous for three events in British naval history: the victories of St Vincent and Camperdown, and the

mutiny at Spithead and the Nore. The *Bellerophon* had left
England before the mutiny had broken out but she could not
help some of her crew being affected by it. The extract in the
log for the 1st April says: 'Punished . . . William Watts and
William Prendergast for Mutinious Expression'. The number
of records in the log during the next few months of boats sent
from the *Bellerophon* 'manned and armed' is considerable. In
fact a great struggle of wills was going on within the fleet. On
one side was Sir John Jervis, and on the other were the much
oppressed crews of his ships goaded by troublesome admirals
and weak-willed captains. Jervis knew of and recognized the
men's grievances but to relax discipline would be to ruin the
Navy; therefore every outbreak of mutiny which occurred he
put down with the greatest severity. A few months later, when
one of the Channel ships arrived with the fleet, a sailor in the
captain's launch which was moored alongside the flagship
started a conversation with a member of the ship's crew who
was looking through one of the lower-deck gun ports. 'Hey',
said the man in the launch, 'what have you chaps been doing
out here while we have been winning your bread and butter?'
'Quiet', replied the man on the flagship, 'or old Jarvie will
hear you and he'll have you dingle dangle from the yardarm
before sunset!' The mutinies in the Mediterranean fleet and
at home broke out almost simultaneously, but there is no
reason to suspect any preplanning of the event. The men of the
Mediterranean were generally considered better off than the
Channel fleet especially as regards prize money.

Soon after the *Bellerophon* arrived Jervis took the fleet to
sea to resume the blockade of Cadiz where the Spanish fleet
was sheltering. The Spanish fleet was a national disgrace and
the Commander-in-Chief at St Vincent, Cordova, was court-
martialled and dismissed the service. It was said by Nelson that
the ladies of Cadiz regarded the naval officers with contempt.

On April 3rd the fleet arrived at its blockading station off
San Sebastian where Admiral Nelson 'joined the fleet with
four of the line, five frigates and a brig'. While cruising off the
port the Spanish 32-gun frigate *Ninfa* was brought into the
fleet by the *Irresistible* after being captured in Conil Bay near
Cadiz on the 26th April. Jervis had by this time been made
Earl St Vincent, while other honours had been distributed
amongst his senior officers. He still had hopes of completing

the defeat of the Spanish fleet and waited for it to give him the chance. He was a man for close blockade and it took very heavy weather to drive him off his station. On the 22nd May he brought the fleet to single anchor off Cadiz, but on the 23rd, while the *Bellerophon* was riding at anchor, her cable broke and the crew spent the next couple of days trying to drag up the anchor! 'found the anchor to be so much sunk in mud as not to be able to catch it by sweeping, tried to weigh it by the buoy rope which broke'. The fleet remained at anchor until the 13th June, when Jervis once again stationed it off San Sebastian to watch the trade routes to Cadiz.

At about this time the Government at home was conceiving many offensive schemes, one of which was an attack on the Spanish island of Tenerife. They hoped to emulate the success of Blake who in 1657 had sacked the capital, Santa Cruz. Jervis was resisting these schemes on the grounds that he could see no use in them and they meant dispersing his forces at the very moment when the Spanish fleet might come out. To force it to do this Jervis planned a series of raids on the port and shipping of Cadiz, employing bomb-vessels and launches of armed men. On the 3rd July Nelson led the first of these boat attacks, and three boats of the *Bellerophon* took part, as she was now attached to Nelson's inshore squadron. The most notable event of this night's work was the capture of the Spanish admiral's launch containing thirty men by Nelson's launch with fifteen men. After eighteen Spaniards had been killed or wounded they decided to call it enough and surrendered. Nelson's life was thrice saved that night by his bos'n Sykes, who interposed his own body to receive sabre thrusts intended for the commodore. These affairs had great nuisance value and kept the Spanish on the alert, and it became a regular practice for boats from the British fleet to row right up to the walls of Cadiz.

Another and heavier attack was made on the 5th July, when an increased number of bomb-vessels succeeded in setting the city alight in three places. Another attack was planned for the 8th, but bad weather intervened and the attack on the 5th July was the last Nelson ever took part in, for on the 15th he left in command of the expedition to Tenerife, where he was to lose his right arm and suffer defeat. The inshore squadron was left to the alternate command of

Sir James Saumarez and Collingwood and the policy of active interference in the port of Cadiz was continued.

Further out the main fleet continued the blockade of Cadiz. It was while the fleet was standing to the westward on the 11th August that Nelson's squadron rejoined, carrying, as well as its cargo of sick and wounded, the dispatches of the Spanish Governor of Tenerife which Nelson had offered to take home for him—becoming one of the first commanders to bring news of his own defeat to the enemy!

While the fleet was at anchor off Cadiz on the 28th August the *Bellerophon* was heeled over and had her bottom scraped and the copper repaired, or as well as could be done while the ship was still at sea.

The crew of the *Bellerophon* had a chance of distinguishing themselves on the 9th September when a strange sail was sighted running for Cadiz. The signal to chase was made and the ship proved to be a Moorish vessel. The Moors anchored under the guns of Cadiz, but Captain Darby sent his boats in after her and cut her out under a heavy fire from the Spanish batteries and gunboats. She was found to be carrying a cargo of wheat. Another Moorish brig was taken on the morning of the 17th September when she was trying to sneak into Cadiz. The main fleet remained moored at single anchor off Cadiz until the 7th October when St Vincent again made sail to the north-west. That day a Genoese schooner was sighted by the *Culloden* and the *Terpischore* which gave chase, but schooner made its escape under fire from the two warships.

The fleet cruised between Cadiz and Cape Trafalgar under easy sail for just over a week before St Vincent took them back to the Tagus. The ships anchored in the Tagus on the 19th October and began to replenish their supplies of water and other necessaries.

The signal to sail again was made on the 5th November; the *Bellerophon* was unlucky and the 'ship missed the stays and got over to leeward on the Lisbon side and came to anchor'. Efforts were made to warp the ship over to the southward, but they were unavailing and only resulted in the loss of three hawsers which broke under the strain. Another attempt was made on the 6th but the hawser broke again, and the ship received slight damage by running foul of a Portuguese vessel. The *Bellerophon* finally got away on the 8th November by reason of a fair wind, and ran down the river to join the rest of the fleet anchored below Belem Castle.

St Vincent detached several of his ships in a squadron under Sir John Orde to maintain a closer watch on Cadiz, and the *Bellerophon* was to be one of the squadron. The rest were the *Minotaur* (flag), *Namur*, *Majestic*, *Gibraltar*, *Hector*, and *Defence*. This squadron was to relieve that of Commodore Collingwood at present watching the port. The squadron arrived off Cadiz on the 16th November, and Collingwood sailed for the Tagus on the 18th November. Two other ships joined the squadron on the 5th December, the *Blenheim*, 90, and the *Princess Royal* of 98 guns. Orde shifted his flag to the latter ship from the *Minotaur* on the 6th December. The sea was calm and the weather good and the squadron ran into no particular trouble while cruising between Cadiz, San Sebastian, and Cape Trafalgar. On Christmas Day the relief squadron of Sir William Parker was sighted comprising eight sail of the line. The two squadrons were briefly united before Orde sailed for the Tagus. After a hurried reprovisioning the squadron sailed again on the 23rd January and rejoined Parker off Cadiz on the 27th January.

Hopes rose high when the inshore frigate *Andromache* signalled that the Spanish fleet were preparing for sea.

At 6.24 the *Andromache* made the signal that the enemy's fleet were weighing. 6.30 saw Spanish Fleet to windward 20 sail of the line and 8 frigates . . . bore up and steered to the northward and westward. At 11.24 the van of the enemy shortened sail. At 1 lost sight of the enemy's fleet and hauled our courses.

No further opportunity occurred of engaging the Spanish fleet before St Vincent rejoined the squadrons off Cadiz with the main fleet on the 9th. St Vincent's arrival off Cadiz brought the force off the port to a total of twenty-nine of the line and frigates.

Rumours were now current of a great expedition preparing in Toulon. No one knew its destination, but guesses were made of Ireland, Egypt, Portugal, or the West Indies. In the absence of any orders from home St Vincent decided to re-enter the Mediterranean. For this job he chose Nelson who had just rejoined the fleet after convalescing in England from the loss of his arm at Tenerife. The decision to use such a junior admiral as Nelson was unpopular with the other admirals, especially Orde and Parker, who both sent angry letters to the Commander-in-Chief. How right St Vincent's decision had been was shown by the letter he received from Spencer which stressed the importance of the appearance of a British fleet in the Mediterranean, and insisted that if he was not able to command in person the command should go to Sir Horatio Nelson. Nelson left St Vincent's fleet on the same day that this letter was written in England.

We have, however, run on ahead of our story, for Nelson did not reach the fleet until the 30th April. Before that time the fleet had been engaged in the routine work off Cadiz, and the *Alexander* had been attacked by several Spanish gunboats and had to be towed out of action. The *Bellerophon* had sailed for Gibraltar on the 5th May, two days after Nelson had left the fleet, bound for the Mediterranean. He had with him only three sail of the line, the *Vanguard* his flagship, *Orion*, and the *Alexander*, all 74s. When the *Bellerophon* anchored at Gibraltar on the 8th May these three ships were almost ready to leave. Nelson had been promised a reinforcement of ten sail of the line as soon as the ships from the Channel Fleet should be sighted from the mastheads of the fleet before Cadiz.

On the 9th May Nelson weighed anchor and set sail from Gibraltar with his three ships of the line, as well as the frigates *Emerald* and *Terpischore* and the sloop-of-war *La Bonne Citoyenne*. The *Bellerophon* sailed to the westward on the 18th May in company with the *Princess Royal* and *Hector* and rejoined the fleet off Cadiz on the 9th May.

The long awaited reinforcements were sighted from the mastheads of the fleet on the 25th May and immediately Sir Thomas Troubridge was dispatched with ten sail of the line and a '50'. Among these reinforcements for Nelson was the *Bellerophon*. The others were *Culloden, Minotaur, Defence, Zealous, Audacious, Goliath, Theseus, Majestic*, and *Swiftsure*, all of 74 guns, and the *Leander* of 50 guns.

Since leaving Gibraltar Nelson had gone far into the Mediterranean. On the 20th May, when near Sardinia, a storm blew up and the *Vanguard* was dismasted. This event, Nelson afterwards wrote, was to check 'my consummate vanity', although the probable cause of the disaster was the inexperience of his flag captain Sir Edward Berry. At one time the

Vanguard seemed sure to be driven on shore, but Sir Alexander Ball in the *Alexander* managed to tow the flagship off. Nelson had once hailed him to cast off the tow, but Ball had replied that he thought he could save her and that by God he would save her! Until this incident, Nelson had entertained a prejudice against Ball ever since he had first met him before the war, in France. This dislike was now converted into a lifelong friendship.

The accident had one unfortunate result in that the frigates, thinking that a ship as badly damaged as the *Vanguard* would have to return to Gibraltar for repairs, set sail thither themselves. Nelson repaired the *Vanguard* from the resources of his squadron and she was fit for service by the time Troubridge joined with his ships. The want of frigates was never remedied, and the only ship below those of the line was the brig *Mutine*, commanded by Captain Thomas Hardy. The consequent lack of observation caused Nelson to miss the French armada on his first trip to Egypt, during which he actually saw the frigates of the fleet, but having none of his own could only press on and leave the frigates alone.

The French armada had sailed from Toulon on the 11th May, and when all the contingents had joined up it totalled thirteen ships of the line, seven frigates, several gunboats and nearly 300 transports of various sizes. On board were 30,000 infantry, 2,800 cavalry, sixty field and forty siege guns, two companies of sappers and miners, and a bridging train. Also on board were several well-known scholars and scientists on their way to undertake work and study in Egypt. Malta had been sighted on the 9th June; the island was summoned and capitulated on the 12th. After landing a garrison and provisions Bonaparte sailed again on the 19th June for Egypt. It was while on their way from Malta to Egypt that, on the night of the 22nd-23rd June, French officers heard British signal guns booming through the night, and steered a slightly more northerly course. Napoleon was one of the few who had no fears of the British fleet; the last news he had heard was that only three sail of the line had been seen in the Mediterranean and that ten more were to join, but he thought that a junction could not yet have been effected.

Nelson had heard on the 17th June of the French landing in Malta, and when he anchored at Sicily he received the news of its surrender. From information obtained from a vessel spoken on the 22nd, Nelson believed the French destination to be Sicily, but from Naples he learned that the French were not interested in that island but in Egypt. He at length decided to go to Alexandria under all possible sail.

The French had arrived off Alexandria on the 1st July, and 5,000 troops were landed to seize the port and give the armada a safe anchorage. The British fleet had been seen off the coast only two days before. Nelson had beaten the French to Egypt because he had steered a direct course while the French had taken a more northerly route to avoid any British fleet in the area. The Pharos Tower had been sighted from the leading British ship on the 29th June. Sir Edward Berry describes the feelings of the fleet: 'We saw the Pharos Tower of Alexandria and continued nearing the land with a press of sail till we had a distinct view of both harbours; and, to our general surprise and disappointment we saw not a French ship in either'.

With his last hope dashed, Nelson decided to cruise in the Levant area to the northward in extended order. One day the *Swiftsure* picked up a buoy which was floating in the sea and had the name 'Artémise' on it, which was known to be that of one of the frigates which sailed with the French from Toulon.

The British fleet passed Cyprus and skirted the coast of Crete, and Nelson, in the depths of depression, wrote: 'Was I to die at this moment, want of frigates would be found stamped on my heart!' As many of the ships had not provisioned since leaving Gibraltar he took the fleet into Syracuse to water and provision, and while there Berry says:

We received vague accounts . . . that the Enemy's fleet had not been seen in the Archipelago nor the Adriatic nor had they gone down the Mediterranean; the conclusion then seemed to be that the coast of Egypt was still the object of their destination, and neither our former disappointment nor the hardships we had endured from the heat of the climate . . . could deter the Admiral from steering to that point where there was a chance of finding the enemy.

The squadron sailed on the 24th July, bound for Egypt. Nelson skirted the southern tip of Greece, and Troubridge in the *Culloden* was sent to the Gulf of Coroni for news and returned with a French brig in tow, whose captain said the

French fleet had sailed SE. four weeks earlier, which could only mean for Egypt.

The coast of Egypt was sighted on the 1st August in the afternoon, and a large number of ships were seen moored in the harbour. Hopes so long frustrated rose again, and the ships prepared for action. Then suddenly all hopes were crushed by the signal from the leading ship, the *Zealous*: 'The Enemy's fleet do not form part of the vessels at anchor.'

Sir James Saumarez of the *Orion* says that they all sat down to dinner with heavy hearts at the thought of once again missing the French fleet. The meal was just being served when the officer of the watch came in, 'Sir, a signal has just now been made that the enemy is in Aboukir Bay'. Where-upon, says Saumarez, 'all sprang to their feet, and only staying to drink a bumper to our success, we were in a moment on deck!'

Once again it was the *Zealous*, commanded by Captain Samuel Hood, which had spotted the enemy. They were moored in line of battle in Aboukir Bay about fifteen miles from Alexandria, and were seen to comprise thirteen of the line with four frigates. Describing the sighting, Berry says:

The enemy's fleet were first discovered by the *Zealous*, Captain Hood who immediately communicated by signal the number of ships, sixteen [sic] laying at anchor in line of battle in a bay on the larboard bow, which we afterwards found to be Aboukir Bay. The Admiral hauled his wind that instant, a movement which was immediately observed and followed by the whole squadron; and at the same time he recalled the *Alexander* and the *Swiftsure*. The wind was at this time NNW. and blew what seamen call a topgallant breeze.

With the sighting of the fleet:

... the utmost joy seemed to animate every breast on board of the squadron ... and the pleasure which the Admiral himself felt was perhaps more heightened than that of any other man as he had now a certainty by which he could regulate his future operations.

Before proceeding with a more detailed report of the battle it would be well here to give a description of the bay and the French line of battle.*

The Bay of Aboukir ... commences about 20 miles to the north-east of Alexandria, and extends from the castle of Aboukir, in a semicircular

* From William James: *Naval History of Great Britain.*

direction, to the westernmost or Rosetta mouth of the Nile, distant from the castle about six miles. Aboukir Bay has no depth for line of battle ships nearer than three miles from the shore, a sand-bank, on which there is not any where more than four fathoms, running out at that distance. Owing also to the width of its opening, the bay affords very little shelter, except on its west-north-west side (that from which the wind commonly blows on this coast) by a small island, situated about two miles from the point whereon the castle stands, and connected with it by a chain of sand-banks and rocks, between which, however, there is a passage for small craft. Aboukir Island is surrounded by a continuation of the shoal that runs along the bottom of the bay; and which extends from the island about 1,650 yards, or nearly a mile, in a north-east direction.

It appears that, on first taking up this anchorage, Vice-Admiral Brueys held a council of flag-officers and captains to determine whether, in case of attack, the fleet should engage at anchor or under sail. All officers, except Rear-Admiral Blanquet, approved of the fleet's remaining at anchor . . . However, finding the majority against him, M. Blanquet requested that the *Franklin* might be placed as one of the seconds to the commander-in-chief. His request was granted, and the ships were formed in line ahead in the following order: *Guerrier*, *Conquérant*, *Spartiate*, *Aquilon*, *Peuple-Souverain*, *Franklin*, *Orient* (flag), *Tonnant*, *Heureux*, *Mercure*, *Guillaume-Tell*, *Généreux*, *Timoléon*; with in an inner line, about 350 yards from the first, and about midway between that and the shoal, the *Sérieuse* frigate, nearly abreast of the opening between the *Conquérant* and *Spartiate* the *Artémise* abreast of the *Heureux* and the *Diane* of the *Guillaume-Tell*.

The leading French ship was about 2,420 yards from Aboukir Island, which was more than double the distance of the shoal which stretched in the same direction. This elementary mistake, combined with only a weak battery on the island, enabled the French line to be turned and doubled by the leading British ships. On the island Brueys had placed four twelve-pounder guns, two thirteen-inch brass mortars and several pieces of a lighter calibre. The distance between each ship was approximately 160 yards, far too wide, and in addition no cables were stretched between the ships as was originally planned. The position had great natural strength, but the French commander did not make the most of it. He left his rear almost in mid air without the benefit of either shoal water or land batteries. His line had a very slight curve in it with the intention of bringing it nearer to shoal water, but did not go far enough and did not help to protect the van. As a precedent for ships at anchor repelling attacks, Brueys had the actions of Barrington at St Lucia in 1778 and Hood at St Kitts in 1782, when both had repelled superior fleets. Hood's action in particular bore many points of resemblance to the position in which Brueys found himself, but he had one advantage over Hood—time, by which he should have made his line impregnable.

In his plan of attack Nelson had assumed that the French flank could not be turned, and his idea was to bring two of his ships to attack one of the enemy. The British ships were to anchor on the bow and quarter of the enemy and fix springs to their cables so that the broadsides could be directed in any direction desired. Then the plan was to proceed along the line blasting it ship by ship, secure in the knowledge that the rear of the French fleet could only await its turn unable to help themselves or the van; but thanks to the distance from the shoal of the leading French ship, Hood in the *Zealous* was able to turn the flank of the line and four other ships followed him.

When the British were first sighted a large contingent from the crews of the French ships were ashore digging for water and only some obeyed the signal for the recall. The French ships were in a disordered state on board, and some were in the midst of painting. The guns on the port side were not ready for action as the admiral considered that it would be impossible for the British to turn his flank.

Seeing the lateness of the hour, Brueys thought the British would wait until morning to make an attack; this, he hoped, would give him time to make all the preparations that he should have made days ago. At one time he considered the idea of engaging under sail, and even gave orders for the top sailyards to be crossed, but seeing some of the leading British ships bring to, he decided to remain at anchor under the impression that the attack would not be made until the morning when the shoals would be more easily avoided. But whatever his reason for giving the order to get ready to sail, he was right in remaining at anchor, for with the wind blowing straight into the bay he could never have got under way. It was also said after the battle by captured French officers that they did not have men enough to man the guns and handle the sails.

On board the British ships all was ready for action. Every man and officer knew what to do and the crews were at a high level of efficiency and morale. Nelson viewed the French line with the 'eye of a seaman determined on attack', and this was what he intended to do. He knew that it would be dark before all his ships could get into action, but on the other hand he knew that the more time he gave the enemy to prepare themselves, the worse it would be for his squadron. From the *Vanguard* fluttered the signal for the recall of the *Alexander* and *Swiftsure* which were away scouting, and for the *Culloden* to drop her prize which she had in tow and rejoin the squadron. Nelson signalled his intention to attack the van and centre of the enemy and for the squadron to form line of battle.

Under easy sail and in a fair wind the British fleet bore down to the attack with the French making frantic preparations to receive them. Numerically the fleets were equal, but it will be seen from the following tables that the French had the heavier weight of metal.

FRENCH FLEET IN ORDER OF BATTLE

Le Guerrier, 74 guns	Capt. Trulet, Sr
Le Conquérant, 74 guns	Capt. Dalbarade
Le Spartiate, 74 guns	Capt. Emereau
L'Aquilon, 74 guns	Capt. Thevenard
Le Peuple-Souverain, 74 guns	Capt. Raccord
Le Franklin, 80 guns	Admiral Blanquet
	Capt. Gillet
L'Orient, 120 guns	Admiral Brueys
	Admiral Ganteaume
	Capt. Casabianca
Le Tonnant, 80 guns	Capt. Dupetit-Thouars
L'Heureux, 74 guns	Capt. Etienne
Le Timoléon, 74 guns	Capt. Trulet, Jr
Le Mercure, 74 guns	Capt. Cambon
Le Guillaume-Tell, 80 guns	Admiral Villeneuve
	Capt. Saumer
La Généreux, 74 guns	Capt. Lejoille

Frigates

La Diane, 48 guns	Admiral de Crepe
	Capt. Soleil
La Justice, 44 guns	Capt. Villeneuve, Jr
L'Artémise, 36 guns	Capt. Estandlet
La Sérieuse, 36 guns	Capt. Martin

BRITISH FLEET IN ORDER OF BATTLE

H.M.S. *Goliath*, 74 guns	Capt. Thomas Foley
H.M.S. *Zealous*, 74 guns	Capt. Samuel Hood
H.M.S. *Orion*, 74 guns	Capt. Sir James Saumarez
H.M.S. *Audacious*, 74 guns	Capt. Davidge Gould
H.M.S. *Theseus*, 74 guns	Capt. Ralph Miller
H.M.S. *Vanguard*, 74 guns	Rear-Admiral Sir Horatio Nelson
	Capt. Edward Berry
H.M.S. *Minotaur*, 74 guns	Capt. Thomas Louis
H.M.S. *Bellerophon*, 74 guns	Capt. Henry Darby
H.M.S. *Defence*, 74 guns	Capt. William Peyton
H.M.S. *Majestic*, 74 guns	Capt. George Westcott
H.M.S. *Alexander*, 74 guns	Capt. Alexander Ball
H.M.S. *Swiftsure*, 74 guns	Capt. Benjamin Hallowell
H.M.S. *Leander*, 50 guns	Capt. Thomas Thompson
H.M.S. *Culloden*, 74 guns	Capt. Thomas Troubridge
H.M.S. *Mutine*, 18 guns (Brig).	Capt. Thomas Hardy

THE BATTLE OF THE NILE

As the British ships approached they formed line of battle as convenient, with the *Goliath* and *Zealous* leading the line. The ten ships hauled sharp to the wind to avoid the shoal ground to seaward of the island and passed into the shallows.

In the French fleet signals were flying to recall the men from ashore who had gone to fetch food and dig for water. Unhappily for Brueys, only a few obeyed the signal and the ships were undermanned when they commenced the action. The British squadron had first been sighted at 2 p.m. and since then frantic preparations had been made in the French ships to prepare them for battle. As the British entered the Bay, Brueys sent the brigs *Alerte* and *Railleur* to reconnoitre them:

The English Fleet was soon off the Island of Bequier. The brig *Alert* then began to put the Admiral's orders into execution, viz. to stand towards the enemy until nearly within gunshot and then to manoeuvre to draw them towards the outer shoal laying off that island. But the English Admiral without doubt had experienced pilots on board as he did not pay any attention to the brig's track but allowed her to go away: he hauled well round all the dangers.

By 5 p.m. the British ships had hauled to the wind in succession and it was plain to Brueys that there was to be an action that night. He therefore flew the signal to engage at anchor.

Nelson hailed Captain Hood on board the *Zealous* to inquire if the ships were far enough to the eastward to bear up. Hood told him: 'I was in eleven fathoms, that I would bear up and sound with the lead, to which I would be very attentive, and carry him as close as I could with safety: he said he would be obliged to me'.

As Hood passed ahead of the fleet, Nelson raised his hat and Hood, in endeavouring to do the same, lost it overboard! 'There it goes for luck', he said. 'Put the helm up and make sail.' In the end it was not Hood in the *Zealous*, but Foley in the *Goliath* who led Nelson's fleet into battle.

According to Admiral Blanquet, the first French ship opened fire at 5.30, but English accounts give a later time. Blanquet records the start of the action thus:

At $\frac{1}{2}$ past 5 the headmost ships of our line being within gunshot of the English, the Admiral made the signal to engage, which was not obeyed until the enemy were in pistol shot and just doubling us, the action then began very warm.

Foley in the *Goliath* had crossed the leading ships of the French line and opened fire, raking the *Guerrier*, the leading ship. The *Goliath* was followed by the *Zealous* which also raked the *Guerrier* before passing inside the line. This raking fire was most damaging to the French ship and within twenty minutes she was dismasted.

The next three ships of the British squadron followed round to the inside of the line, the *Orion* and *Theseus* passing the head of the line and the *Audacious* passing between the *Guerrier* and the *Conquérant*, thereby raking both. Once inside the line the *Goliath* dropped her stern anchor to bring her up alongside the *Guerrier* but it failed to hold and she ended by the *Conquérant*, and Hood in the *Zealous* took her place by the *Guerrier*. Nelson, in the sixth ship the *Vanguard*, stood down the outside of the line and fetched by the larboard bow of the *Spartiate*. Berry describes the start of the action in a few short words:

These two ships [*Zealous* and *Goliath*] with the *Orion, Audacious* and *Theseus* took their stations inside of the Enemy's line and were immediately in close action.

An officer of the *Zealous* says:

Goliath passed the Van ship and anchored alongside the second, and we anchored athwart the larboard bow of the Van ship, $\frac{1}{3}$ of a cable distant and engaged her, in 7 minutes we shot away her Foremast and in 20 she had not a mast standing.

Blanquet describes the position of the van thus: 'All the Van attacked on both sides by the enemy who ranged close along our line.'

Captain Gould in the *Audacious* had placed his ship to rake the *Conquérant* and the destruction in that ship was so great that the officers could not get the men to stand to their guns. Saumarez passed down the line and anchored the *Orion* opposite the *Peuple-Souverain*, the fifth ship. Miller in the *Theseus*, after raking the *Conquérant*, had dropped anchor opposite the *Spartiate* and opened a destructive fire. Troubridge in the *Culloden*, in hurrying to join the action, had grounded on a shoal at the entrance to the bay, and had the mortifying experience for a man of his temperament of having to stand by the whole night and watch the battle. However, his mishap acted as a warning to the last two English ships the *Alexander* and *Swiftsure* which, seeing the grounded ship ahead of them, were able to haul well clear of the shoal.

Nelson in the *Vanguard* was engaged with both the *Spartiate* and the *Aquilon*, and was hard pressed until Captain Louis in the *Minotaur* arrived to engage the latter. The *Defence* arrived to attack the *Peuple-Souverain* which was already engaging the *Orion* on the inside and was soon in close action. Saumarez in the *Orion*, seeing that the *Peuple-Souverain* was almost finished, shifted his position farther down the line. The *Bellerophon* began to engage at 6.45: '$\frac{3}{4}$ past 6 engaged running down the enemy line. At 7 let go [anchor] alongside the *L'Orient*, Commander-in-Chief of the French Fleet.'

By 7 p.m. when the *Bellerophon* arrived alongside the towering *Orient* it was completely dark, and the scene was only lit by the flashes of the guns. The *Bellerophon* should have brought up on the bow of the *Orient* but the anchor failed to hold and she came to rest square alongside the French flagship. This was the chance which Captain Casabianca had been waiting for, and before the *Bellerophon* could fire a shot she had received two broadsides from the French ship. These must have been some of the most destructive blows ever received by her during her long career, for they killed or wounded seventy men and dismounted eight guns. Captain Darby was among the wounded and had to be carried below. The action then commenced in earnest for the *Bellerophon*, and a close action it was, with both ships touching. On the French ship, Casabianca and Brueys were directing the battle and were showing great gallantry. A hot fire was kept up on the decks of the *Bellerophon* from the *Orient*, and it was not long before the first lieutenant who had taken command after the fall of Captain Darby was wounded, and as he was being carried below a further shot killed him. Lieutenant Lander, who was in charge of one of the gun decks below, was now sent for to take charge of the ship. Obviously such a contest could not go on without serious damage being suffered by the smaller ship, and at 8 o'clock the mizen mast was shot away followed shortly after by the main mast. Lander, who had just arrived on deck, was killed by the falling main mast.

Elsewhere in the battle Captain Westcott in the *Majestic* had lost his bearings in the smoke and darkness, and had run into the *Heureux* in such a position that she was unable to bring all her guns to bear. In this situation Westcott was killed and the ship was commanded thereafter by Lieutenant Cuthbert, who managed to get her free and to get into action with *Le Mercure*. This was about 8 o'clock, at which time Nelson was standing on the deck of the *Vanguard* when he was hit by a flying piece of shrapnel. He was momentarily blinded and believed himself mortally wounded. Berry caught him as he fell and he was taken down to the cockpit.

The *Bellerophon* now found her situation more than she could bear, and as she was totally dismasted and many of her guns were dismounted, Lieutenant Hindmarsh, the sole surviving officer on deck, ordered the crew to cut her cables, and she drifted out of action. She had engaged the *Orient*, a ship of twice her force, for over an hour and had reduced her foe to such a state that she was a comparatively easy prey for the following ships. Admiral Blanquet in the *Franklin* noticed her withdrawal with great satisfaction:

At 8 o'clock at night the ship which was engaging the *L'Orient* on her Starboard Quarter, notwithstanding her advantageous position was dismasted and so roughly treated that she cut her cables and drifted from the line.

According to the log of the *Bellerophon*:

At 10 observing our antagonist on fire on the middle deck, cut the cable and wore clear of her by loosing the spritsail. Shortly after cutting the foremast was shot away.

A time discrepancy will be noted in the British and French accounts, but the accepted time is generally 8 p.m. or just after. As she drifted away from the action the *Bellerophon* received a broadside from *Tonnant* and a few distant shot from the *Heureux*.

The next two ships in action were the *Alexander* and *Swiftsure*. The *Alexander* anchored inside the enemy line opposite the space between *Orient* and *Tonnant* and the *Swiftsure* anchored on the outside of the line opposite the space between *Orient* and *Franklin*. A signal from the *Vanguard* had summoned *Leander* to the fight from where she had been trying to tow off the *Culloden*, and she took up her station in the gap vacated by the *Peuple-Souverain* in which the little ship was able to rake both the *Franklin* and *Orient*.

The *Bellerophon* was on fire in several places because the wreckage which hung over the side of the ship became ignited by the flashes of the guns as they were fired. This was soon extinguished and the task of clearing the wreckage continued under the command of Lieutenant Robert Cathcart, the senior surviving officer. There was a tense moment as the ship was drifting when she was nearly fired upon in error by the *Alexander* and *Swiftsure*. Luckily Captain Hallowell of the *Swiftsure* was not certain that the dismasted wreck before him was a French ship and hailed her, 'What ship is that?' to which he got the reply, *Bellerophon* leaving the action dismasted!' The crew of the *Swiftsure* gave the crippled ship a cheer and sailed on into the fight.

The fire on the *Orient* had been seen by other ships, French and British, and the British ordered their guns to be trained on that spot to thwart all attempts to extinguish it. On shore the glow had also been noticed by a group of French observers who were watching from a nearby hilltop. One of them says: 'The Cannonading was very heavy until about a quarter of nine o'clock when favoured by the night we perceived an immense light which announced to us that some ship was on fire.' By this time Brueys had been killed and Captain

Casabianca was wounded. Desperate efforts were made to get the blaze under control, but the firing from the British ships foiled any attempt to close with the flames.

The *Bellerophon*, still drifting out of control, was seen by Villeneuve in the *Guillaume-Tell*, but believing her to be a dismasted French ship he let her go. The task of clearing the wreckage on the *Bellerophon* was no light one, as the entry in her log shows:

Employed clearing the wreck clear of the guns and heaving the dead overboard. Extinguished the fire which caught in several places of the ship and rigging which hung over the side, occasioned by the guns.

While the men of the *Bellerophon* were fighting their smaller fires, the crew of the *Orient* were now losing the fight against their conflagration. One half of the ship was now a mass of flames and some of the crew were already jumping overboard to escape the final explosion which was certain to come. The flagship was now under the fire of three British ships, the *Swiftsure* on her starboard bow, the *Leander* on her bow, and the *Alexander*, which had dropped into the space on her larboard quarter vacated by the *Tonnant*. Under such conditions proper fire fighting was impossible and it was evident to everybody on board and to all spectators that the ship was lost. Boats were launched from neighbouring ships to help pick up the crew. Nelson, when told of the fire, came on deck on the *Vanguard*, and ordered the one remaining boat of his ship to be sent to the rescue of the survivors. Nearby ships began cutting their cables to escape the effects of the blast. One who did not move was the *Swiftsure*, whose captain, Hallowell, conjectured that the blast would lift the majority of the wreckage over the ship. In this he was proved right, and only one or two pieces finally descended on the deck of the *Swiftsure*. Among these pieces was part of the mainmast, which Captain Hallowell ordered the ship's carpenter to turn into a coffin for Nelson, and which the admiral much admired!

One of the youngest participants in the battle was John Theophilus Lee, a midshipman of the *Swiftsure*, who was only eleven years old. He had already seen one action, the battle of Cape St Vincent, in the *Barfleur*, and in the present engagement he was acting as Captain Hallowell's A.D.C. Writing his account of the action years afterwards he said:

... the French nothing daunted still gloriously maintained the honour of their flag ... The brave Brueys having lost both his legs, was seated with tourniquets on the stumps in an armchair facing his enemies and giving directions for extinguishing the fire when a cannon ball from the *Swift-sure* ... cut him in two.

Following the example of their captain, the crew of the *Orient* continued to serve their guns and keep up a sporadic fire on the British 74s. The end was now very near for the giant ship, and just after ten she blew up with an explosion that was heard in Rosetta, ten miles away. John Nicol, whom we have met before, was serving in the powder room of the *Goliath*, and when he and his comrades heard the explosion they thought it was their own ship blowing up. The log of the *Bellerophon* records the occurrence in a few brief words: 'At 11 the *L'Orient* blew up!' A letter written home by an officer of the *Zealous* after the battle is more graphic: 'At 10 *L'Orient* blew into the air!'

The French observer ashore says: 'The thunder of the cannon was heard with redoubled fury, and the ship on fire blew up with the most dreadful explosion which was heard at Rosetta.'

Admiral Blanquet describes the event thus: '¾ past 10 the ship [*L'Orient*] blew up. The explosion was dreadful and spread the fire all round to a considerable distance.'

The *Franklin*'s decks were covered with red hot pieces of timber and rope on fire ... immediately after the explosion the action ceased everywhere and was succeeded by a most profound silence. .... It was a quarter of an hour before the ships crews recovered from the kind of stupor they were thrown into.

Sir Edward Berry, observing the explosion from the deck of the *Vanguard*, writes:

The cannonading was partially kept up to leeward of the centre till 10 o'clock, when *L'Orient* blew up with a most tremendous explosion. An awful pause and deathlike silence for about three minutes ensued, when the wreck of the masts, yards etc. etc. which had been carried to a vast height fell down into the water and on board the surrounding ships.

As will be seen, no two accounts seem to agree exactly as to when the *Orient* did blow up, but the generally accepted time seems to have been some time after ten. All observers accounted it the most terrifying experience of their lives and remembered it vividly for years afterwards. The silence of the night, until the battle was resumed, was one of the most impressive incidents of the engagement. The destruction of the giant ship was the climax of the battle, and the issue could no longer be in doubt. The French van was smashed and the centre was almost destroyed, only the rear was, so far, virtually untouched.

The French were the first to resume firing after the destruction of the *Orient*, and it was Admiral Blanquet's ship, the *Franklin*, which fired the first shots in the second half of the battle. The gallant resistance of the *Franklin* was, however, nearly at an end and she struck soon afterwards:

At ½ past 11 o'clock having only three Lower Deck Guns that could defend the Honour of the Flag it became necessary to put an end to so disproportional a struggle, and Citizen Martin, Captain of a Frigate, ordered the colours to be struck.

To complete his victory, Nelson was trying to get the ships which had been engaging the French van and were comparatively undamaged to drift down and attack the rear. The signal lieutenant of the *Vanguard*, Capel, was sent in a boat to the ships to impress on their captains the necessity of getting into action with the rear as soon as possible. The *Tonnant* was the only French ship now engaging the British with spirit, and at 3 a.m. she brought down the main and mizen masts of the *Majestic*, her own masts followed soon after and she temporarily ceased firing, but did not strike. She had slipped her cable to escape the blast of the *Orient* and was now firmly aground. Many French seamen from other ships had climbed aboard her and she had nearly 1,600 men on board. Her captain, Dupetit-Thouars, had fought her most gallantly, until fatally wounded.

A second lull occurred in the firing about 3 a.m. and this lasted until about 5 a.m. It was occasioned by the exhaustion of both parties after nearly twenty-four hours of unparalleled effort. On both sides men dropped asleep by the side of their guns, and a period of silence reigned over the embattled scene. It was noted by the French observer ashore: 'The firing . . . continued without intermission until 3 o'clock in the morning when it ceased almost entirely until 5 o'clock when it commenced again with as great a vivacity as ever.'

Just as day broke over the mouth of the Nile the firing began again, with the *Majestic* and *Alexander* on one side and the *Tonnant*, *Généreux*, *Timoléon*, and *Guillaume-Tell* on the other. The British ships were soon joined by the *Theseus* and *Goliath* and sporadic firing continued on both sides. Of the French fleet which had existed twenty-four hours before, six ships had been taken and one had been destroyed. Of the six survivors, *Tonnant* was grounded as also was the *Heureux*, while the *Mercure*, *Généreux*, *Guillaume-Tell*, and *Timoléon* were comparatively undamaged. Viewing the scene from the tower on shore the French observer says:

I placed myself on a Tower which is about a cannon shot from Rosetta ... from thence I could plainly see the whole battle. At 8 o'clock I perceived a ship on fire and in about half an hour blew up similar to that last night.

A note of optimism enters his account as he records:

... the two squadrons so mingled among each other that it was impossible to distinguish French from English nor on whose side the advantage was. The firing continued with unavailing vivacity until about 2 o'clock after midday ... when we perceived two sail of the line and two frigates under a press of sail standing eastward. We perceived the whole four were under French Colours no other vessel made any movement and the firing ceased entirely.

Dawn saw the crew of the *Bellerophon* still repairing their damaged ship. During the latter part of the night they had picked up some survivors from the *Orient*, as had most ships in the vicinity. Dawn also brought her a fresh alarm when the French frigate *La Justice* bore down on her, sent by Villeneuve to take possession of the lone dismasted British 74. The log states: 'At 7 one of the enemy's frigates bore down on us, beat to Quarters and saw the Lower Deck Guns clear and the Larboard side of the Main Decks, the Quarter Deck guns being rendered useless.' Nelson had seen the peril of the *Bellerophon* and had detached Hood in the *Zealous* to her assistance. Seeing that the British were prepared, the French retreated. Nelson signalled for the *Zealous* to stay with the *Bellerophon* to protect her from any further forays on the part of the French.

Just before midday Villeneuve seized his chance to get away and made sail to the eastwards. Of the battleships only the *Guillaume-Tell* and the *Généreux* were able to escape; the

Timoléon was too far to leeward and ran herself on shore, losing her foremast by the shock of collision. Her captain, Trulet, abandoned her and set her on fire, her crew making off inland. The two frigates made their escape with the battleships. Hood in the *Zealous* was the nearest British ship in a position to intercept them and immediately stood towards them. Gould in the *Audacious* was also suitably placed, but as he made no move in answer to Nelson's signals the *Zealous* was recalled, and the four French ships stood out of the bay. They passed the *Bellerophon* but did not fire on her.

The battle was now over, the enemy completely defeated. In the words of Nelson: 'Victory is not a name strong enough for such a scene.'

The escape of the French was noted in the log of the *Bellerophon*: '. . . at 2 p.m. two ships of the French Line and two frigates . . . stood out from the fleet exchanging their broadsides with the *Zealous* who covered us.'

When the crew came to check the hammocks which had been erected before the battle as protection against shot and splinters, they found them 'entirely shot to pieces by the enemy's shot'. Besides this minor damage, the hull was in a very shattered state, all the masts had been shot away, and sixteen guns had been dismounted or destroyed. As soon as the deck was reasonably clear of wreckage a muster was held to find the number of dead or wounded. The log states:

We had killed 3 lieutenants, 1 Masters Mate, 32 Sailors and 13 Marines; the captain of Marines, Master Boatswain, 1 Midshipman, 126 Sailors and 17 Marines wounded, making in all 49 killed and 149 wounded.

Many more sailors died from their wounds within the next few weeks, and among the later deaths was the captain of Marines.

The crew had erected jury masts by the morning of the 3rd August, and rigged them by the 4th. With temporary repairs made to the hull, the *Bellerophon* was ready to sail, and at 1 a.m. on the morning of the 5th she stood back to the fleet.

On the 3rd August Nelson had had copies made of his dispatch to Lord St Vincent, the wording of which rang round Europe:

My Lord,
    Almighty God has blessed His Majesty's Arms in the late Battle by a Great Victory over the Fleet of the enemy . . .

After the repair of the British ships, the next step was to make the prizes seaworthy for transport to Gibraltar. The ships considered worth taking into the British service were *Le Franklin, Le Spartiate, L'Aquilon, Le Tonnant, Le Peuple-Souverain,* and *Le Conquérant.* The rest were stripped down and useful material from them was removed before the hulks were destroyed. The problem of French prisoners and wounded was also pressing, and a truce was arranged with the commandant of Aboukir so that the wounded could be sent on shore to receive attention from their own surgeons. The first outsiders to realize the extent of the victory and its full consequences were the Bedouins who had lined the shore during the battle, for they immediately attacked the French parties on shore. Nelson had sent off his dispatches on the 6th in the *Leander,* also sending Captain Berry with her. A message was sent to the Governor of India to let him know of the defeat of the French, as fears had been entertained in that country ever since hearing of the landing of the French. A duplicate set of dispatches was sent by the *Mutine,* for Nelson feared the French might intercept the *Leander.* In this he proved right, for on the 18th August she was attacked by the *Généreux,* one of the survivors of the Nile. Against the 900 men and 74 guns of her opponent, the *Leander* could only reply with 343 men and 50 guns. Notwithstanding this she fought the French ship for six and a half hours before surrendering. Captain Thompson was wounded four times and Berry slightly wounded. Her loss was thirty-five killed and fifty-seven wounded, or nearly one-third of the crew. The loss of the *Généreux* was reported to be 100 killed and 188 wounded.

The total British casualties in the battle of the Nile were 218 killed and 678 wounded. No count was ever taken of the number of French casualties, but guesses in the British Press afterwards ranged from 2,000 to 5,000. The latter is the more likely figure judging by the number of ships engaged and the shattered state they were in after the battle.

On the 12th August three strange sails were sighted from the bay, but they proved to be the frigates *Emerald* and *Alcmene* and the sloop *Bonne Citoyenne.* At first they were chased by the *Swiftsure* in error for French frigates, but having got over their fright they rejoined next day. On the 14th Sir James Saumarez took part of the squadron back to Gibraltar with the prizes. His squadron included *Orion*, *Theseus*, *Majestic*, *Minotaur*, *Defence*, *Audacious*, and *Bellerophon*, with the prizes *Franklin*, *Tonnant*, *Aquilon*, *Conquérant*, *Peuple-Souverain*, and *Spartiate*, all the prizes being rigged with jury masts.

On the 16th Captain Hopkins of the Marines died on board the *Bellerophon* and was buried at sea with full military honours. Progress was very slow, Sicily being reached only on the 16th September, and Malta (where the French commandant was summoned to surrender) on the 26th. The squadron finally moored in Rosas Bay on the 19th October, to the cheers of the populace and garrison, and the salutes of the ships moored in the bay.

Of the rest of the squadron, Nelson in the *Vanguard*, accompanied by the *Culloden* and *Alexander*, sailed for Naples on the 19th August and Hood was left to blockade the coast of Egypt with the *Zealous*, *Goliath*, *Swiftsure*, *Emerald*, *Alcmene*, *Bonne Citoyenne*, and the newly joined frigate *Seahorse*.

Such was the famous battle of the Nile, one of the most complete victories ever gained at sea. Even the four ships that escaped were all taken by 1801, the last to fall being *La Justice*. Of the prizes captured, only *Tonnant*, *Spartiate*, and *Franklin* were taken into the Royal Navy, the latter being given the name of *Canopus*.

The victory completely cut off the French army in Egypt from France, and the Mediterranean once again became a 'British lake'. It resolved the Porte to declare war on France again and to prepare for an invasion to reconquer Egypt. It heartened the powers of Europe to form the Second Coalition, which had such striking success before Napoleon came back from Egypt to reanimate the French resistance. It brought the name of Nelson to the very top of his profession, and gave to the people and Government of Britain a champion to look up to in the long struggle ahead. The execution of the battle was near perfect, and Nelson in his dispatch said that everyone did his best. Some complaints were heard about Captain Gould of the *Audacious* for not supporting Hood in cutting off the retreat of the French ships on the morning of the 2nd, but Gould's reply was that his ship was too badly damaged to get under way.

Napoleon rose to the emergency and conducted a successful invasion of Syria, defeating the armies of the Porte. He advanced as far as Acre, where a British naval force under Sir Sidney Smith and an émigré French military engineer named Phelippeaux held the town against all the efforts of the French. From there he had to retreat to Egypt, and the French met defeat there at the hands of Sir Ralph Abercromby in 1801. After defeating one more Turkish army, Napoleon learnt of the crisis in France, and on the 18th August 1799 he embarked in the frigate *Le Muiron* and finally reached France on the 9th October landing at Fréjus. His career from then on is well known: he rose to be First Consul and later Emperor, and conqueror of nearly all Europe before his final defeat on the plains of Waterloo in 1815.

While the squadron of Sir James Saumarez was at Gibraltar, celebrations took place to honour the representatives of the victor of the Nile. The prizes and the ships of the British squadron underwent repairs for the hoped for voyage to England. The wounded were taken ashore to be cared for by the hospitals of Gibraltar.

At the time of Saumarez's arrival, St Vincent also happened to be ashore at Gibraltar, and warmly congratulated the victorious captains, paying special attention to Captain Darby of the *Bellerophon*. The condition of the *Bellerophon* was the cause of much comment, and St Vincent said she was 'more mauled than any ship I ever saw'. Another onlooker said her side was like a 'honeycomb' with shot holes. Captain Darby was also loquacious on the condition of his ship! The crew of the *Bellerophon* as well as the rest of the squadron were looking forward to being back in England by Christmas, and worked hard at the repairs to get their ships ready in time.

Just before the refitting was complete and the ships ready to sail, an announcement from St Vincent fell like a thunderbolt on the men of the fleet. His order was that none of the ships of Sir James Saumarez's squadron was to leave the command, and the prizes were to be taken round to the Tagus where the main Mediterranean Fleet was based. This announcement stunned everybody; Sir James Saumarez was too diplomatic to comment, but Captain Darby was not and his Irish temper came to the boil. He told numerous people, civilians and army and navy officers alike, that the condition

of his ship was such that a dockyard like Gibraltar's could not
hope to repair it well enough to take part in any major operations. He thought a post-chaise could be driven through the
holes in its sides, and that it was a shameful way to treat the
sailors who won Britain's naval victories for her if they were
to be sent to sea in virtual wrecks afterwards with a good
chance of drowning!

St Vincent's decision was based on the notion that world
moral opinion would be struck by the fact that a French fleet
had been destroyed, but not one of the British ships was so
badly damaged that it had to leave its station for repairs. Both
men had a certain amount of right on their side, but on the
whole it must be considered that St Vincent held the balance.

Captain Darby's lack of restraint soon reached St Vincent's
ears, but appreciating the position of Darby and his compat-
riots, he kept quiet as long as possible. It was only when Darby
began airing his opinions in army messes that he decided to
take unofficial action. This is the way he did it, according to
the story handed down to posterity by his flag-lieutenant.

One night, after a long party at which both St Vincent and
Darby were present, St Vincent called round to the house
where Darby was staying. Darby had just retired to bed when
he heard a knocking on his window. Feeling rather annoyed,
he asked who the blazes was there at that time of night! He
was much surprised to recognize St Vincent's voice saying,
'Open up! Open up Darby! 'Tis I! I have something which I
must say to you.' Darby opened the window and there below
was the Commander-in-Chief in full-dress uniform. He told
Darby that he had had a dream which he felt he must recount
to him. He said he dreamed he was watching the battle of the
Nile and was much struck by the noble part played by the
Bellerophon, contending alone against the mighty *Orient*.
The scene of his dream then changed to the Rock where people
were saying what a fine fellow that Darby was and what a great
fight he put up. But, said St Vincent, he dreamed that Darby
himself was saying that the Rock lacked the shipwrights to
repair his ship, and that there would be a dreadful catastrophe
when the ship next put to sea. St Vincent said to himself that
this surely could not be the same Darby he had seen fighting
so nobly at the Nile; he must have turned chicken-hearted! A
rather exasperated Darby burst in at this point, and asked

what he meant by such a term, but St Vincent continued calmly and said that in his dream the reports of the bad condition of the *Bellerophon* were soon all over the Rock. Then the scene of the dream changed to a court martial and the officer being tried was Darby, and the blade of his sword was pointed towards him. St Vincent finished his story with these words: 'Now remember, this was only a dream, Darby; but now I have told you I hope I shall be able to rest, so good night!' He then strode away leaving Darby to spend a rather restless night! Whatever the truth of this story, the ships and prizes did remain on the station; for on the 24th October Sir James Saumarez sailed for the Tagus with the *Orion*, *Theseus*, and *Thalia* (frigate) escorting with the prizes *Franklin*, *Spartiate*, *Aquilon*, *Tonnant*, and *Conquérant*.

To speed repairs on the *Bellerophon* and the other badly damaged ships, St Vincent gave orders for every ship at Lisbon to send a carpenter and shipwright to the Rock to aid in the repair of the remaining ships.

On the 1st January the *Prince* arrived, flying the flag of Rear-Admiral Sir Roger Curtis.

The new year of 1799 saw the *Bellerophon* still at Gibraltar under repair, with carpenters and shipwrights from the fleet and dockyards swarming all over her. On the 7th January all the workmen were discharged from the ship, and on the 8th she weighed anchor and ran out to sea under orders to escort a convoy to Port Mahon. Besides the *Bellerophon*, the escort consisted of the frigate *La Minerve* and the brig *San Leon*. The convoy was made up of four transports and eight merchantmen. The ships, proceeding under all sail, rounded Cape Malaga and stood to the east with a fine breeze. Although no one on board knew it, this was to be the first of many voyages as convoy escort before the *Bellerophon* was next engaged in a fleet action at Trafalgar in 1805. During this period she served in three theatres, the Mediterranean, Channel and West Indies, on the hard unremitting grind which drew from the American naval historian the famous remark about the 'far distant storm-beaten ships on which the Grand Army never looked which stood between it and the dominion of the world'.

On the 25th January the convoy and its escort anchored at Port Mahon and Captain Darby went ashore with chests of money for the garrison. The four transports went into the harbour, while the escort and the merchantmen stayed outside awaiting the return of Captain Darby to the *Bellerophon*. After this the ships moved eastwards once more; this time they were headed for Palermo where they anchored on the 30th January. Outside the mole the signal was flown for a pilot to guide them in to the anchorage. At Palermo they found Nelson in the *Vanguard*, which was still in a battered condition after her efforts at the Nile. On the arrival of the *Bellerophon* Nelson shifted his flag to her, while the *Vanguard* underwent further repairs. The crew of the *Bellerophon* assisted in the re-rigging of the flagship, whose condition had been worsened by the violent storm which had raged during the crossing from Naples while evacuating the Neapolitan Royal Family. The work was soon completed, however, and Nelson re-hoisted his flag on board of the *Vanguard* on the 13th February.

The *Bellerophon* stayed several more weeks at Palermo, before leaving with a convoy for Leghorn on the 7th March. She then returned to Palermo on the 21st March, bringing with her another convoy of twenty-seven sail of merchantmen. On the 1st April they were sent out again, this time to the westwards to Port Mahon which was reached on the 12th April. Just over a week was spent at Port Mahon before the ships sailed again on the evening of the 20th April. This time she had for company the *Leviathan*, flying the flag of Rear-Admiral John Thomas Duckworth, and the 16-gun sloop *Peterel*. The *Peterel* spoke a Portuguese frigate on the 23rd April in the position 40′ 42″ N. and 2° 36″ E. The weather was hazy and the sea had a steady swell. The ever active *Peterel* chased and boarded a Spanish merchantman on the same day; she was bound from Majorca to Barcelona carrying a cargo of wheat. The sloop took her prize in tow and returned to Port Mahon.

The 30th April saw the *Bellerophon* and *Leviathan* approaching the passage between Cabrera and Majorca which was covered by a Spanish fort. To ensure a trouble-free passage the ships hoisted Spanish colours and this, combined with the poor visibility, enabled them to get through unmolested. The next day the frigates *Santa Teresa* and *Aurora* joined the two battleships.

Duckworth returned his squadron to Port Mahon on the 10th May for provisioning. It is notable that at this period the log kept by the first lieutenant, John Hadaway, in its careful record of each cask of beef opened, invariably records that it was so many pounds short of the stated weight.

On the 21st May the Commander-in-Chief anchored at Port Mahon with a fleet of sixteen sail of the line. He was in search of the French fleet which had escaped from Brest on the 25th April, past the lax watch of the Channel Fleet under Lord Bridport. The French had numbered twenty-five of the line when they escaped from Brest, and had appeared to be heading for Ireland. Lord Bridport fell back to cover that route, but in reality they were heading south. On the 4th May the French had appeared off Cadiz where Lord Keith was blockading the Spanish fleet with a force of fifteen sail of the line. The French now numbered only twenty-four ships, but the force in Cadiz of twenty-two sail of the line could not proceed to join because of a gale which was blowing directly into the port. Lord Keith's position outside made it impossible for the French to enter the port without an engagement which would have seriously crippled their force. Bruix therefore determined to enter the Mediterranean without delay. On the 5th May St Vincent, who was still ashore on the Rock, saw the line of French ships running before the gale through the Straits, and on the 11th he sailed from Gibraltar in his flagship the *Ville de Paris* of 110 guns, with fifteen other sail of the line.

Lord Keith, who had been cruising off Cape Spartel, had steered for Gibraltar on the 9th and it was his force which sailed under St Vincent's orders on the 11th. The Spaniards had seized the chance to get out, and on the 14th they sailed with seventeen sail of the line, including six three-deckers. They had a rough passage and by the time they reached Cartagena on the 20th eleven of the fleet had been partially or totally dismasted.

St Vincent sailed from Port Mahon on the 22nd taking Duckworth's division with him, thereby raising his force to twenty sail of the line. News had reached him that the French fleet had been seen to the north of Minorca steering for Toulon. He sent this news to Nelson at Palermo and set course for Toulon. Learning on the way of the escape of the Spaniards, he decided to cruise off Cape San Sebastian to prevent a junction of the enemy fleets. On the 30th May he heard that Bruix had sailed from Toulon on the 27th for an unknown destination, and believing that it might be eastwards to Egypt or Sicily he sent Duckworth with four sail of the line as reinforcements to Nelson. With his force temporarily reduced to sixteen sail of the line, he was inferior to any opposing fleet, but on the evening of the same day Rear-Admiral Whitshed joined with five sail of the line, including the three-decker *Queen Charlotte*.

On the 2nd June St Vincent's health, which had been poor for some months, broke down completely and he handed over the command to Lord Keith and sailed for Port Mahon in the *Ville de Paris* to supervise operations from there.

Keith continued on the same course until the 5th June, when he received information that the French fleet had been seen in Vado Bay on the 4th. A detachment of the French fleet had sent supplies into Genoa, which was besieged by the Austrians, and then Bruix steered along the coast of Piedmont and Provence to avoid the British; he passed Toulon and made for Cartagena where he joined the Spanish fleet already there. On the 8th June Keith received orders from St Vincent to take up a position in Rosas Bay. On the previous day the *Bellerophon* and *Powerful* had left the fleet to reinforce Nelson at Palermo. This gave Nelson a force of seventeen sail of the line and Keith eighteen, to foil any French attempt to go west or east. Unfortunately for Keith he did not obey St Vincent's order to remain in Rosas Bay and steered for Minorca, believing that place to be in danger of attack by the French. Had he remained in the bay he would undoubtedly have met the French for they were then only sixty miles away.

The *Bellerophon* and *Powerful* had left the fleet on the 7th June, and a week later they joined Nelson at Palermo. Nelson now had thirteen English and four Portuguese sail of the line and sailed from Palermo on the 16th June with the *Bellerophon* stationed in the rear division. The fleet moored in Naples Bay on the 25th June. Cardinal Ruffo came on board to consult with Nelson as to the best method of annoying the French and restoring the power of Their Sicilian Majesties, a subject on which they violently disagreed. Nelson's flagship was now the *Foudroyant* and he had as his flag-captain, Captain Hardy. The *Bellerophon* spent nearly six weeks at Naples before she sailed on the 3rd August with the *Zealous* for Gayette Bay. They anchored there on the 5th August and found the *Minotaur* already there, and the Neapolitan frigate *San Leon* with Neapolitan transports containing French troops. The Frenchmen were to be evacuated by sea to Toulon under the terms of a treaty recently signed by Cardinal Ruffo and the Russian general on the coast, which had been reluctantly concurred in by the British naval representative on the spot, Captain Foote of the frigate *Seahorse.* Nelson disapproved of the treaty and soon brought it to nought by refusing to allow the French troops to be evacuated.

The *Bellerophon* and *Zealous* left Gayette Bay on the 6th August and sailed for Sardinia with two English transports and a merchant vessel. They arrived at Port Mahon on the 19th, and the *Vanguard* arrived the following day. From then until the 17th October, all three ships were engaged in guard duty at the port. On that day the *Bellerophon*, accompanied by the frigate *Bulldog*, sailed for Gibraltar. From Gibraltar, where she arrived on the 3rd November, she sailed for the Tagus. From the Tagus she operated in Spanish seas for three months, sometimes going as far north as Cape Finisterre. It must have been with some joy that Captain Darby finally received orders to sail for Britain, and the *Bellerophon* left the Tagus on the 17th March. The Lizard was sighted on the 1st April and the ships dropped anchor at Spithead on the 3rd.

To cover briefly events in the Mediterranean from the receipt of St Vincent's order to Keith on the 8th June, will give a complete picture of the state of naval affairs at the end of the eighteenth century.

On the 14th June Lord Keith shifted his flag from the *Barfleur* of 98 guns to the *Queen Charlotte* of 100 guns, and Whitshed entered the former vessel. He stayed only a few days at Minorca, but during that period St Vincent finally turned over the whole command of the Mediterranean to Keith and sailed for home in the first available ship which happened to be the frigate *Argo*, commanded by Captain James Bowen, who had been master of the *Queen Charlotte* at the Glorious First of June.

Keith sailed for Toulon on the 15th but was now out of contact with the French, and from then until the 6th July the fleet scoured the area between Genoa, Toulon, and Minorca for any sign of Bruix. On the latter date Keith returned to Port Mahon and found awaiting him the force dispatched by Lord Bridport from the Channel on the 1st June. This was a force of twelve ships of the line, including five three-decked ships of 98 guns, under Rear-Admiral Sir Charles Cotton; among its commanders were Rear-Admiral Collingwood and Captain Sir Edward Pellew. Immediately after his arrival Keith received news that the French had reached Cartagena, and after refilling with water he steered to the westward on the 10th July with a force of thirty-one sail of the line. They were already too late to catch the French either in port or just as they were leaving, for Bruix had sailed on the 29th June with forty sail of the line. On the very day that Keith reached Minorca after his fruitless search off Toulon, the combined fleet of French and Spanish passed the Straits. By a coincidence it was again St Vincent who saw them gliding through the Straits and out into the Atlantic. He had arrived only twenty-four hours earlier and was waiting for a frigate to take him home. The combined fleet entered Cadiz on the 11th July, the day after Keith had sailed from Minorca in pursuit. On the 21st July they sailed again, this time to the north and bound for Brest. Keith reached Gibraltar on the 30th and sailed to the north without delay. The final leg of the long chase to Brest saw the British gradually closing the gap, and they arrived outside Brest only twenty-four hours after the French and Spanish ships had dropped anchor. This was on the 13th August, and for four days Keith remained outside, holding the port in close blockade, but when his frigates reported that the enemy were beginning to take down their top masts preparatory to a refit, he took twenty-seven of his fleet to Torbay and the four most in need of repair to Spithead.

With the departure of Lord Keith and the retirement of Lord St Vincent, the chief command in the Mediterranean now fell upon Nelson, and he remained in this capacity until the return of Lord Keith in December 1800.

The cruise of the French and Spanish fleets almost free from interference by the Royal Navy greatly boosted the morale of the allies. In the words of the naval historian James:

The Brest Fleet, although it had not signalised itself by a battle, had shown to the world, and particularly to the Spaniards, what could be effected by energy and address. It had traversed without molestation an immense extent of sea; that sea beset on every side, by the powerful fleets of England. If no other advantage was gained by the four months cruise, it had exercised the seamen, and could not fail to inspire a confidence, that would long continue to exert its encouraging influence over the French Marine.

To return to the *Bellerophon*: we left her at Spithead. She went into Portsmouth harbour for a refit, a lengthy process, and was out of commission until the 1st July 1801. A change of command occurred during the time the *Bellerophon* was not on active service, Captain Darby being replaced by Captain Lord Garlies in May 1801. Lord Garlies, later Earl of Galloway, was a well known officer of the Navy who subsequently became a Lord of the Admiralty, and to him befell the task of once again preparing the *Bellerophon* for sea. The ship was recommissioned on the 1st July, and was moved to Spithead on the 20th August to await a fair wind to join the Channel Fleet. This fleet was now under the command of Admiral Cornwallis, who had succeeded to the command on the promotion of St Vincent to the Admiralty. The change of command was of little significance, for both admirals held the same ideas on the subject of blockade.

The *Bellerophon* sailed with a fair wind on the 21st August, and ran down the coast to Cawsand Bay where she was to pick up some passengers for the Channel fleet. She anchored in Cawsand Bay on the evening of the 22nd August, and lay at single anchor taking aboard more supplies of vegetables while awaiting her passengers. On the 28th August these passengers came aboard; they included Rear-Admiral Campbell, who was on his way to the Channel fleet to hoist his flag in the famous *Téméraire* preparatory to sailing with a squadron for the West Indies. He was accompanied by his flag-captain Eyles, Lieutenant Douglas, and a French pilot for operations off the stormy coast of Brittany. The *Bellerophon* got under way at 8.15 a.m. that day and in two days had sighted the Channel fleet cruising off Ushant. On being signalled from the flagship, the *Ville de Paris*, the *Bellerophon* replied with her number, and began to work to windward to join the fleet. The first sighting had been made at 5.15 a.m., but it was not until 2.45 p.m. that the ship came up with the fleet. Her first task was to unload the supplies of vegetables and meat that she had brought for the other ships. Each vessel posted to join the

Channel fleet usually picked up a large supply of victuals for the use of the fleet before setting out. This practice considerably eased the supply situation, and enabled the ships to stay longer at sea.

Rear-Admiral Campbell joined the *Téméraire* at 5.15 p.m. and, after hoisting his flag, left with his squadron for the West Indies.

The *Bellerophon*, after unloading her supplies and her passengers, took her place in the fleet, and began what Lord Garlies called 'the dismal drudgery of the Bay'. The 'Bay' was of course the Bay of Biscay, and the station of the Channel fleet when blockading the French ports of Brest, Rochefort, and Aix Roads was off Ushant. Lord St Vincent's maxim was 'Well up with Ushant in an easterly wind', and Admiral Cornwallis was of a similar frame of mind. The close blockade, as practised by St Vincent and Cornwallis in this war and by Hawke and Anson in the Seven Years' War, had many detractors in its day, who said it was wearing on the ships and on the men, and that in a westerly gale the French could escape at any time they wanted. It was contrasted with the system of the earlier years of the war as used by Lords Howe and Bridport, which kept the main fleets in Spithead or Torbay in a high state of readiness, with only detachments of frigates or 74s watching the enemy in port. Against these arguments it can be said that keeping the fleets at sea gave a terrific boost to the public morale in Britain. People in the towns along the coast, and senior officers in the Navy, remembered the panic in August-September 1779 when the French and Spanish combined fleet had escaped and joined up to gain command of the Channel for three weeks. When St Vincent had assumed the command of the Channel fleet in 1800 he had kept a close blockade, and this policy had thereafter been maintained.

The *Bellerophon* was detached from the main fleet on the 10th September and went to join Admiral Thornborough's inshore squadron, a similar position to that which she had held at the blockade of Cadiz four years earlier. It was the policy of Cornwallis to relieve the inshore squadron frequently as the work was very wearing on the officers and men involved. St Vincent had said that Sir James Suamarez had got 'as thin as a herring' during his spell as commander of the inshore squadron. Thornborough's squadron at present consisted of the *Mars*, *Robust*, and *Brunswick*. The relieving force consisted of the *Bellerophon*, *Saturn*, *Edgar*, *Captain*, and *Elephant*.

The squadron was moored off the Black Rocks, in what Fraser calls the 'very jaws of Brest Harbour', and for the next six weeks they stayed cruising around the most dangerous shore on the whole Channel coast. During this hazardous and difficult work, occasional glimpses were caught of the main fleet in their relatively secure station farther out to sea. Eventually the squadron was relieved and rejoined the main fleet on the 20th October. The gales of late October forced the ships to run for the shelter of Torbay where the fleet anchored on the 1st November—in fact the *Bellerophon* spent the rest of the year in Torbay, along with several other ships of the Channel fleet. Lord Garlies was replaced in command of the *Bellerophon* in December 1801, when Captain John Loring took over. Loring, it will be remembered, had been acting captain for six months in 1796, after Lord Cranstoun had left and before Darby was available.

The new year of 1802 arrived and with it hopes of peace. Negotiations were going on at Amiens between a British and a French delegation. The British party was led by Lord Cornwallis, elder brother of Admiral Cornwallis, and known to history for his surrender at Yorktown in 1782 and his victories in India. The officers and men of the *Bellerophon* did not hear the news of the peace treaty, which was signed at Amiens on the 25th March, for they sailed for the West Indies on the 2nd March and anchored in Port Royal, Jamaica, on the 29th. Here they joined Rear-Admiral Campbell's squadron of eight of the line. By the time the *Bellerophon* sailed from Port Royal again it was the 6th April, but the time lag was well spent in overhauling the rigging and in reprovisioning. She then sailed in company with the *Audacious* (74) and the *Désirée* (40). The latter was a large frigate of 1,010 tons which had been captured by the *Dart* of 28 guns in a smart action off Dunkirk in 1800. A sudden gale blew up next day which carried away the mizen mast of the *Audacious*, but she did not leave the squadron. The tip of Santo Domingo was sighted on the 9th and the ships stayed for a while cruising along the coast before turning back for Port Royal.

When the three ships arrived at Jamaica they found already in port the squadron of Rear-Admiral Campbell who had just been joined by the *Leviathan*, flying the flag of Sir John Thomas Duckworth. The arrival of the *Bellerophon* and her consorts raised the force in West Indian waters to fourteen of the line, two frigates and a brig at Port Royal, and other cruisers scattered about the islands looking for privateers and on escort duties. The main fleet sailed some days before the *Bellerophon* was ready, and it was not until the 22nd April that she quitted Port Royal. It is certain that some time during April the news of the Peace of Amiens must have reached the West Indies, though the log of the *Bellerophon* makes no note of the actual date. A fast ship could have carried the news of the treaty across the Atlantic in approximately two to three weeks, arriving in the West Indies some time between the 11th and the 20th April. The *Bellerophon* sighted a French frigate on the 25th April and showed French colours to her—something she would not have done if she had not heard of the peace. Two days later she joined the fleet of Rear-Admiral Campbell, and for some time the force cruised between the island of Navaza and Donna Maria, which was the westernmost tip of Santo Domingo.

The island of Santo Domingo had recently been in revolt against the French, and Napoleon took advantage of the Peace of Amiens to send a large naval and military force under General Leclerc, his brother-in-law, and Admiral Villaret-Joyeuse. The army comprised 21,200 men and the fleet thirty-three sail of the line. The Spanish were allowed to co-operate in the venture since the leader of the rebellion, Toussaint L'Ouverture, had also gained possession of the Spanish half of the island including the important port of Santo Domingo.

The first contingent of this armada sailed on the 14th December 1801, and consisted of ten French and five Spanish sail of the line, six frigates, four corvettes and smaller vessels, and two transports containing the troops. James gives the total number of men on this first expedition as 7,000. During the next week further ships and men crossed the Atlantic under the command of Rear-Admiral Latouche-Treville, and by the end of January 1802, 10,500 men were ready to land on the island. This force, with the aid of further supplies of men, was enough to put down the rebellion in most areas, but by the summer yellow fever and enemy action had made large inroads into the strength of the garrison on the island. Toussaint, after the defeat of his forces, was arrested by the French and conveyed to France where he died mysteriously in prison. The death of Leclerc of yellow fever on the 2nd November and the absence of a large number of French troops in Guadeloupe repressing another rebellion were the signal for the coloured revolt to break out again. The resumption of the war between France and England in April 1803 was the death blow for the French hopes of retaining the colony, and they were soon restricted to Santo Domingo and its immediate vicinity. We have rather gone ahead of our chronicle, and we must now return to the operations of the *Bellerophon* and her consorts in the West Indies.

The British ships in the West Indies, although at peace with France, had the task of acting as a squadron of observation on the French forces in Santo Domingo. Reinforcements had raised the force to sixteen sail of the line, three frigates, and a brig by the 13th May, but that very evening seven of the ships of the line sailed for England. This was one of the inevitable results of the peace, when a large naval establishment was no longer required, and the processes of reducing the forces were hurried along by St Vincent at the Admiralty, where he was waging his one-man war against corruption.

The destructive effect of the climate of the West Indies on Europeans is demonstrated by the frequent entries in the *Bellerophon*'s log which begin with the words: 'Departed this life . . .' or 'Committed his body to the deep'. On the 28th May the surgeon of the *Bellerophon* died of yellow fever and was buried at sea. Three days later on the 31st May the log reads: 'A.M. . . . sold the effects of Mr. Young (Surgeon)'. This was the usual procedure when an officer or man died. The effects of their deceased comrades made life slightly more comfortable for the survivors for a few more weeks. There were often arguments between men as to the disposal of their belongings when a ship was about to go into action.

The *Bellerophon* left the squadron on the 4th June to return to Port Royal, and anchored there on the 5th June. She was there for nearly three weeks and the log makes mention of several tasks performed while the ship was in port, including scrubbing the lower decks with vinegar to clear up any possible infection. She sailed again on the 25th June to rejoin the squadron, which she did in a couple of days. On the 10th July the entry in the log reads; 'Mustered the people . . . and read the thanks of Parliament.' This would be about all the thanks the seamen could expect from the government of Addington, who were already discharging hundreds of their fellows on to the streets of Britain as soon as their ships entered port. No doubt the sailors were glad to leave the service, but such a large influx of labour on to an already declining economy meant real hardship for many, especially those who knew no other life than the sea.

By the 18th July the squadron under Admiral Duckworth comprised ten of the line and a frigate. They were still in their wartime cruising area in the seas off the island of Navaza, which enabled a watch to be kept on French operations in Santo Domingo. A squall on the 21st July sprung the *Bellero-phon*'s mizen topmast, but the damage had been repaired by the 22nd.

The squadron was now sailing north as the hurricane season was due in the West Indies very soon. There was no danger in leaving the French unwatched in Santo Domingo as they would be as hard hit by the weather as any British ships which stayed to watch them. There is a very interesting piece of sailors' doggerel which puts the facts rather prettily:

> July—Stand By.
> August—Go you must.
> September—Remember.
> October—All over!

With the passage north the sightings of American ships became more common, and on these occasions the squadron always showed French colours. This was also done whenever a Spanish ship came into view. Whether these manoeuvres fooled anyone it is difficult to say, but they are indicative of a certain coolness between British and American naval officers which in ten years would lead to the war of 1812-14. The squadron anchored at Halifax on the 14th September where they found the commander of the station, Vice-Admiral Sir Andrew Mitchell, flying his flag in the *Leander*, one of the *Bellerophon*'s old comrades of the Nile. It will be remembered that she had been captured off Crete by the *Généreux*; since then she entered the French navy, and had been recaptured by the Russians and Turks at the surrender of Corfu and restored to Britain by the Emperor of Russia.

It will be seen from the above rhyme that the hurricane only lasted until October, and the West India squadron left Halifax on the 11th October, bound for their proper station. It was a long trip to the West Indies under sail, and it was not until the 8th November that the squadron dropped anchor in Port Royal. To conclude briefly this period of the *Bellerophon*'s career, it is only necessary to mention the cruise which the squadron undertook from the 4th December to the 3rd January 1803. No events of importance happened, and with the peace still in progress it looked as if the ship's fighting days were over.

Many people in Britain hoped that the peace, now that it had come, would be permanent and that having proved themselves unconquerable they would be able to sit back and enjoy the profits of their industries. Others thought differently and combined an ardent patriotism with a violent hatred of Napoleon. They said he was only biding his time until the navies of the Continent had been rebuilt, when he would form a grand naval coalition to overwhelm England. Certainly the events in the dockyards of France supported this view, while the activity in Britain was directed towards reducing rather than increasing naval strength.

7

Trafalgar

THE new period of six years in the life of the *Bellerophon* began with her still in the West Indies, and the Peace of Amiens still in operation. This state of affairs did not seem likely to last very long, for the British Government was asking for some security before it released its hold on Malta, and Bonaparte was seeking to extend French influence in India and America.

Much of this, however, was unreal to the men of the *Bellerophon* and the other ships of the British West Indian squadron. Their immediate task was to keep a watch on French doings in Santo Domingo and their other West Indian possessions; their next was to ensure that they themselves kept as comfortable and as healthy as the hot climate would allow. The strict naval discipline would have been slightly relaxed under peace-time conditions, and most of the crews on the ships serving in the overseas stations of the Navy at that time were volunteers.

To continue our narrative, we left the *Bellerophon* and the squadron of Rear-Admiral Campbell moored in Port Royal where they had arrived on the 3rd January. There they remained, with different ships going out for a reconnaissance of the French, and the *Bellerophon* sailed in company with the *Elephant* and the *Charlotte* packet, with an easterly wind, on the 17th January. These three ships were joined by the *Vanguard* on the 19th January and followed the other ships of the squadron that were already on patrol. From then the daily routine varied little, with the ships cruising off Navaza until the 28th February when they returned to Port Royal.

By the 24th they were once again off Navaza, but this time when the weather forced them to go for shelter Campbell decided to run for Cumberland harbour in Cuba. This harbour had been discovered by Admiral Vernon's fleet during their operations against Cartagena in 1741. The fleet often used this port in future whenever their ships needed careening or repairs to the rigging. As they ran into the harbour, with the frigate *Désirée* leading the battleships, they must have made a fine sight set against the tropical background and the blue sky. The date when they moored in the bay was the 12th April and they remained there for four days.

The fleet returned to Port Royal on the 4th May, and, although they did not know it, they were making their last anchorage in peace-time for the next eleven years, for before they sailed again on the 24th, war had been declared between France and Britain. The actual starting date was the 16th May, when the Government issued letters of marque to privateers, but the declaration did not come until two days later. The blockade of Brest was resumed immediately, and a fleet of ten sail of the line and frigates sailed from Spithead on the 17th May under the command of Cornwallis.

The squadron at Port Royal sailed on the 24th May with a south-easterly wind for their old cruising ground. The news of the resumption of the war had not reached Jamaica by this time, but there can be little doubt that the report of further French reinforcements of 2,000 troops for Santo Domingo was the immediate cause of the squadron's sailing once again. The news of the war must have been relayed to them some time during the first week in June, for by that time practices with great and small arms are mentioned more frequently in the log.

The relative state of the opposing forces in the West Indies at the outbreak of war was as follows: The French had two ships of 74 guns in Santo Domingo, the *Duguay-Trouin* and the *Duquesne*, with several frigates and corvettes. The British force in the area comprised the 74-gun ships *Bellerophon, Hercule, Cumberland, Goliath, Elephant, Theseus,* and *Vanguard* with their attendant frigates. The British force was therefore definitely superior.

The first shots of the war were fired in the West Indies, when on the 29th June the French Corvette *Mignonne* was captured by a squadron from Port Royal including *Bellerophon*. The French frigate *Poursuivante* nearly shared the same fate when the *Hercule* 74 was detached to chase her. The British ship was the faster sailer of the two, but was badly handled and the frigate escaped. A second capture on the same day was that of a French brig from Santo Domingo. This brig returned next day to Port Royal with a prize crew. Another French vessel was taken on the 30th June—the 40-gun frigate *Créole*. She was taken into the Navy, but foundered on the 2nd January 1804 on a voyage from Jamaica. With the war now started, the Navy was entitled to impress men from merchant ships, and an entry in the *Bellerophon*'s log for the 30th June records that fourteen men were impressed from a merchant vessel encountered by the squadron. The capture of French ships continued, with a schooner taken on the 1st July and a brig on the 3rd. Both were returned to Port Royal with prize crews. The new Commander-in-Chief, West Indies, Sir John Duckworth, joined on the 10th July in the *Leviathan* and took over command of the squadron off Santo Domingo. Yet another French schooner was captured on the 11th July, which must have been most gratifying for the officers and men of the squadron, for most if not all of the prizes would have been purchased into the Navy. A famous British ship joined the squadron on the 21st July, when the schooner *Pickle* was sighted. This was the ship which later carried home Lord Collingwood's dispatches from the battle of Trafalgar.

On the 25th July the two remaining French 74s in Santo Domingo tried to escape to sea. They were accompanied by the 40-gun frigate *Guerrière*. Once clear of the harbour they steered to the westward, but they were seen by part of the blockading squadron which immediately gave chase. The ships in pursuit comprised the *Bellerophon, Elephant, Theseus, Vanguard,* and the frigates *Tartar* and *Aeolus*. The *Bellerophon* and *Elephant* were the fastest ships of the squadron, and when the French ships parted company, the *Duquesne* going along the shore to the west and the *Duguay-Trouin* to the east, the *Bellerophon, Theseus, Vanguard,* and frigates pursued the former, and the *Elephant* the latter. During the early morning the *Theseus* was detached to investigate some heavy firing heard from the east, while the *Vanguard* and

Tartar had now drawn ahead of the *Bellerophon* in a fluke wind and closed on the *Duquesne*. At 8 a.m. a rebel battery on shore opened fire on the *Duquesne*, which the French returned. By 3.30 p.m. the two leading British ships were close enough to open fire with their bow chasers, which they did, and after an exchange of several shots the French ship struck her colours. The French had no one killed or wounded on board and the British loss was only one man killed on the *Vanguard* and one wounded.

The *Elephant* was not so lucky as her sister ships. At daylight the *Duguay-Trouin* was about a mile ahead of her. Around 6 a.m. the French ship opened fire with her stern chasers and scored one or two hits on the *Elephant*'s hull. The British ship reserved her fire until she was on the starboard quarter of the French 74 when she fired her broadside, which the French returned. The firing was at long range and no damage was done to either ship. Two sails appeared on the horizon at this time: one was the British sloop *Snake* to the north-west, and the other was the French frigate *Guerrière* to the windward. The *Elephant* was unable to hold on to the *Duguay-Trouin* and the consequence was that both the French ships escaped. They steered straight for Europe where they arrived on the 2nd September off Cape Prior. Here they were attacked by a British squadron under Sir Edward Pellew, but once again their luck held and they escaped into Corunna.

After their action with the French 74s the British squadron were in complete control of the seas around Santo Domingo, and the last hopes of the French garrison's holding out against the rebels was gone.

The watch on Santo Domingo was continued, and by the end of October the French only held the port of San Nicolas and Cap Français. Both were blockaded by sea and land and the garrisons were almost at starvation point. The commander at Cap Français, General Rochambeau, proposed to Captain Loring of the *Bellerophon* that the French garrison should be allowed to evacuate the cape and be carried to France on board one of the ships of war remaining in the port. Loring rejected these terms, as the Frenchman no doubt expected him to do. They both knew who held the whip hand, for the French would have to surrender to the British if they wanted to stay alive. Luck, however, was temporarily on the

side of the French, and General Rochambeau made an agreement with the local coloured commander, Dessalines, agreeing
to evacuate Cap Français and its dependencies within ten days
from the 20th November. By the 30th November the French
had not left, and the negroes prepared to sink the ships in the
harbour with red-hot shot from the forts overlooking the bay,
which they now controlled.

Captain Loring, blockading the port, sent in Captain John
Bligh to reach an agreement with the French, and the final
terms were that the French should be allowed to depart in
their ships, fire one broadside for the honour of their flag, and
then surrender to the British ships outside. That day the log
of the *Bellerophon* records the final exit of French power in
Santo Domingo:

A.M. . . . Light Breezes observed the enemy's frigates and other vessels
getting under weigh, made the signal for a general chace . . . At 8 arrived
on board Captain Bligh to inform me the Cape and ships had surrendered
to Articles of Capitulation . . . At 10 the *Surveillante* frigate, *Cerf* brig and
two or three small vessels joined the squadron after discharging their guns.
Sent Lt. Thomas with an officer of Marines, two Petty Officers and 100
men to take possession of the *Surveillante*.

Having no further business at Cap Français, Captain Loring
took the squadron to the mole of San Nicolas to treat with
General Noailles commanding the last French garrison in the
island. On receiving the demand to surrender Noailles said
he had enough provisions to last for five months and would
not surrender until these were exhausted. His reason for not
treating with the British was that he had already made his
arrangements to escape that night, and as soon as the British
ships were out of sight on the way to Jamaica with their prizes,
he embarked his force in seven small vessels and escaped to
Cuba which was still controlled by neutral Spain. Why
Captain Loring left the port entirely unwatched is one of the
mysteries of the war. A few frigates and other small vessels
would have been enough to keep an efficient watch on the last
remaining French ships in Santo Domingo. Whatever the
reason, the squadron arrived back in Port Royal on the 7th
December, and stayed there repairing and reprovisioning the
ships for the rest of the year; but the frequent coming and
going of other small ships shows that the Royal Navy was
still on the hunt for French merchantmen and for any stray

ships of war which might try to reach the remaining French islands.

It was not until the 3rd February that the *Bellerophon* sailed from Port Royal for her cruising station off Cape Navaza, where the squadron was joined by the frigates *Tartar* and *Aeolus*. Loring brought the squadron to anchor in Manchincal Bay, Santo Domingo, the squadron consisting at that time of *Bellerophon*, *Elephant*, *Tartar*, and *Aeolus*. The ships sailed from the bay in the evening of the 4th March and Loring detached the *Elephant* and *Aeolus* to probe further down the coast. The *Tartar* was sent on escort duty with a convoy leaving for England.

A strange sail sighted on the 11th March proved to be an American schooner which had been taken by French privateers; it was brought to after a short chase.

The *Bellerophon* brought her prize to Port Royal on the 22nd March, the same day that her former prize, the *Duquesne*, left for England. The *Bellerophon* herself was only in port a couple of days before she was sent out to escort a convoy into Port Royal. This convoy was sighted on the 2nd April and the *Bellerophon* joined the escort that day, then with her consort the *Elephant* and the existing escort, composed of the frigate *Franchise* and the sloop *Renard*, she steered for Jamaica. The two light vessels parted company from the convoy the next day as it entered the windward channel. Having a convoy under her escort was too good a chance for the warships to miss, and the *Bellerophon* impressed several men from the convoy to supplement her crew with a few more trained seamen.

A fierce gale blew up on the 14th which lasted until the 16th, during the course of which the main topmast and topsail were carried away and the convoy and its escort greatly scattered. No losses occurred among the ships, however, and the majority of the convoy was in sight from the *Bellerophon* by the 18th, and they resumed their interrupted journey to Port Royal, dropping anchor on the 1st May. The gale which had scattered the convoy and damaged the *Bellerophon* had also blown the *Duquesne* back into port, for she was already at anchor when the *Bellerophon* and her charges came in. Her arrival was opportune, however, for it enabled her to sail as escort to the next homeward-bound convoy with the *Bellerophon*, which was also returning to England after two years' service in the West Indies. The convoy and its escort left Port Royal on the 17th June and for the first few days suffered from frequent rain storms.

The 22nd June brought another addition to the convoy when the schooner *Pickle* joined with a further fifteen sail of merchantmen, and parted company herself the next day. The convoy was taking the long upwards loop usual to sailing ships at that time of year, and by the 7th July were in the position 27° 56′ N. and 80° 22′ W.—a total distance of twenty-one leagues north-west of Cape Canaveral, which was to become famous as the American missile station, but in those days was only a point of navigation.

A Spanish ship of the line had passed through the convoy on the 29th June, and no doubt the captain eyed longingly the rich ships which were gliding by before his gaze, and probably cursed the fact that England and Spain were still at peace!

A count from the *Bellerophon* on the 8th July revealed 178 sail in sight, covering the sea for miles around. The position recorded in the log for midday 12th July states, 'Grand Bank of Newfoundland Dist. 347 Leagues. 34° 24′ N. 72° 20′ W.', and the convoy was well on the homeward path. A total of 163 sail was sighted from the *Bellerophon* on the 15th July, but the numbers always fluctuated according to the vagaries of the wind over such a large area of sea as that covered by the convoy, and the different sailing qualities of the ships. By the 30th July the convoy was 367 leagues NW. of St Agnes Point, and by the 9th August Start Point was seven leagues away. The convoy finally came to anchor in the Downs on the 11th August, where they found the fleet of Admiral Lord Keith who was entrusted with the task of watching the French invasion preparations at Boulogne.

The *Bellerophon* sailed from the Downs on the 18th August on her way to Spithead for a refit, and she anchored in St Helen's Roads on the 21st August, going into Portsmouth harbour next day. It was the 8th October before she came out of harbour, and the 1st of December before she was considered fit to sail. Her latest orders were to place herself under Admiral Cornwallis, who was in command of the Channel Fleet entrusted with the blockade of Brest and Rochefort—a service which he carried out with exactness and precision, always hoping for a chance to meet a French fleet at sea while in independent command; but to him, as to Lord Collingwood after him, the chance never came.

The *Bellerophon* joined the fleet on the 3rd December, and it was decided by Cornwallis to detach her to the inshore squadron under Sir Thomas Graves that was blockading Rochefort. Cornwallis records in his Journal his use of the new arrival: 'I detached the *Bellerophon* to join Rear-Admiral Sir Thomas Graves off Rochefort, and I sent orders for the *Queen* to proceed to Cawsand Bay to replenish and afterwards to rejoin me'. The *Bellerophon* left the main fleet on the 5th December, and had reached the squadron of Sir Thomas Graves by the 11th December. The squadron at that time consisted of the following ships: *Foudroyant*, *Queen*, *Hero*, *Tonnant*, *Mars*, and *Colossus*. The *Bellerophon* was of course to replace the *Queen*, as stated in Cornwallis's Journal.

Out on the Atlantic one more event had happened which was to add to the list of enemies against Great Britain. The Government, having news that Spain was almost certain to join the war against them, had determined to seize the consignment of gold and bullion which was sent across the Atlantic every year. It would mean a serious loss to the Spanish treasury and perhaps delay or even prevent the entry of Spain into the war on the side of France. The ships sent on this service were the *Indefatigable* (44), *Lively* (38), *Amphion* (32), and the *Medusa* (32). The officer in charge of this operation was Captain Graham Moore, brother of Sir John Moore, the general who was to become famous for his retreat to Corunna in 1809.

The treasure fleet was bound to Cadiz from Monte Video in South America, and the British ships assembled off Cape St Mary on the morning of the 3rd October. Early on the 5th October the Spanish squadron was sighted, and was seen to consist of the *Medea* (40), *Clara* (34), *Fama* (34), and *Mercedes* (34). As soon as they sighted the British ships, the Spanish ships formed line of battle ahead in the order *Fama*, *Medea*, *Mercedes*, and *Clara*. The British made full sail in chase, and by five past nine both lines were running parallel to each other with the British on the weather beam in the order *Medusa*, *Indefatigable*, *Amphion*, and *Lively*. Captain Moore in the *Indefatigable* hailed the *Medea* to heave to but received no response, so a shot was sent across her bows—upon which the Spanish ship obeyed. Moore sent a message aboard the Spanish frigate that his mission was to obtain without bloodshed, if possible, the cargo the Spanish ships were carrying. The officer carrying the message returned with an unsatisfactory answer, Moore fired a second shot across the bows of the *Medea* and bore down close to the Spanish ship's weather bow. Whether or not this was mistaken for a general engagement, it caused the *Mercedes* to fire into the *Amphion*, and within a few seconds the *Medea* had fired into the *Indefatigable*. Captain Moore flew the signal for close action, and this continued for about nine minutes before tragedy struck. The *Mercedes*, which had been engaging the *Amphion*, suddenly blew up with a tremendous explosion and only forty-one persons out of her passengers and crew were saved. The loss of the ship was made even more tragic by the loss of the entire fortune and most of the family of a South American merchant who was travelling as a passenger on the ship. He himself had a short time before gone on board the *Medea* with one of his sons, leaving his wife, four daughters, and four other sons on board the *Mercedes*; this saved his life, but gave him the terrible agony of seeing his family destroyed in an instant. It is good to relate that the British Government fully compensated him for the loss of his money although they could make no reparation for the loss of his family.

A few minutes after the *Mercedes* blew up, the *Fama* struck her colours to the *Medusa*, but when the latter ship ceased fire she rehoisted them and attempted to make her escape. The *Medusa* gave chase, assisted by the *Lively* which had forced the *Clara* to surrender. The *Fama* soon struck to her two pursuing enemies. *Medea* had been engaging the *Indefatigable*, but after the destruction of the *Mercedes*, the *Amphion* too opened fire on her and she was soon forced to strike.

The value of the cargo on the three remaining frigates was little short of £1 million sterling in cash as well as kind. The cost in Spanish lives had been 300 killed and eighty wounded, and the British two killed and seven wounded. The argument raged at the time, and still does rage, as to whether Britain had any right to seize the ships. The British force, however, was of such a superior nature that the Spaniards could have surrendered without any loss of honour. The affair naturally led to the war which had been expected, but which it had been hoped would be avoided by the seizure of the treasure fleet. Spain declared war on Britain on the 12th December 1804, and on the 11th January 1805 the British Goverment issued letters of marque to ships to operate against Spanish property.

The Spanish declaration of war meant that a much greater area had to be kept under observation by the Royal Navy, and there was a considerable increase in the number of ships of the line at the disposal of Napoleon. There were Spanish and French squadrons in most of the Continental ports, and new ones to be watched included Cadiz and Cartagena. The port of Ferrol was already being guarded as it contained a French squadron.

At the time of the Spanish declaration of war the *Bellerophon* was cruising off the Roches Bonnes and Belleisle with the squadron of Sir Thomas Graves. On the 2nd January Admiral Graves took his squadron into Quiberon Bay to water, and the admiral commanding the French squadron at Rochefort, Admiral Missiessy, was able to get to sea on the 11th January. Fortunately they were observed by two British light vessels, the frigate *Doris* and the schooner *Felix*.

Captain Campbell of the *Doris* knew that Sir Thomas Graves was at Quiberon Bay, and as soon as he saw the preparations of the French to move out he hastened to warn Graves, leaving the *Felix* to watch the movements of the French when they eventually got to sea. His passage was interrupted by storms and he did not arrive in Quiberon Bay until the 11th, the day the French sailed and the day after Graves had left. The following day he received definite news that the French were at sea from an American schooner which had been boarded by them on the 11th. While he was attempting to work out of Quiberon Bay to get this news to Graves, the *Doris* struck a rock and began to take in water. The situation was looking desperate, for the French were of such a force that they would probably be able to fall on Sir Thomas Grave's lighter squadron and drive it before them. Further confirmation of the American's news arrived with the schooner *Felix* which had been left to watch the French at Rochefort.

The crew worked all through the night to save the ship, and were just about holding their own when a gale blew up next morning. Once again the *Doris* began to take in water faster than the pumps could control it, and Campbell took the decision to abandon. The American schooner and the *Felix* were still in sight, and he stood over towards them to save the crew. By 3 o'clock on the morning of the 21st January the water filled the lower deck, and the crew were immediately transferred to the waiting schooners before Captain Campbell set the *Doris* on fire to destroy her. The failure of Captain Campbell to reach Admiral Graves with the intelligence of the French novements enabled Missiessy to get away from Rochefort with no one in Britain having any certain idea of his destination.

With the year 1805, and the escape of Missiessy, we now come to one of the most critical years in naval history. Fleets moved over the surface of the oceans of the western hemisphere in move and countermove in the great plan of Napoleon to invade the British Isles, and to end the war at one stroke before the British Government could raise up another coalition against him. Napoleon and many other Frenchmen regarded it as the opportunity to end once and for all the 600-year struggle between England and France, and to crush the hereditary enemy.

The year saw the art of sailing-ship warfare brought to perfection by Nelson at the battle of Trafalgar. It saw the end of the active war at sea, leaving the Royal Navy only the passive and infinitely more wearing work of the blockade of Europe. It saw the complete destruction of any challenge to Britain's maritime supremacy. It saw England 'save herself by her exertions', but not yet 'save others by her example'.

To understand the following pages it is necessary first of all to outline the various schemes which were hatched in Napoleon's mind for the invasion of the British Isles, culminating with his 'Grand Design' and the defeat at Trafalgar. Ever since the renewal of the war in 1803, Napoleon had sought a way of dealing a death blow which would cause the British governing and commercial classes to sue for a quick peace. His first plan was made in 1804, based on the escape of the Toulon fleet. This fleet was to be raised to a force of ten sail of the line, and at a fitting moment was to sail with a NW. wind to give the impression to the watching British frigates that another descent on Egypt was planned. This, it was hoped, would leave Nelson and his fleet chasing a fleet at the eastern end of the Mediterranean which had altered course and headed west.

The Brest fleet was to embark 20,000 men as though to be ready for an attempt at an invasion of Ireland. The French hoped that when Cornwallis saw this he would close in to the port and leave the main Channel passage free of a British force. Once the Toulon fleet was unobserved it was to turn and make for Cadiz, to be joined there by the Rochefort squadron, making a total of fifteen or sixteen sail of the line. The combined fleet was then to make its way up-Channel, dodge Cornwallis who would be close in to Brest, and appear off Boulogne to escort Napoleon's army to England.

This plan was impracticable and the French admirals recognized it, but none of them would dare to tell the Emperor that he would have to think again! Its most glaring fault was that it relied upon all the squadrons getting away at a given time and meeting at a given point. It further assumed that none of the squadrons would meet a British force before they had united.

Napoleon decided to go ahead with his plan, and appointed the foremost French admiral of the day to command the key Toulon fleet; this was Latouche Treville, a disciple of Suffren. The plan folded up with the death of Latouche Treville in June 1804.

In Napoleon's next plan the key role was given to the Brest fleet under Admiral Ganteaume, which had before only served to hold down the blockading squadron of Cornwallis while the combined Toulon and Rochefort squadrons made their way up Channel unopposed. This time the Irish invasion scheme received priority and Marshal Augereau was given command of 18,000 men. Ganteaume was to embark these troops, escape from Brest without fighting, proceed up the west coast of Ireland and land the troops in Northern Ireland. He was then to make his way to the Channel by which ever way was the more convenient, either round Scotland or down the Irish coast, and sail up the Channel to Boulogne. As soon as the Brest fleet arrived off Boulogne, if the wind was favourable it was to rush the Grand Army across to land in England. Napoleon realized that with only 18,000 men in

Ireland he was running a great risk, and said that whether they were increased to 40,000, or whether he was himself in England with the Grand Army while 18,000 were in Ireland, the war was almost won.

To assist the Brest fleet in its operations the Toulon and Rochefort squadrons were to cause a diversion by sailing for the West Indies on separate dates. The Toulon squadron was to detach a couple of ships of the line on the way across the Atlantic and seize the British island of St Helena. The squadrons were then to cruise for three months in the West Indies, attacking British commerce and possessions and doing all the damage they possibly could to British interests. They were then to unite and with a force of twenty sail to return to European waters, relieve the French ships in Ferrol, and proceed to Rochefort. Napoleon calculated that the British would have to send thirty ships in pursuit of the combined squadrons. The Toulon fleet commanded by Villeneuve was to sail by the 12th October and the Rochefort fleet commanded by Missiessy by the 1st November. The Irish expedition was not to sail until word arrived that both other squadrons were away.

This second plan was more vast in its conception than the previous one, and therefore much more difficult to put into operation. It too was never embarked upon, as Napoleon postponed it with the entry of Spain into the war on the side of France. The Spanish declaration added a further twenty-five sail of the line to the force available to Napoleon in his efforts to destroy Britain. He already had the aid of the Dutch navy, which was situated on his right flank and was admirably placed for either an invasion of Britain or an attack on her commerce.

The third plan was made towards the end of December 1804, and fresh orders were issued to Villeneuve and Missiessy in the form of a modified second plan. Missiessy was to leave Rochefort and steer a course between the Canaries and the Azores to avoid any British squadrons off the coast of Spain or in the Bay of Biscay. Once clear of European waters he was to go direct to Martinique, taking on the way the British islands of St Lucia and Dominica. Villeneuve was to escape from Toulon, go to Cayenne, recapture Dutch Guiana and link up with Missiessy. The combined squadrons were then to relieve Santo Domingo (the Spanish half of which was still in French hands) and return to Europe after spending not more than sixty days in the West Indies. The combined squadrons were to appear off Ferrol, release the squadrons blockaded therein and proceed up-Channel to Rochefort.

The first part of this plan succeeded, as we have seen, with the escape of Missiessy from Rochefort on the 11th January. He reached Martinique on the 20th February, and on the 24th of the same month Rear-Admiral Cochrane was sent in pursuit with six sail of the line, which would raise the British force in the West Indies to ten of the line. Cochrane's place off Ferrol was filled by a detachment from the Channel Fleet. Missiessy's mission to the West Indies was a comparative failure, for after causing only slight damage to the British possessions he returned to Rochefort, where he anchored on the 26th May and was promptly blockaded by a force of five or six ships.

Villeneuve was ready to sail in early January and managed to get away on the 18th of that month. He steered a course for Sardinia, watched by British frigates. These frigates reported his course to Nelson who was at anchor in Maddalena Bay. Nelson immediately put to sea and steered along the east coast of Sardinia, sending frigates ahead to regain touch with the enemy. A vain search was made for the elusive French fleet by Nelson always keeping to the east of Toulon to bar their path to Egypt. What Nelson could not achieve the weather could, and a violent storm blew up which forced Villeneuve to the decision that neither his ships nor his crews were fit for sea, and he returned to Toulon suffering from severe storm damage. It was in Toulon that Nelson found them the next time he looked into the port.

With one detachment at large, but another detachment stormbound in port, it was obvious that the plan would have to be changed, and fresh orders were drafted. Missiessy was ordered to remain in the West Indies until at least the end of June, and to be ready to join any other forces from Europe which should come to Martinique.

Admiral Gourdon, commanding at Ferrol, was told to hold himself in immediate readiness for sea, and to sail and join the Brest fleet when that appeared off the port.

Admiral Ganteaume was ordered to embark 3,000 troops and to sail with twenty-one sail of the line to release Gourdon from Ferrol. The combined force was then to proceed to Martinique. Here he was to join forces with Missiessy and Villeneuve and with a force of forty sail of the line to return to the Channel, overwhelm any force he might find in his path, and arrive off Boulogne. The expected time of arrival of the combined force off Boulogne was mid-July. If Villeneuve failed to break out of the Mediterranean, Ganteaume was to wait thirty days and then with twenty-five sail of the line to try to fight his way up-Channel to Boulogne. If he had less than this number, he was to rendezvous off Ferrol with all the French and Spanish forces then free, and then make for the Channel.

Admiral Villeneuve at Toulon was to break out of the Mediterranean and relieve the Spanish squadron blockaded in Cadiz. The combined squadrons were then to proceed to Martinique where they were to wait forty days for the arrival of Ganteaume. At the end of that period, if Ganteaume had not arrived in the West Indies, they were to do all the damage they could to British interests before proceeding to the Canaries. Here had been fixed another possible rendezvous for Ganteaume, and Villeneuve was to wait for him for a further twenty days. If Ganteaume still failed to appear, the combined squadrons were to return to Cadiz and await further orders.

This plan has been widely criticized by both Frenchmen and Englishmen as unworthy 'both of Napoleon and his genius'. It has been suggested that there never was any plan for the invasion of the British Isles, and that the great camp at Boulogne and the naval manoeuvres were only a blind for military operations on the Continent. This seems unlikely, as none of the senior marshals who were corps leaders in the invasion forces has shown himself aware of the fact that they were only there at Boulogne to fool the English, and not as part of a great concentration for an invasion. With the loss of Napoleon's fleet at Trafalgar and the almost complete extinction of French sea power that this entailed, it would seem a very expensive method of lulling his Continental enemies into a sense of false security. The plan itself was almost outrageous in its ignorance of the basic facts of war at sea, such as wind, and the disregard of any possible counter-move by the British.

Napoleon's final plan to subdue Britain—the one which he put into operation—is woven into the story of the *Bellerophon* and the salient features of it will be related as they occur.

Sir Thomas Graves's squadron was back in Quiberon Bay by the 17th January, and was joined that same day by the schooner *Felix* with the news of the escape of Missiessy from Rochefort. Graves received reinforcements by the arrival of the three-decker *Windsor Castle* (98), transferred from the Channel Fleet to the inshore squadron by Cornwallis as soon as he heard of the escape of the French squadron. He had also detached Admiral Calder with six sail of the line to help Cochrane off Ferrol. Calder carried orders from Cornwallis that he was to pursue Missiessy to the West Indies, as this was now suspected to be his destination.

Graves was unable to get away from Quiberon Bay until the 21st January, and fell back, under orders, to join the Channel Fleet off Brest. He joined Cornwallis on the 29th January, cruising between Ushant and Belleisle, then the winter gales forced even Cornwallis to run for the shelter of Torbay. The fleet was brought to anchor in Torbay on the evening of the 10th February, but it was able to sail again next day. The following day the *Prince of Wales* (98) flying the flag of Sir Robert Calder, and his squadron rejoined the main fleet, followed later in the day by the *St George* (98). Calder left with his squadron, reinforced by the *St George*, a week later on the 19th, his force consisting of the *Prince of Wales* (98), *St George* (98), *Atlas* (98), *Eagle* (74), *Spartiate* (74), and *Veteran* (64).

Cornwallis was forced to bring the fleet back to Torbay on the 27th of February, but sailed again on the 7th March. The weather was still very bad and he was unable to assume his blockading station off Ushant and by the 16th of March the fleet was riding at single anchor in Torbay once more. Recently Cornwallis had been feeling the strain of his prolonged blockade, and had applied for a period of shore leave to the Admiralty. He had had a period of twenty-two months of arduous blockading service including two very stormy winters, and his health had broken down under the strain. Permission was received for him to go ashore on the 19th March, and on that day he took his flagship, the 110-gun *Ville de Paris*, and the 98-gun *Queen* round to Spithead for repairs, where they anchored next day. Until the arrival of the new Commander-in-Chief, who was to be Admiral Lord Gardner, the command of the fleet resolved upon Vice-Admiral Sir Charles Cotton with his flag flying in the 110-gun ship *San Josef*. Gardner was at that time at Cork flying his flag in the frigate *Trent*, but the new three-decker *Hibernia* (110) was allotted to carry his flag.

The fleet left Torbay immediately the gale eased on the 20th March and took their station off Ushant. At this point in our story we begin what is known to history as:

THE TRAFALGAR CAMPAIGN, MARCH-OCTOBER, 1805

We have seen how Napoleon had modified his ideas yet again on the projected invasion of England, and that under the new orders Villeneuve was to break out of the Mediterranean, collect the Spanish squadron in Cadiz, and cross to the West Indies. The Brest fleet under Ganteaume was to break out, relieve Ferrol, and also cross to the West Indies, link up with Villeneuve, and return to European waters with a force of forty sail of the line.

The Admiralty in London suspected nothing of any of the Emperor's plans at the beginning of the year, but they became aware that 'something was up' when reports of increased activity came from the squadrons blockading the enemy ports. The *Bellerophon* had been sent by Cotton to form part of the inshore squadron off the Black Rocks near Brest. On the 26th March the look-outs spotted the fleet in Brest beginning to move out of the inner harbour, and this information was immediately signalled to the main fleet farther out. Ganteaume had been told to get to sea without an action, but seeing only a force of seventeen British ships before the port, he signalled to the Emperor for permission to sail. 'Success is not doubtful', he said. 'I await Your Majesty's orders.' Napoleon, however, still clung to the idea of escape without an action, such as Villeneuve achieved in the Mediterranean, and signalled back to Ganteaume: 'A naval victory in these circumstances would lead to nothing. Have but one object, to fulfil your mission. Go without fighting.'

As soon as the French movements were reported to him, Cotton brought his whole force up to Brest, and it was this fleet of seventeen battleships which compelled Ganteaume to stay in port.

On the 27th March, he made an effort to leave port without an action, and his movements were spotted by the inshore squadron. The events are reported in the log of the *Bellerophon* in the following words:

Observed the Enemys ships coming out of harbour, made all sail towards them, cleared for action. At noon observed the Enemys Fleet consisting of 21 sail of the line, 6 frigates and two Brigs under sail standing out of Brest Harbour.

Once again Cotton brought the fleet close into Brest:

A.M. . . . . Saw our Fleet standing towards us and the enemy anchoring in Bertheaume Roads as they came out of Brest. At 5.30 a.m. Fleet joined immediately after which, observed the Enemy hoist their topsails and several of them under weigh returning to Brest Roads.

Ganteaume had been waiting for a spell of thick mist before sailing, but when this came the signal stations reported that the British were off the port in strength. He had therefore to abandon his plan of sailing without an action, and when he saw the British fleet bearing down on him he thought that Cotton was going to make an attack on the French at anchor, as Nelson had done at the Nile, and he prepared to make sail to engage the British in open sea. Cotton, seeing this, hauled out again and stood out for the sea hoping the French would follow him. A change of wind, however, forced the French back into the harbour of Brest.

The next day, March 30th in the Mediterranean, Villeneuve made his second attempt to get to sea, and this time was successful. We will not follow the details of Nelson's long chase after Villeneuve except in so far as it affects the *Bellerophon*.

In the Channel on the 3rd April a sail was sighted in the distance and when signalled answered that it was the *Hibernia* carrying the new Commander-in-Chief, Lord Gardner. The *Bellerophon* received orders from the Commander-in-Chief to return to port for a change of command. Captain Loring was leaving the ship and Captain John Cooke was taking over. The ship moored in Cawsand Bay on the 23rd April, and Captain Cooke took command on the 24th. In his log he writes: 'I came on board—my commission read, and superseded Captain John Loring in the command of the ship.' Captain Cooke was considerably more of a disciplinarian than Captain Loring and from his assumption of command until his death at the battle of Trafalgar, hardly a week goes by without at least one flogging recorded in the log.

With the change of command completed and the ship reprovisioned, the *Bellerophon* sailed to rejoin the fleet on the 8th May, and after a quick run across the Channel was up with the main fleet on the 9th.

With Villeneuve away but Ganteaume still securely locked in Brest the Emperor sent new orders to his admiral. If he (Ganteaume) could not get away by the 20th May he was to remain where he was in Brest but to move to the outer anchorage which had been heavily fortified in case the British decided to attack the French at anchor.

By this time Villeneuve had been away for several weeks, had crossed the Atlantic, and Nelson had sailed in pursuit. The Government had certain news that the French had gone to the West Indies, but no one knew where Nelson had gone and there was much criticism of the admiral. It was not until 4th June, the same day that he reached the West Indies, that Nelson's letters arrived in London telling of his decision to sail there. Earlier, with the knowledge that both Villeneuve and Missiessy had gone to the West Indies, the Admiralty had dispatched Admiral Collingwood to pursue them unless he found that Nelson had already left—in which case he was to send two of his ships to the West Indies and with the rest to blockade both Cadiz and Cartagena. For this mission they gave him the following ships for his squadron: *Dreadnought* (98), *Tonnant* (80), *Achilles* (74), *Colossus* (74), *Mars* (74), *Illustrious* (74), and the *Bellerophon*. Accompanying the line ships was the frigate *Endymion*.

Off Cape Finisterre on the 27th May Collingwood fell in with Sir Richard Bickerton in the *Queen* (98). Bickerton informed him that Nelson had gone to the West Indies after Villeneuve and the Combined Fleet, and Collingwood sent his two fastest ships, the *Ramillies* and *Illustrious* to catch up with him. With the rest of his force he proceeded to the blockade of Cadiz and Cartagena, and Bickerton joined his squadron with the *Queen*.

With the blockade of Cadiz and Cartagena by Collingwood this was the position of the various British Naval forces in early June 1805:

Lord Gardner was blockading a force of twenty-one sail of the line in Brest under Admiral Ganteaume.

Lord Nelson, with eleven of the line, was in the West Indies pursuing Villeneuve with the combined fleet, with a force of twenty of the line.

Admiral Calder, with nine sail, was blockading a force of ten French and Spanish ships in Ferrol under Admirals Gourdon and Grandellana.

Admiral Stirling, with five of the line, was blockading Admiral Allemande with five sail in Rochefort.

Admiral Collingwood, with seven sail of the line, was blockading a Franco-Spanish force in Cadiz and Cartagena of approximately ten sail.

Collingwood sent the *Bellerophon* to blockade Cartagena with Sir Richard Bickerton, and with reinforcements arriving from home the force before each port was as follows: before Cadiz, *Dreadnought* (98), *Mars* (74), *Colossus* (74), *Achilles* (74), and the frigates *Hydra* and *Endymion*. Before Cartagena were the *Queen* (98), *Tonnant* (80), *Bellerophon* (74), and *Minotaur* (74), with the *Lively*, *Ambuscade*, and *Seahorse* frigates. One battleship was detached to Cape Spartel, and there were two of the line in the Mediterranean, making a total of nine of the line, one 50, and ten frigates as well as various light craft. Collingwood was engaged in blockading Cadiz from the 8th June, and stopped several neutral vessels to gain intelligence of the movements of the ships in Cadiz and the Combined Fleet without.

The month of June 1805 saw much activity out on the Atlantic. Nelson, thanks to wrong information, had missed Villeneuve in the West Indies. Villeneuve, hearing of Nelson's arrival in the area and believing him to be superior both numerically and qualitatively, decided to return to Europe. He had been reinforced by the arrival of Admiral Magon with two battleships on the 4th June, and the following day he captured part of a large fleet of British merchantmen. With Nelson's arrival he and the Spanish admiral, Gravina, decided to return to Europe and try to effect the concentration of force which Napoleon desired in the Straits of Dover. By 11th June the Combined Fleet was once again on the move, this time eastwards. By the 13th June Nelson had sailed in pursuit, but he was destined to miss them once again for they were heading north for the Bay of Biscay, while Nelson thought they would make south for Cadiz. He had sent the *Curieux* ahead to warn the Admiralty of his intentions, and luckily this vessel spotted the Combined Fleet on its passage and raced on to warn the Admiralty, arriving at Plymouth on 7th July. The First Lord, Lord Barham, as soon as he received the news sent orders to reinforce Admiral Calder's fleet off Ferrol.

On the 22nd July the clash between Calder and Villeneuve occurred. It was indecisive, and both British and French admirals claimed a victory. It had, however, the effect of forcing Villeneuve to seek shelter in Vigo instead of carrying on his way up the Channel.

Nelson brought his fleet to anchor at Gibraltar on the 19th July, having passed his friend Collingwood who was off the Rock with three of the line. When he reached Gibraltar Nelson went ashore for the first time since the 16th June 1803. As soon as the news of the sighting of the Combined Fleet by the *Curieux* reached him, on 25th July, he took his fleet north. He left his ships with Admiral Cornwallis, who was once again in charge of the Channel fleet, and with only the *Victory* and the *Superb* made his way to Portsmouth. Here the great sailor passes out of our story until he arrives off Cadiz to take command of the fleet blockading that port.

On the 2nd July, Collingwood had written a letter to a friend, the Rev. Dr Carlyle, in which he gives his opinions on what object the Combined Fleet had in view by their manoeuvres. It is worth quoting some of it:

... I sent 2 ships to strengthen my friend [Nelson] in the West Indies and the rest are divided between the two ports here [Cadiz and Cartagena]. Such is my employment at present, without any means of giving much annoyance to the Spaniards while they keep snug, and little expectation of their coming out. But I think it is not impossible that I shall have all those fellows coming up from the West Indies again before the Hurricane months, unless they sail from thence direct to Ireland, which I have always had an idea was their plan. For this Bonaparte has as many tricks as a monkey. I believe their object in the West Indies to be less conquest than to draw our force from home. The Rochefort squadron seem to have had nothing else in view. If the Toulon people can put the Spaniards in possession of Trinidad, and cause a great alarm, and draw a great force

Bellerophon figurehead at the Victory
Museum Portsmouth.

Admiral Lord Howe.

The launching of a two decker.

Admiral Sir Thomas Pasley.   Captain William Johnstone Hope.

The Approach of the British Fleet at the Nile.

The Glorious 1st of June.

A British '74' (H.M.S. *Warrior*)

Captain John Cooke.

Captain Edward Rotheram.

Napoleon boarding the *Bellerophon*.

ord Nelson.

Vice Admiral Sir Richard Keats.

he Battle of Trafalgar, *Royal Sovereign* in action.

The Battle of the Nile.

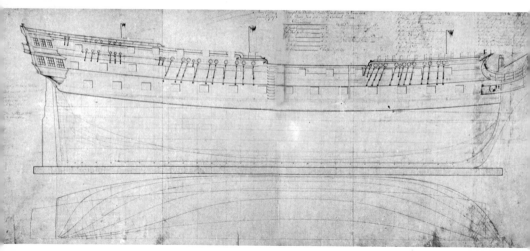

Sheerdraught of a '74' of the *Bellerophon* type.

Cornwallis's Retreat. *Royal Sovereign* bearing down to aid the *Mars*.

he *Bellerophon* at Trafalgar. (L. to R.) *Bahama*, *San Juan Nepomuceno*, *Bellerophon*, *Aigle* and
r. *Swiftsure*.

he Battle of the Nile. Plan based on information of Capt. Miller. The *Audacious* is shown in
rong position, she should be raking *Conquérant*.

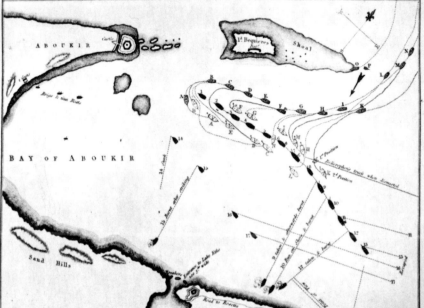

PLAN of the BATTLE of the NILE, August 1ˢᵗ 1798.

Napoleon and the *Bellerophon* at Torbay.

Captain Frederick Maitland.

Lord Keith.

there from England they will have so much less to oppose them in their real attack which will be at home in harvest time.

From this letter it will be seen that at least one British admiral was not so stupid as Napoleon believed, and with Nelson's return from the Indies the Emperor's plan was ruined. Being a dictator, he refused to recognize this, and sent orders to Villeneuve in Vigo to make his way up the Channel. The Combined Fleet did manage to get as far as Ferrol, but there they had to stop because of the rotten condition of the ships and crews.

Far away in England, at Merton, Nelson received news of the Combined Fleet from Sir Henry Blackwood. 'I am sure you bring me news of the French and Spanish Fleets, and I think I shall yet have to beat them.' Soon after these words he was on his way to the Admiralty to see Lord Barham and arrange a force for the destruction of the enemy fleet. He had a strong presentiment that this was to be his last voyage and would end in his death, and he spoke of this to many friends and acquaintances.

To many officers in the next few days went out the letters from the Admiralty for which they had been so eagerly waiting:

You are hereby required and directed to put yourself under command of the Rt. Honble Lord Vt. Nelson K.B. Vice Admiral of the White, and follow his lordship's orders for your proceedings.

Given &c 5th September 1805.

> J. Gambier
> P. Patton
> Garlies

In Ferrol, Villeneuve found his situation worse than before, and despite having a force of thirty of the line he was unable to complete the Emperor's plans. He did in fact make an effort to get up-Channel to Brest, but contrary winds decided him to turn for Cadiz where he hoped to get the stores and men he wanted to re-equip his fleet. With this reversal, the last hope of Napoleon for the invasion of the British Isles failed. Like the great man he was, he realized it and began to break up his camp by the Channel and organize the march into Europe which was to end in the battles of Ulm and Austerlitz and the destruction of yet another coalition. Of course, the blame for the failure of the invasion plan could not be attached to him, nor could the destruction of the combined navies of France and Spain. That all belonged to the incompetence and pusillanimity of 'the Admirals'.

Villeneuve arrived off Cadiz on the 20th August while the *Bellerophon* was at anchor at Gibraltar, but Collingwood was there with his three of the line to see them safe into port. He wrote to his wife afterwards:

I must tell you what a squeeze we had like to have got yesterday. While we were cruising off the town, down came the Combined Fleet of 36 sail of men of war. We were only three poor things with a frigate and a bomb and drew off towards the straights.

To his sister in England he wrote:

They are in port like a forest, I reckon them now to be thirty-six sail of the line and plenty of frigates What can I do with such a host? But I hope I shall get a reinforcement, suited to the occasion and, if I do, well betide us!

On the day that the Combined Fleet entered Cadiz he wrote to Captain Gambier:

They are gone into Cadiz for the purpose of replenishing their ships and are expected to sail again soon, reinforced by eight from that port.

On the 21st he wrote to his wife:

We have been looking into Cadiz where their fleet is now as thick as a wood. I hope I shall have somebody come to me soon. In the meantime I must take the best care of myself I can.

Only eleven days after the arrival of the Combined Fleet at Cadiz, the door is slammed on them by the arrival of Sir Robert Calder's squadron from the Channel Fleet. The detachment of this powerful force had been much criticized, notably by Mahan and by Napoleon himself, but it was not such a risk, and a high proportion of the ships remaining with Cornwallis were three-deckers.

By the 4th September the fleet before Cadiz consisted of twenty-four sail of the line, four frigates and one bomb. A week later two more ships joined; these were the *Mars* and the *Conqueror*. The former was under the command of Captain George Duff, who was to meet his death in the action which followed. The captain of the *Conqueror* was Israel Pellew, brother of the more famous Sir Edward Pellew and a gunnery expert.

The scarcity of all sorts of provisions and stores at Cadiz was a very great embarrassment to Villeneuve. The city of Cadiz and the immediate area surrounding it had not yet recovered from an epidemic which had raged there that summer. As well as food, naval supplies were almost unobtainable —the port authorities refused to issue any without direct orders from Madrid. The French themselves were not popular, as the two ships which had been lost at the battle of Finisterre had both been manned at Cadiz, and stories of their desertion by the French during the action were going around. The situation was so serious that Villeneuve appealed to the French Ambassador in Madrid and to Manuel Godoy the Prime Minister. In answer to these appeals, instructions were sent to Cadiz to supply the Combined Fleet with all the items they required. The Cadiz authorities, however, refused to obey! Their main reason for refusal was that they would not accept French paper money, and would only supply the stores if the French paid cash down; and it was only by the intervention of a French business man that this problem was overcome. With further prodding from Madrid the Cadiz authorities were at last forced to hand over the naval stores which were so urgently required by the Combined Fleet. Feelings between the two nations still ran high over the loss of the two ships to Calder, and several French seamen were murdered in the back streets of Cadiz. Rumours were going round that Gravina had accused Villeneuve of treachery and wanted to resign. This was partly true: Gravina did want to resign, not because of a direct dispute with Villeneuve, but because he felt that the loss of the two ships impugned his honour as a flag officer. His resignation was not accepted by Godoy, and he was persuaded to stay on.

The French were by no means united among themselves, and there was a considerable feeling of ill will towards Villeneuve. Many considered his actions were dictated by a haunting fear of meeting with Nelson. This was perhaps true, for he had witnessed the holocaust of the Nile and felt himself inadequate to meet such a challenge whenever it should come. Perhaps the best tribute that can be paid to this man was that when the day did come at Trafalgar, the fight he put up against Nelson and his superbly trained fleet was out of all proportion to that which might have been expected when the condition of the

French and Spanish ships is taken into account. He even worked out in advance the manner in which Nelson might attack his fleet, and the best way of combating it. It was due partly to his own indecision and partly to the Combined Fleet's lack of sea training that he was unable to put his plan into operation.

The remaining French flag officers, Dumanoir and Magon, were not on good terms with their Commander-in-Chief, the former from professional jealousy, and the latter from contempt for Villeneuve's actions since leaving Toulon.

On the 14th September, before leaving Paris for the Danube campaign, Napoleon sent his last orders to Villeneuve. These were to take the Combined Fleet into the Mediterranean and join the ships at Cartagena. With this augmentation to his force he was to go to southern Italy and land the troops to reinforce General St Cyr. In a letter to his Minister of Marine, Decres, he said that if 'Villeneuve's excessive pusillanimity will prevent him from undertaking this, you will send to replace him Admiral Rosily, who will bear letters directing Villeneuve to return to France and give an account of his conduct'.

On the 15th September, Nelson left home in the *Victory* to join the fleet off Cadiz, accompanied by Sir Henry Blackwood in the frigate *Euryalus*.

By the 24th September the Combined Fleet had received all its six months' provisions and was ready to carry out any tasks assigned to it. On the 28th Villeneuve received the orders which Napoleon had dictated on the 15th, telling him to take his fleet into the Mediterranean. Included in the dispatch were the words: 'Attack wherever you find the enemy in inferior force, attack without hesitation, and make a decisive affair of it.' It was perhaps with these words ringing in his ears that the admiral gave the order to make sail on the 19th October. In Paris, Napoleon had already taken the decision to replace Admiral Villeneuve with Admiral Rosily, for on the day after his orders giving the new plan for the Combined Fleet, he sent a letter to Decres saying: 'As his [Villeneuve's] pusillanimity will prevent his undertaking the plan, you will dispatch Admiral Rosily to take command of the fleet, and give him letters directing Villeneuve to return to France forthwith and account to me for his conduct.' Decres, however in his letter to Villeneuve said nothing of this, possibly to spare his fellow admiral's feelings, for they were friends. Admiral Rosily was to take the letter to Cadiz personally and was presumably to explain the new situation to the unhappy Commander-in-Chief.

On the receipt of Napoleon's orders giving his new plan, Villeneuve replied to Decres that he was ready to sail with the first fair wind. Leaving with his dispatch were two generals, Lauriston and Reille, who had commanded the troops on board the fleet. They arrived at Napoleon's headquarters in Germany just after Austerlitz, to congratulate Napoleon on his victory and hear the news of the disaster which had struck the fleet which they had just left. The officer now in charge of the troops was Brigadier de Contamine.

While there was dissention and unrest in the Combined Fleet, there was a certain amount of boredom in the blockading British fleet. Admiral Collingwood was not a man to be understood at first glance, and was compared unfavourably with Nelson as regards his relations with his subordinates. Captain Edward Codrington summed up the feelings of many officers when he wrote in his diary: 'For Charity's sake, send us Lord Nelson, ye men of power!' His prayer was answered on the 28th September, when Lord Nelson arrived in the *Victory*, accompanied by the *Ajax* and *Thunderer*. Blackwood had been sent ahead in the *Euryalus* to inform Collingwood that Nelson did not want his arrival to be saluted in the usual way because of the warning it would give the enemy. Villeneuve, however, knew the same day of the arrival of the *Victory* and her consorts, although he did not know that Nelson was aboard. The *Bellerophon* spotted the three ships approaching and recorded in her log for the day: 'Saw three sail of the line in the N.W. 4.40 shortened sail and hove to. Joined Co. H.M. Ships *Victory*, Vice Admiral Lord Nelson, *Ajax* and *Thunderer*.'

With the arrival of Nelson off the port the blockading force was twenty-seven sail of the line, disposed in the usual close blockade. Nelson, who did not like this form of blockade, substituted his own method, keeping his main force out of sight over the horizon, and leaving a squadron of faster 74s and frigates to watch the enemy's port and report on his movements. Under his command were two vice-admirals, Collingwood and Calder, and two rear-admirals, Louis and the Earl of Northesk. He was soon to lose two of these, for he brought orders for the recall of Calder for a court martial on his action against the Combined Fleet in July, and Louis was sent to Gibraltar to escort a convoy and restock with water. Nelson's orders were to send Calder home in a frigate, but as a generous gesture he allowed him to remain in his flagship the *Prince of Wales*, which seriously weakened his fleet and was a loss not made good until the arrival of the *Royal Sovereign* on the 8th October.

Soon after his arrival Nelson had his captains and admirals on board to explain his plan for attacking the enemy. This plan, the 'Nelson touch', was contained in the 'Fighting Memorandum' which he issued to the fleet after his initial talks with the captains.

Calder was due to leave the fleet on the 13th October, and had requested that the captains who were in his action might go home to give evidence at his court martial. There were three officers involved, Captain William Brown of the *Ajax*, Captain William Lechmere of the *Thunderer* and Captain Philip Durham of the *Defiance*. When the *Defiance* had joined the fleet, Nelson said he was glad to see Durham, but that his stay would be short as Calder was sailing tomorrow and was taking with him all the captains who were in his action to give evidence at the court martial. When Durham went aboard the *Prince of Wales* he found that the order stated that captains were only to return home 'if willing', and Captain Philip Durham was definitely not willing. Both Captain Brown and Captain Lechmere were apparently willing to go home, and had left their ships under the command of their first lieutenants, John Pilford and John Stockham. It is clear that Calder was better off without the evidence of Durham at his court martial as the two men disliked each other, and it had been Durham who had first sighted the Combined Fleet and signalled to the admiral for permission to renew the engagement on the second day.

Ships were now joining Nelson's fleet at a fairly regular rate, as fast as the dockyards in Britain and Gibraltar could fit them out. Admiral Louis left on the 2nd October and took with him five sail of the line (*Canopus, Queen, Spencer, Tigre,* and *Zealous*). On the 7th *Defiance* joined, on the 8th *Leviathan* and *Royal Sovereign*, and on the 13th *Agamemnon* joined. The captain of the latter vessel was Nelson's old flag-captain from the battle of the Nile, Sir Edward Berry, one of the most famous fighting men in the Fleet. As soon as the *Agamemnon* was signalled, Nelson cried: 'Here comes Berry! NOW we shall have a battle!' The same day saw the arrival of another 64, the *Africa*, so that after the departure of Sir Robert Calder to England and the *Donegal* to Gibraltar, a total was left of twenty-seven sail of the line.

The position of the British fleet at this time was sixteen to eighteen leagues west of Cadiz, which enabled them to steer for the Straits in case the Combined Fleet tried to get into the Mediterranean. Close inshore was the squadron of frigates under Sir Henry Blackwood, comprising the *Euryalus, Naiad, Phoebe, Sirius*, and *Amazon* accompanied by the schooner *Pickle* and the brig *Weazle*. Further out to sea was the communicating chain of battleships which Nelson had placed under the command of Captain Duff of the *Mars*; these were the *Defence, Agamemnon*, and *Colossus*.

Meanwhile, in Cadiz, Villeneuve had heard rumours of his replacement through travellers who had arrived in the port and letters from Bayonne. He did not apparently realize at this time the depth of the Emperor's displeasure. He knew that Admiral Rosily was employed by the French Admiralty on special missions, and he remained confident of his own position. Further news arrived from Madrid that Admiral Rosily had arrived there, and was to proceed to Cadiz as fast as possible, and only then did the first suspicion cross Villeneuve's mind that he might be in danger of losing his post, as the rumours in the port had asserted for some time. He realized that he, with the supreme command of the Combined Fleet, had not received any news direct from Paris, not even from his immediate superior in the Ministry of Marine, Decres. Anxiously he wrote to Decres: 'I shall be happy to yield the first place to Rosily, if I am allowed to have the second; but it will be too hard to have to give up all hope of being vouchsafed the opportunity of proving that I am worthy of a better fate.' It was at this juncture that he decided to sail with the Combined Fleet as soon as there was a fair wind, to carry the Emperor's latest plan into action. His own fighting instructions were already issued, and he had received news of the dispatch of five English ships to Gibraltar. He reasoned that the time would never be better for the Combined Fleet.

Writing to Decres he said that he wanted to get to sea and run out about 200 leagues into the Atlantic, then double back and make for the Straits. As the watch of the British fleet was so close, he feared he would be spotted getting away, especially as the ships he commanded were not well enough trained to creep out of port in the dark. Some of his vessels were slow, and he thought that he would be brought to action before he had got far out into the Atlantic. His second alternative was to pass down the coast to the Straits, but here also the risks were enormous and he was certain they would be caught half-way and destroyed. Villeneuve, however, considered the last plan the more reasonable of the two, and as the Emperor had ordered the fleet into the Mediterranean, they must try and get into the Mediterranean. Admiral Rosily, whose ever nearing presence had forced Villeneuve to get to sea to vindicate his honour, was delayed at Madrid for two days for repairs to his carriage. He only arrived at Cadiz to take command of the shattered remnants of the Combined Fleet after Nelson had finished with it.

Once his mind was made up, Villeneuve sent orders to Admiral Magon to sail from the port with the first fair wind to sweep away the British cruisers which were watching the Franco-Spanish ships. He was then to make a reconnaissance out to sea to ascertain the position of Nelson and his exact strength. While he was thus engaged the rest of the fleet would be working out of harbour, a task that Villeneuve hoped would be completed within twenty-four hours. All that was wanted now was a change in the wind which had blown from the west for the last ten days.

The first signs of a change in the wind began to show on the 17th when it began to veer to the east. That day he also received news from farther down the coast that the five British vessels detached from Nelson's fleet were passing the Straits of Gibraltar, and realized that his moment had come. He called the Spanish admiral, Gravina, on board of the *Bucentaure* and apprised him of his decision to sail at once. Gravina expressed himself ready to sail that afternoon, and to follow the movements of the French fleet. As Gravina rowed back to his ship the *Principe de Asturias*, the signal 'Prepare to make sail' flew from the masthead of the *Bucentaure*. Before the movement had properly begun, however, the wind began to die away and by four o'clock there was a dead calm. Orders were sent to the ships to be ready to put to sea the next morning.

The next day, the 19th, was fine and clear but the wind was light, and getting away from the harbour was a lengthy process. So slow, indeed, was the progress that by midday there were only nine ships outside the harbour, and once again the wind died away. Everyone on the Combined Fleet could see the British frigates signalling to the fleet out at sea, and were aware that in a few hours the British would be closing in on them while they were still struggling out of port or only half formed outside. The British fleet had been formed into two divisions, the *Bellerophon* being in the larboard division under Admiral Collingwood. On board ship a keen watch was being kept on the chain of battleships which formed the link between Nelson and Blackwood. The nearest ship, the *Mars*, was so far away that only her topgallant masts were visible above the horizon.

The *Victory* was signalling to various ships of the fleet to close with the flagship and Nelson was asking their captains to lunch. He had just sent a message to Collingwood and had signalled the *Bellerophon* to close, when from the deck of the latter the first lieutenant spotted a signal flying from the *Mars*. Focusing his telescope on it he was able to make out that it was the signal for the enemy to come out of port.

Lieutenant Cumby relates the sighting of the fleet in an account written after the battle:

Early in the forenoon of Saturday, the 19th of October, 1805, the captain of the *Bellerophon* was invited with some other captains by signal to dine with the Commander-in-Chief, and on our answering in the affirmative, *Bellerophon*'s signal was made to close the Admiral, which we immediately made sail to accomplish, our station being in the lee column, the fourth astern of the *Royal Sovereign* bearing the flag of Vice-Admiral Colling-wood, who led our division. While carrying sail for this purpose I perceived flags flying at the masthead of the lookout ship towards Cadiz, the *Mars*, and distinctly made out to my own satisfaction the numeral 370, signifying 'The enemy's ships are coming out of port, or getting under weigh.' This I immediately reported to Captain Cooke, and asked his permission to repeat it. The *Mars* at this time was so far from us that her top gallant masts alone were visible above the horizon.

The distance, however, was so great for the discovering the colour of the flags that Captain Cooke said he was unwilling to repeat a signal of so much importance unless he could clearly distinguish the flags himself, which on looking through his glass he declared himself unable to do. The conviction of the correctness of my statement, founded on long and frequent experience of the strength of my own sight, induced me again to urge Captain Cooke to repeat it, when he said if any other person of the many whose glasses were now fixed upon the *Mars* would confirm my opinion, he would repeat the signal. None of the officers or signalmen, however, were bold enough to assert positively, as I did, that the flags were 370, and I had the mortification to be disappointed in my anxious wish that the *Bellerophon* should be the first to repeat such delightful intelligence to the Admiral.

Soon afterwards the *Mars* hauled down the flags, and I said, 'Now she will make the distant signal 370' which distant signal was made with a flag, a ball, and a pendant, differently disposed at different mastheads by a combination totally unconnected with the flag or pendant used. She did make the distant signal No. 370 as I had predicted. This could not be mistaken, and as we were preparing to repeat it the *Mars* signal was answered from the *Victory*, and immediately afterwards the dinner signal was annull'd, and the signal was made for a general chase ESE.

The appearance of the Combined Fleet getting ready for sea was seen with the greatest joy by the officers and men of the British fleet. They felt that at last the period of waiting was over. They never doubted gaining the victory, and bringing peace to Europe.

The Combined Fleet meanwhile was making a painful effort to get outside the port. All through Saturday evening the work went on, and during the night there was no rest for anybody on the French and Spanish ships, for Villeneuve had ordered the vessels to be towed or warped out. About dawn on the 20th, a Sunday, the first morning breeze from the land caught the sails and Villeneuve was able to work out his entire fleet and have them under way by noon. The crowds on the quay watched them go with some trepidation, for many people had relatives or friends on the ships and it was expected that there would be a hard and bloody battle outside. Prayers were offered in all the churches in the city for the safety of the great ships, and there were queues of people to get in.

Once the fleet was outside the wind veered to the south-west, and the weather became thick and squally, effectually shortening the range of vision of the British frigates. The signal was made for the fleet to tack to the southward and to form in five columns in accordance with Villeneuve's Fighting Instructions. The weather cleared up in the afternoon and the wind changed again to the north-west, but the breeze was so light that the pace of the fleet was painfully slow. However there was no sign of Nelson and his fleet and that gave some cause for satisfaction, although the British frigates were still holding the Combined Fleet under observation.

As we have already seen, as soon as the signal was made for the enemy coming out of port, Nelson ordered his fleet to chase to the south-east. By doing this he was steering for the Straits of Gibraltar to stop the Combined Fleet from entering the Mediterranean, and he also hoped to meet Admiral Louis on his way back from escorting the Malta convoy. In the afternoon he began his last letter to Emma Hamilton:

> Victory.
> October 19th, 1805, Noon.
> Cadiz, ESE. 16 leagues.

> My dearest beloved Emma, the dear friend of my bosom. The signal has been made that the Enemy's Combined Fleet are coming out of port. We have very little wind, so that I have no hopes of seeing them before tomorrow. May the God of Battles crown my endeavours with success; at all events, I will take care that my name shall ever be most dear to you and Horatia, both of whom I love as much as my own life. And as my last writing before the Battle will be to you so I hope in God that I shall live to finish my letter after the Battle.

> May Heaven bless you prays your
> Nelson & Bronte

He did not finish the letter at that moment, for he was to add a postscript to it the next day.

All the week-end the British fleet carried every stitch of sail it possibly could to catch every breath of wind. The *Bellerophon* was part of an advanced squadron of fast sailing two-decked ships. Lieutenant Cumby records the events of the Saturday night on board:

> Captain Cooke said to me that he should not feel comfortable unless either he or I were constantly upon deck, until we either brought the enemy to action or the chase was ended, on which I volunteered taking two watches on deck that night. I accordingly remained on deck till midnight, when the captain relieved me, as I did him again at four o'clock. So the night pass'd and morning came, but with it no sight of the enemy's fleet.

The same arrangements existed on the Sunday night with the two officers relieving each other every four hours. There was nothing to be seen of the enemy from the main fleet, but lights could be seen burning from the frigates which meant that they were still in sight from them.

On Sunday evening Villeneuve received a note from Gravina telling him that eighteen sail had been sighted to the south-west, and he added to his last dispatch to Paris:

They have just signalled me that eighteen of the enemy are in sight . . . In leaving port I have only consulted my anxious desire to conform to the wishes of His Majesty, and to do everything in my power to remove that feeling of dissatisfaction with which he has regarded the events of my previous cruise.

Later that evening after his dispatch had been sealed, one of his frigates brought in the report that the number of enemy in sight was now twenty.

As darkness fell, the signal lights of the British frigates were to be seen from the decks of the French and Spanish ships, lights which they knew to be reporting their course and position to Nelson. A French officer wrote afterwards:

Lights were continuously seen at various points of the horizon. They were the signals of the English Fleet and the look-out ships that felt the way for them. The reports of cannon, repeated from time to time and blue lights casting a bright and sudden glare in the midst of profound darkness, were soon added to the earlier signals, and convinced Admiral Villeneuve that he would vainly attempt to conceal his course from his active foes.

During the night a report came from Gravina that the enemy were only two miles off. This seemed incredible to Villeneuve, but he signalled to his ships to form line of battle, and to clear for action. The forming of line of battle at night was more than the seamanship of the Combined Fleet could manage, and some confusion arose. In his report after the battle, Captain Lucas of the *Redoutable* wrote:

About nine o' clock at night the flagship made the general signal to the fleet to form in the order of battle, without regard to the stations of individual ships. To carry out this evolution those ships most to leeward ought to have shown a light at each masthead, so as to mark their positions. Whether this was done I do not know: at any rate I was unable to see such lights. At that moment, indeed, we were all widely scattered. The ships of the battle squadron and those of the squadron of observation were all mixed up. Another cause of confusion was this. Nearly all the ships had answered the Admiral's signals with flares which made it impossible to tell which was the flagship. All I could do was to follow the motions of other ships near me which were closing on some to leeward.

The long night finally passed and dawn broke on the memorable morning of the 21st October. Before another twenty-four hours had gone by thousands of men were to fight each other, hundreds were to be killed and hundreds more wounded, and the 'Empire of the sea' was to become Britain's for over 100 years without challenge. The dawn was described by an officer on the *Bellerophon*:

Monday morning dawned with a haze over the sea which gradually cleared off as the clouds broke away and the rays of the sun gleamed through, with every promise of a fine autumn day. It brought with it the longed for sight. It revealed the whole horizon to leeward thickly studded with masts.

Less romantically written was the log kept by Captain Cooke:

A.M. Do. Weather. 4 Light airs inclinable to calm with a heavy swell from the westward. Answ'd signal to wear. 4.15 Wore ship. At daylight saw the Enemy's fleet ENE. Ans'd 72 & 76 General. Compass ENE. Out all reefs and made sail towards them. 6.20 Answ'd No. 13 General (Prepare for Battle). 6.42 Answ'd 76 General. Compass East. Beat to quarters & cleared for action.

On the French flagship the signal was received, 'The enemy in sight to windward'. The frigates were signalled by the admiral to reconnoitre and report the numbers of the enemy.

At 7.00 a.m. the signal of the previous night was repeated to form line of battle on the starboard tack and clear for action. This signal was greeted with shouts and cheers throughout the Combined Fleet. At last the long night was over, the long months of running and being blockaded, at last they were face to face with the fleet which had hunted them from one side of the Atlantic to the other and back again—the fleet which had so insolently flaunted itself off Cadiz. All over the fleet, drums were beating the Générale. Bulkheads were cleared, sand was scattered over the decks, furniture was stowed away in the hold, hammocks were rigged round the decks, shot and powder were made ready. In many breasts hearts were beating a little faster, and by the end of the day many of them would have ceased to beat altogether. One

Spanish account describes the scene aboard the 130-gun *Santisima Trinidad*:

Early in the morning the decks were cleared for action, and when all was ready for serving the guns and working the ship, I heard some one say: 'The sand—bring the sand'. A number of sailors were posted on the ladders from the hatchway to the hold between decks, and in this way were hauling up sacks of sand. Each man handed one to the man next to him and so it passed on. A great quantity of sacks were thus brought up from hand to hand, and they were emptied out on the upper decks, the poop, and the forecastle, the sand being spread about so as to cover all the planking. The same thing was done between decks. My curiosity prompted me to ask a lad who stood next me what this was for.

'For the blood', he said very coolly.

'For the blood!' I exclaimed, unable to repress a shudder. I looked at the sand—I looked at the men who were busily employed on this task—and for a moment I felt I was a coward.

Aboard the *Bellerophon* Cumby had been asleep when the Combined Fleet was first sighted on the horizon, but was roused by the master:

'Cumby, my boy, turn out; here they all are ready for you, three and thirty sail of the line close under our lee and evidently disposed to await our attack!' You may readily conclude I did not long remain in a recumbent position, but springing out of bed, hurried on my clothes, and kneeling down by the side of my cot put up a short but fervent prayer to the Great God of Battles 'for Glorious Victory' to the arms of my country, committing myself individually to His all-wise disposal, and begging His gracious protection and favour for my dear wife and children, whatever, in His unerring wisdom, He might see fit to order for myself. This was the substance, and, as near as my memory will serve me, the actual words of my petition.

I was soon on deck, whence the enemy's fleet was distinctly seen to leeward standing to the southward under easy sail, and forming a line on the starboard tack.

At six o'clock the signal was made to form the order of sailing, and soon after to bear up and steer ENE. We made sail in our station and at twenty minutes past six we answered the signal to prepare for battle, and soon afterwards to steer East. We then beat to quarters, and cleared ship for action.

A month after the action Midshipman Walker, writing to his mother, summed up the days previous to the sighting of the Combined Fleet and the great day itself; he begins with the first sighting on the 19th:

The Admiral immediately made signals for a General Chase and to prepare for action. You may easily conceive with what alacrity this was obeyed. In a quarter of an hour 26 of the finest ships in the Navy were under all sail and formed a glorious sight, the wind was favourable, and in a short time the *Bellerophon, Belleisle, Orion, Leviathan,* and *Polyphemus* showed their superiority of sailing, and got far ahead of the fleet, which continued under a press of sail the whole ensuing night steering for the straits which was supposed to be the enemy's destination.

He records the sighting of the Combined Fleet on the morning of the 21st:

... at daylight, we saw them to leeward, and immediately beat to quarters and bore down on them in two columns with all sail set, Lord Nelson in the *Victory* leading one line and Admiral Collingwood in the *Royal Sovereign* the other, in which the *Bellerophon* was the fifth ship.

Walker was also impressed with the bearing of the French and Spanish:

Whilst we were bearing down on them they formed in a close order of battle, French and Spaniards alternately, and awaited for us with great intrepidity.

At eight o'clock, Villeneuve decided that the prevailing wind was too light for them to reach the Straits, and signalled for each ship to go about, so as to have Cadiz harbour under his lee for crippled ships to enter after an action. The task, however, seemed to prove of some difficulty, for the light winds and the strong swell from the westward complicated the situation for some of the sketchily trained crews of the Combined Fleet, and it was two hours before the manoeuvre was completed, and well past ten before anything like a regular order of battle was formed. The final formation was shaped like a crescent with the centre sagging away to leeward in a great curve. The squadron of observation under Gravina, which was supposed to be separate from the rest of the fleet, had become involved in the manoeuvre, and had now been incorporated in the main body, being joined on to the rear to prolong the line. No signal from Villeneuve could move Gravina from his station and that was where he stayed to fight the battle. This was a serious blow to the hopes of Villeneuve for countering the English attack.

The Combined Fleet had now assumed the final positions in which it was to meet the onslaught of the British fleet, and

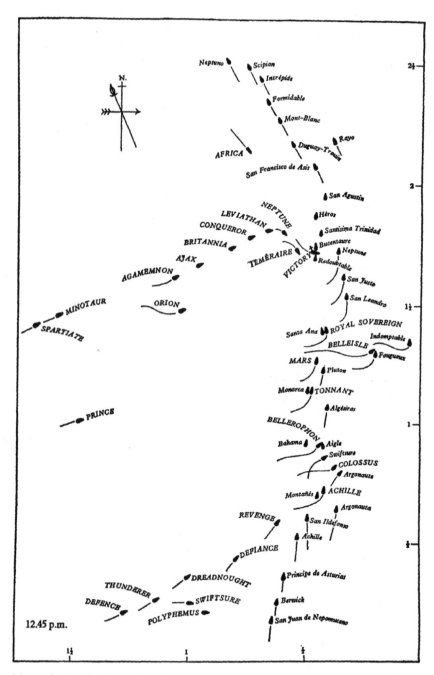

Plan of the Battle of Trafalgar at 12.45 p.m. (By permission of Rear Admiral A. H. Taylor and The Society for Nautical Research).

on board several ships, of both fleets, breakfast was taken.
Aboard the *Bellerophon* Captain Cooke had decided to show
Lieutenant Cumby Nelson's plan of attack, in case he himself
was killed or wounded.

He wished me to be acquainted with it, that in the event of his being
'bowled out' as he said, I might know how to conduct the ship agreeably
to the Admiral's wishes. On this I observed that it was very possible that
the same shot which disposed of him might have an equally tranquillizing
effect upon me, and under that idea I submitted to him the expediency of
the Master (as being the only officer who in such a case would remain on
the quarter deck) being also apprised . . . Overton the sailing master of the
Bellerophon was thereupon sent for to the captain's cabin, and given the
Memorandum to read. Of the three officers who carried the knowledge
of this private Memorandum into the action, I was the only one who
brought it out.

On board all the ships of both fleets everything was ready
for the coming conflict. The magazines were all open, pistols
and cutlasses were ready to repel boarders, the shot was
stowed close to the guns. The powder monkeys stood ready to
begin their task, and the officers were pacing the quarter-deck
or at their respective stations. The effect which some ships had
on their crews had been noted by an officer of the *Bellerophon*
when he had written a few days earlier, 'No man can be a
coward on board of the *Bellerophon*!' and it was true that
aboard a good many of the ships the utmost high spirits
prevailed, with singing and dancing of hornpipes.

Nelson was on the poop deck of the *Victory*, taking a look at
the enemy he had waited so long to find. He was dressed as
always in his frock-coat with the four orders of knighthood
embroidered on the chest. He had resigned himself to his
death in the coming battle and had made a new will to provide
for Lady Hamilton and his brothers. The massive figure of
Captain Hardy, Nelson's great friend and fighting companion,
was also visible on the quarter deck.

On the *Royal Sovereign* Collingwood had dressed and gone
up on deck, after pointing out the Combined Fleet to his
steward Smith. On deck he met Lieutenant Clavell who, he
noticed, was wearing high leather boots. Collingwood said to
him, 'You had better put on silk stockings as I have done, for
if one gets a shot in the leg, they are so much more manage-
able for the surgeon.' The captain of the *Royal Sovereign*,

Rotheram, also had a sense of what was proper for a battle at sea, and was wearing his cocked hat. When certain persons remonstrated with him he growled in reply that he had always worn a cocked hat in battle and always would! Fortunately for him his dress sense, unlike Nelson's, did not lead him to his death.

The wind was still very light and was carrying the British fleet into action at no more than walking pace. To anyone viewing from a distance, the ships looked like great white swans gliding down the stream. All eye-witnesses agree that it was the most magnificent sight they ever saw in their lives; in fact it was the last time that two large sailing fleets came together for battle upon the open sea.

From the Combined Fleet the stately advance of the British fleet was noted by Captain Lucas:

On the 29th Vendemaire [21st October] at daybreak, the enemy were sighted to windward. . . . The Combined Fleet was spread out from south-east to north-west; the ships being much scattered and not forming any apparent order. The enemy also were not in any order, but their ships were fast manoeuvring to close. Their force was now reconnoitred and reported exactly. It comprised twenty-seven sail of the line, of which seven were three-deckers, besides four frigates and a schooner. . . .

By nine o'clock the enemy had formed up in two columns. They were under all sail—they even had studding sails out—and heading directly for our fleet, before a light breeze from the west-south-west . . .

Towards eleven o'clock the two columns of the enemy were drawing near us. One was led by a three-decker, the *Royal Sovereign*, and headed towards our present rear squadron. The other led by the *Victory* and the *Téméraire*, was manoeuvring as if to attack our centre.

Aboard the *Victory* Nelson was on the point of sending one more signal to the fleet, and for that purpose he walked across to the signal lieutenant, Pasco, and said, 'Mr Pasco, I wish to say to the Fleet, "England confides that every man will do his duty." ' After a moment's thought, Pasco replied, 'If your Lordship will permit me to substitute "expects" for "confides" the signal will soon be completed, because the word "expects" is in the vocabulary, and "confides" must be spelt.' Nelson replied that that would do, and to make it directly, for he had one more signal to make which was for 'Close Action'.

As Captain Blackwood was preparing to leave the *Victory* to go back to the *Euryalus* he noticed the signal for close action being hauled up the halliards. He expressed the hope that he would be able to come back after the battle and congratulate Nelson on a great victory. To which Nelson replied, 'God bless you, Blackwood, I shall never speak to you again'.

The effect of the 'England Expects' signal on the fleet varied according to the ship in which it was received. In the *Bellerophon* it was received by Midshipman Franklin, later famous as an Arctic explorer, and passed to Captain Cooke, who had it read to the men. According to Walker, it was 'received on board our ship with three cheers and a general shout of "No fear of that" '. On board the *Defiance*, according to Midshipman Campbell, 'Captain Durham then turned the hands up and made a short but very expressive speech to the ship's company which was answered by three cheers. Everything being then ready, matches lit, guns double shotted with grape and rounds, and decks cleared we piped to dinner and had a good glass of grog'. On the *Neptune* and the *Britannia* it was welcomed with cheers, and on the *Ajax* after a moment of puzzled silence the crew broke into three cheers, 'more from love and admiration of the Admiral than from a full appreciation of his signal'. On board Collingwood's ship the *Royal Sovereign*, Collingwood, before its significance was explained to him, said that he wished Nelson would make no more signals for they all knew what they had to do. Once it was explained to him, he was delighted, and desired it to be read to the ship's company.

When Cumby made a final inspection of the *Bellerophon*'s decks before the battle, Lieutenant Saunders pointed out to him how some of the men had chalked 'Bellerophon—Victory or Death' in large letters on the sides of their guns. Midshipman Walker, writing home after the battle, noted the high spirits of the majority: 'One would have thought they were preparing for a festival rather than a combat.'

THE BATTLE OF TRAFALGAR, 21st OCTOBER 1805

The Two Fleets in order of sailing

BRITISH

Van Squadron—Starboard Division

Victory, 100 guns	Vice Admiral Viscount Nelson, K.B.
	Captain Thomas Masterman Hardy

Téméraire, 98 guns	Captain Eliab Harvey
Neptune, 98 guns	Captain Thomas Francis Fremantle
Conqueror, 74 guns	Captain Israel Pellew
Leviathan, 74 guns	Captain Henry William Bayntun
Ajax, 74 guns	Lieutenant John Pilford
Orion, 74 guns	Captain Edward Codrington
Agamemnon, 64 guns	Captain Sir Edward Berry
Minotaur, 74 guns	Captain Charles John Mansfield
Spartiate, 74 guns	Captain Sir Charles Laforey, Bart
Britannia, 100 guns	Rear Admiral the Earl of Northesk
	Captain Charles Bullen
Africa, 64 guns	Captain Henry Digby

Rear Squadron—Port Division

Royal Sovereign, 100 guns	Vice Admiral Cuthbert Collingwood
	Captain Edward Rotheram
Mars, 74 guns	Captain George Duff
Belleisle, 74 guns	Captain William Hargood
Tonnant, 80 guns	Captain Charles Tyler
Bellerophon, 74 guns	Captain John Cooke
Colossus, 74 guns	Captain James Nicoll Morris
Achilles, 74 guns	Captain Richard King
Polyphemus, 64 guns	Captain Robert Redmill
Revenge, 74 guns	Captain Robert Moorsom
Swiftsure, 74 guns	Captain William George Rutherford
Defence, 74 guns	Captain George Hope
Thunderer, 74 guns	Lieutenant John Stockham
Defiance, 74 guns	Captain Philip Charles Durham
Prince, 98 guns	Captain Richard Grindall
Dreadnought, 98 guns	Captain John Conn

Also present were the following light craft and frigates:

Euryalus, 36 guns	Captain the Hon. Henry Blackwood
Sirius, 36 guns	Captain William Prowse
Phoebe, 36 guns	Captain the Hon. Thomas Bladen Capel
Naiad, 38 guns	Captain Thomas Dundas
Entreprenante, 12 guns	Lieutenant Robert Benjamin Young
Pickle, 8 guns	Lieutenant John Richard Lapenotiere

FRENCH

Bucentaure, 80 guns	Vice-Admiral P. Ch. J.B.S. de Villeneuve
	Captain Jean Jacques Magendie

Formidable, 80 guns	Rear-Admiral P.R.M.E. Dumanoir Le Pelley
	Captain Jean Marie Letellier
Neptune, 80 guns	Commodore Esprit Tranquille Maistral
Indomptable, 80 guns	Commodore Jean Joseph Hubert
Algésiras, 74 guns	Rear-Admiral Charles Magon
	Captain Gabriel Auguste Brouard
Pluton, 74 guns	Commodore Julien M. Cosmao
Mont-Blanc, 74 guns	Commodore G. J. Noel La Villegris
Intrépide, 74 guns	Commodore Louis Antoine Cyprian Infernet
Swiftsure, 74 guns	Captain C. E. L'Hospitalier
Aigle, 74 guns	Captain Pierre Paul Gourrège
Scipion, 74 guns	Captain Charles Berenger
Duguay-Trouin, 74 guns	Captain Claude Touffet
Berwick, 74 guns	Captain Jean Gilles Filhol Camas
Argonaute, 74 guns	Captain Jacques Epron
Achille, 74 guns	Captain Gabriel de Nieport
Redoutable, 74 guns	Captain Jean Jacques Étienne Lucas
Fougueux, 74 guns	Captain Louis Beaudouin
Héros, 74 guns	Captain Jean B. J. Remi Poulain

SPANISH

Santisima Trinidad, 130 guns	Rear-Admiral don B. Hildago Cisneros
	Commodore don Francisco de Uriarte
Principe de Asturias, 112 guns	Admiral don Frederico Gravina
	Rear-Admiral don Antonio Escano
Santa Ana, 112 guns	Vice-Admiral don Ign. Maria de Alava
	Captain don Josef Guardoqui
Rayo, 100 guns	Commodore don Enrique Macdonell
Neptuno, 80 guns	Commodore don Cayetano Valdés
Argonauta, 80 guns	Commodore don Antonio Parejas
Bahama, 74 guns	Captain don Dionisio Galiano
Montañés, 74 guns	Captain don Josef Salzedo
San Augustin, 74 guns	Captain don Felipe Xado Cagigal
San Ildefonso, 74 guns	Captain don Josef Bargas
San Juan de Nepomuceno, 74 guns	Captain don Cosme Churraca
Monarca, 74 guns	Captain don Teodoro Argumosa
San Francisco de Asis, 74 guns	Captain don Luis de Flores
San Justo, 74 guns	Captain don Miguel Gaston
San Leandro, 64 guns	Captain don Josef Quevedo

Also present:

Frigates: *Cornélie*, *Thémis*, *Rhin*, *Hermione*, and *Hortense*.
Brigs: *Argus* and *Furet*.
Total: British —27 sail of the Line
Combined Fleet—33 Sail of the Line

The leading ships of the British fleet were by now drawing near the range of the guns of the Combined Fleet, and many officers and men on both were calculating when the first shot would be fired. The ships of the British fleet all had their studding sails set to bring them to action more quickly.

The outstanding ship in the enemy line as far as the British seamen and officers were concerned was the huge *Santisima Trinidad*, the largest warship in the world, and far larger than any ship in the Royal Navy. She had once before been a prize of the Navy, at St Vincent, but in the confusion had rehoisted her flag and escaped. Now she was observed by many eyes as the British ships bore down for the attack, and remarks were passed about what a fine prize she would make. Aboard the British ships the bands had been ordered to play to relieve the tension and to hearten the men, and the strains of 'Hearts of Oak', 'Britons Strike Home', and 'Rule Britannia' were to be heard drifting across the water.

The leading ship of the port division, the *Royal Sovereign*, had drawn well ahead of her next in line, the 74-gun *Mars*. It was obvious to many officers and men in the fleet that the advance into battle was becoming a race between Nelson and Collingwood. Collingwood would not shorten sail to let his other ships come up, and Nelson would not shorten sail to let the *Téméraire* pass and lead the line. The *Royal Sovereign* was one of the cleanest bottomed ships in the fleet, and was slowly widening the gap between herself and the *Mars*. Her captain had his eye upon the space between a Spanish three-decker and a French two-decker—the *Santa Ana* and the *Fougueux*—and aboard them the range between themselves and the *Royal Sovereign* was being closely watched. The extreme range of the old cannon was about 1,000 yards, and when this range was calculated aboard the *Fougueux* the order was given to fire. The time was 12.10 and the battle of Trafalgar had begun.

At about the same time Collingwood fired the first shot from the British side to give his ship a cover of smoke and hide her from the enemy gunners.

A French officer aboard the *Fougueux* describes the opening of the action:

The *Fougueux* on board of which I was master-at-arms, had for her immediate leader the Spanish man-of-war *Santa Ana* of 110 guns. By bad handling that ship left a gap of at least a cable across, between herself and the next astern, ourselves; thus offering the enemy an easy passage through. It was just on this point that Admiral Collingwood directed his attack, as he advanced to break the line. It necessarily resulted that he crossed right in front of our bows, and so our first antagonist was Admiral Collingwood.

At a quarter past twelve o'clock the *Fougueux*, a man-of-war of seventy-four guns, fired the first gun in the fleet. As she did so she hoisted her colours. She continued her cannonade, firing on the English flagship, which was a greatly superior vessel in size, height, guns, and the number of the crew. Her main-deck and upper-deck guns, in fact, could fire right down on to our decks, and in that way all our upper-deck men employed in working the ship, and the infantry marksmen posted on the gangways, were without cover and entirely exposed. We had also, according to our bad habit in the French Navy, fired away over a hundred rounds from our big guns at long range before the English ship had practically snapped a gun lock. It was, indeed, not until we found ourselves side by side and yardarm to yardarm with the English ship that she fired at all. Then she gave us a broadside from five and fifty guns and carronades, hurtling forth a storm of cannon balls, big and small, and musket shot.

The opening fire of the *Fougueux* was followed by that of the *Santa Ana* and then by the *Monarca, San Justo, San Leandro, Pluton,* and *Algésiras*. At the last moment Captain Beaudouin of the *Fougueux* had made an effort to close the gap between his ship and the *Santa Ana*, but backed up when he saw the *Royal Sovereign* was going to carry away his bowsprit.

As the *Royal Sovereign* crashed through the line, she poured her full treble-shotted broadside into the stern of the *Santa Ana*, the weakest part of the ship. Her other broadside was fired into the *Fougueux*, and the effect on both ships was staggering. Captain Rotheram then luffed his ship and brought her alongside the *Santa Ana*, but as the *Royal Sovereign* turned, Beaudouin took the chance to fire his broadside into the starboard quarter of the three-decker. The *Indomptable* also added her fire to the quota. As soon as the

Royal Sovereign was alongside the Spanish ship, the Spanish gunners fired their own broadside, and the British ship heeled over with the impact. Two more Spanish ships, the *San Justo* and *San Leandro*, and one more French ship, the *Neptune*, also began firing on the *Royal Sovereign*, making a total of three French and three Spanish ships firing into her at the same time. For some three minutes the *Royal Sovereign* fought alone, and succeeded in causing the Spanish ship to slacken her fire. The French officer on the *Fougueux* describes the act of the *Royal Sovereign* breaking the line, from the moment she fired her first broadside:

I thought the *Fougueux* was shattered to pieces—pulverized. The storm of projectiles that hurled themselves against the hull on the port side made the ship heel to starboard. Most of the sails and rigging were cut to pieces, while the upper deck was swept clear of the greater number of seamen working there, and of the soldiers sharpshooters. Our gun decks below had, however, suffered less severely. There not more than thirty men in all were put hors de combat. This preliminary greeting, rough and brutal as it was, did not dishearten our men. A well-maintained fire showed the Englishmen that we too had guns and could use them.

Several British eye-witnesses describe the *Royal Sovereign* breaking the line. The log of the *Bellerophon* records it thus:

At 10 minutes past noon the *Royal Sovereign* opened fire on the enemy's centre. At 12.13 answ'd 16 General (Closer Action). At 12.20 the *Royal Sovereign* broke through the enemy's line astern of a Spanish three-decker & engaged to leeward being followed by H.M. Ships *Mars*, *Belleisle* & *Tonnant* which engaged their respective opponents.

Midshipman Walker in his letter writes:

At 10 minutes past twelve the *Royal Sovereign* opened fire on the enemy's centre; at 12.20 she broke their line and engaged a Spanish 3-decker to leeward.

Collingwood had a narrow escape from death when the master of the *Royal Sovereign* was killed by a cannon shot while standing next to him, The only wound the admiral received in the battle was a slight splinter wound in the leg, which he did not mention until five months later in a letter to his wife.

The second ship of Collingwood's division was now app-roaching the Combined Fleet. This was the 74-gun *Belleisle*, a French prize captured by Lord Bridport in his action off

L'Orient in 1795. As with most French ships, she was a fast sailer, and she had overtaken two ships to take second place in line. The first ship she had passed had been another prize, the *Tonnant*, taken at the Nile. As the *Belleisle* forged past the *Tonnant*, Captain Hargood ordered her band to play 'Rule Britannia', and Captain Tyler of the *Tonnant*, in order not to be outdone, ordered his band to reply with 'Britons Strike Home!' and hailed across to Captain Hargood, 'A glorious day for old England! We shall have one apiece before night!' Having passed the *Tonnant*, the next ahead was the *Mars* commanded by Captain George Duff. There were quite a family of Duffs on board for Captain Duff had brought his thirteen-year-old son Norwich as a midshipman, and Norwich was accompanied by his cousin Thomas and Thomas's elder brother Alexander. It was an unlucky day for the Duff family for George and Alexander were to meet their deaths in the forthcoming action. Nelson had signalled to Duff to overtake the *Royal Sovereign* and lead the line, when the 98-gun *Prince* had dropped back while shifting a topsail, but try as he might Captain Duff could not get up enough speed to overtake the *Royal Sovereign*, and now the *Belleisle* was gaining on him!

Three minutes after the *Royal Sovereign* had broken the line, the *Belleisle* followed her through. During her run down she had been subjected to a heavy raking fire from the ships of the Combined Fleet, and had suffered a loss of between fifty and sixty men in killed and wounded by the time she had broken the line. Aboard the British ship, however, complete silence prevailed, only broken by the crash of a shot striking home or the shriek of some wounded man. Captain Hargood had been hit by a splinter during the approach, but had refused to be taken below and continued to direct the ship. There seems some considerable doubt as to the actual time which elapsed between the *Royal Sovereign* and the *Belleisle* breaking the line. Some accounts give up to fifteen minutes and others give only three minutes, here the latter figure is adopted as being the most commonly accepted.

Lieutenant Nicolas, who described the scene on the *Belleisle* as she approached the line, says:

My eyes were horror struck at the bloody corpses around me, and my ears rang with the shrieks of the wounded and the moans of the dying.

At this moment, seeing that almost everyone was lying down, I was half disposed to follow their example, and several times stooped for the purpose, but—and I remember the impression well—a certain monitor seemed to whisper 'stand up and do not shrink from your duty.'

Turning round, my much esteemed and gallant Senior [Lt. Owen] fixed my attention; the serenity of his countenance and the composure with which he paced the deck drove more than half my terror away; and joining him, I became somewhat infused with his spirit, which cheered me on to act the part it became me.

Lieutenant Nicolas reports that the tension was relieved on the ship by the order to prepare to fire. Captain Hargood said to his officers on the quarter deck, 'Gentlemen, I have only this to say: that I shall pass under the stern of that ship', pointing to the *Santa Ana* which was now looming up out of the smoke ahead and from which red flashes could be seen rippling down her sides. After exchanging a few shots with the *Monarca*, the *Belleisle* passed through the allied line astern of the *Santa Ana* and ahead of the *Fougueux*, then hauled up and fired some shots into the larboard quarter of the *Santa Ana*. Seeking an opponent in the smoke and dust, Captain Hargood brought his ship astern the French 80-gun ship *Indomptable* and raked her. She then crashed into the *Fougueux* and began a fast and furious action at point-blank range. The *Indomptable* came to her companion's rescue and fired a broadside into the *Belleisle* before drifting away and vanishing in the smoke.

The next British ship into action was the *Mars*. Captain Duff was steering to break the line between the *Monarca* and *Pluton* from which ships she had suffered severely as she approached. The captain of the *Pluton*, seeing her intention, closed up on the *Monarca* and Duff altered course to pass ahead of the *Monarca*. Once again the *Pluton* followed the move and soon the ships were in close action. When the *Mars* had to luff up to avoid hitting the *Santa Ana*, the *Pluton* stationed herself on her starboard quarter and began firing from a position to which the gunners aboard the *Mars* could make no serious reply. With his ship being raked from astern, Duff was in a desperate position, but he kept calm and asked if any guns could be brought to bear on the *Pluton*. A reprieve came in the form of the *Tonnant* entering action, for Captain Tyler immediately bore down to rake the *Pluton*, and the

French captain, seeing him coming, luffed up to try to rake him first. Temporarily relieved from the fire of the *Pluton*, the *Mars* was still badly shattered and out of control. Just then the *Fougueux*, which had been engaging the *Belleisle* and had had the good fortune to shoot away her opponent's mizen-mast, drifted down on the *Mars* and Captain Beaudouin brought his ship into a perfect position to rake the already shattered *Mars*.

As the *Fougueux* was pointed out to Captain Duff he again enquired if any guns could be brought to bear on her. The answer was that they probably could not, but no one could be sure because of the smoke. Duff then said: 'Then we must point our guns on the ships on which they will bear. I shall go and look, but the men below may see better as there is less smoke there.' Having just sent orders below for the guns to be pointed farther aft to engage the *Fougueux*, the first broadside from that ship killed him, and word was sent to his son below that his father had been killed.

As stated earlier, the *Tonnant* had entered the action and gone to the help of the *Mars* by firing into the *Pluton*. Captain Tyler had taken his ship into action steering straight for the larboard bow of the *Algésiras*, then passing between that ship and the *Monarca* raked the latter vessel. The *Algésiras* tried to cross the stern of the *Tonnant*, but Captain Tyler defeated the intention of the Frenchman by running her on board. The two ships had been brought together in such a position that it was impossible for the *Algésiras* to return any fire to the *Tonnant*, and the British gunners loaded and fired as fast as they could. Admiral Magon was flying his flag on board the *Algésiras* and was killed in this stage of the battle. A French naval historian describes the clash of the two ships:

The *Algésiras* had already exchanged fire with several vessels, when she fell in with the *Tonnant*. The British ship crossed her bows and got entangled with her bowsprit. Then holding her antagonist fast, the *Tonnant* began firing broadsides into the *Algésiras* that raked the French ship from end to end, and to which she could only reply with a few of her foremost guns. The position for the *Algésiras* was that of a pugilist held fast 'in chancery'. Admiral Magon, as the only thing to do, gave orders to board. He would, he shouted, lead the boarders himself.

Within a few minutes of making his gallant pronouncement, Admiral Magon was dead, killed by a cannon ball from the

Tonnant. His life might have been spared if he had quitted the deck after he had been wounded in the shoulder a few minutes previously.

A witness aboard the *Tonnant* describes the opening of the action with the *Algésiras*:

A French ship of eighty guns with an Admiral's flag came up, and poured a raking broadside into our stern which killed and wounded forty petty officers and men, nearly cut the rudder in two, and shattered the whole of the stern with the quarter galleries. She then, in a most gallant manner, locked her bowsprit in our starboard main shrouds and attempted to board us with the greater part of her officers and ship's company. She had riflemen in her tops, who did great execution. Our poop was soon cleared and our gallant captain shot through the left thigh and obliged to be carried below. During this time we were not idle. We gave it her most gloriously with the starboard and main deckers, and turned the forecastle gun, loaded with grape, on the gentlemen who wished to give us a fraternal hug. The marines kept up a warm destructive fire on the boarders. Only one man made good his footing on our quarter-deck, when he was pinned through the calf of his right leg by one of the crew with his half pike, whilst another was going to cut him down, which I prevented, and desired him to be taken to the cockpit.

The action between the *Tonnant* and *Algésiras* lasted for more than half an hour, with the ships gradually swinging round until they were broadside to broadside, and the British were firing their guns without being able to run them out. During the action both ships caught fire from the blazing wads thrown from the guns, but the fire fighting crew of the *Tonnant* extinguished the blaze on both ships. The *Algésiras* eventually struck to the *Tonnant* at 2.15 p.m.

The next ship of Collingwood's line bearing down on the enemy was the *Bellerophon*. As the wind was gradually failing it was not until fifteen minutes after the *Tonnant* had broken the line that the *Bellerophon* followed her through. Her log states: '12.20 opened our fire on the enemy. At 12.30 engaging on both sides in passing through the enemy's line astern of a Spanish two-decker.'

Captain Cooke was aiming to bring his ship to pass under the stern of the Spanish two-decker *Bahama* and ahead of the French *L'Aigle*, raking both ships as he went through. The wind was light by now and the advancing ship was hardly moving above walking pace, so suffered much from the fire of the ships of the Combined Fleet. Just after the *Royal Sovereign* had broken the line, one of the midshipmen on the *Bellerophon*'s quarter deck tripped over a trigger line and set off one of the guns. The enemy ships must have thought this some kind of a signal from one of the British flagships, for four of them, *Aigle*, *Montañés*, *Bahama*, and *Swiftsure* opened a heavy fire. This fire was very galling and was damaging the hull and rigging, so Captain Cooke ordered some of the forward guns to be fired to cover the ship in smoke. Not, however, until they were under the stern of the *Bahama* and ahead of the *Montañés* was a broadside fired. Lieutenant Cumby, who was on the quarter-deck, describes the moment of passing through:

At half-past twelve we were engaged on both sides, passing through their line close under the stern of a Spanish seventy-four, into whom, from the lightness of the wind being still further lulled by the effect of the cannonade, we fired our carronades three times, and every long gun on the starboard side, at least twice.

The effect of this first broadside into the *Bahama* was most destructive, and almost put the Spanish seventy-four out of action. Captain Cooke ordered the master to lay the *Bellerophon* alongside the *Bahama* and make an end of the business As the ship started to swing round, however:

... we saw over the smoke the topgallant sails of another ship close under our starboard bow, which proved to be the French seventy-four *L'Aigle*, as the name on her stern showed us, and although we hove all aback to avoid it, we could not sufficiently check our ship's way to prevent our running her on board with our starboard bow on her larboard quarter, our foreyard locking with her mainyard.

The *Bellerophon* was now engaged on both sides, having the *Bahama* on one side and the *L'Aigle* on the other, and in a short time three more ships, the *Algésiras*, *Swiftsure*, and *Montañés* were also firing into her. The *Swiftsure* had almost blundered into the *Bellerophon* and *L'Aigle*, which were locked together, and in luffing up to avoid a collision, presented her bows to the gunners on the *Bellerophon* who did not miss the chance to rake her. The *Algésiras* had now drifted on out of the fight, but the *Bellerophon* was still being fired at by four enemy ships. Her main opponent was *L'Aigle* one of a new class of French 74s, considerably bigger than the British 74, and mounting heavier guns. The log mentions the tricky position of the ship in a few words:

At 12.35 while hauling to the wind, fell on board the French two-decked ship *L'Aigle* with our starboad bow on her larboard qtr. our fore yard locking with her main one. Kept up a brisk fire on both her and the Spanish ship on the larboard bow, at the same time receiving the fire of two ships, one astern, the other on the larboard qtr.

There were several soldiers on board of *L'Aigle* and these were lining her bulwarks and stationed throughout the tops firing on to the English ships, and causing great confusion. A storm of musket bullets was sweeping the decks of the *Bellerophon* from end to end, the only protection being the smoke of the engagement. There were no men in the *Bellerophon*'s tops, in accordance with an order from Nelson who considered them a greater fire risk to their own ship than a danger to the enemy. The *San Juan Nepomuceno* now opened a distant fire on the *Bellerophon* and brought the ship's antagonists back to five. Within eighteen minutes of the start of the engagement the fire from the tops of *L'Aigle* had killed or injured all but four of the people on the quarter deck of the *Bellerophon*. The only people uninjured were the captain, master, first lieutenant and a midshipman. Midshipman Walker gave his version of the action in his letter home:

The action soon after became general. *L'Aigle* was the best manned ship in the Combined Fleet, and was full of picked grenadiers, who annoyed us most dreadfully with musketry. The *Bellerophon* was equally well manned and had she been fairly alongside her opponent, would soon have carried her, and even in the disadvantageous situation in which we were placed, we very soon drove them from the lower deck; and though we could only bring our foremost guns to bear upon her, whilst we received her whole broadside and the fire of four other ships, we had nearly silenced her fire when she dropped astern of us.

Those few lines, however, cover a very hot and hectic action! At about one o'clock, a shot from one of her opponents sent the mainmast over the side and the mizen topmast followed soon after. The master, Overton, was killed by musketry soon after, and at 1.11 p.m. Captain Cooke was struck by two musket balls in the chest. Asked if he wanted to go below for treatment, Cooke replied: 'No, let me lie quietly one minute.' Before that minute had passed, however, he was dead, and the command of the *Bellerophon* resolved on Lieutenant Cumby. One of the greatest sources of annoyance besides the musketry was the number of grenades thrown from the tops. One of these, exploding on the lower deck, killed or disabled upwards of twenty-five men. Another almost finished the ship when thrown in at a lower-deck port, for it set fire to the storeroom and forced open the door into the magazine passage. The door was so designed, however, that if it was blown open the door to the magazine closed. The fire was soon got under control by the gunner and a few spare hands.

Up on the quarter-deck Midshipman Franklin was severely tried by the French musketry, and related the following episode to his brother-in-law afterwards:

Very early in the engagement the *Bellerophon*'s masts became entangled with and caught fast hold of a French line of battleship. Though the masts were pretty close together at the top there was a space between them below, but not so great as to prevent the French sailors from trying to board the *Bellerophon*. In the attempt their hands received severe blows, as they laid hold of the side of the ship, from whatever the English sailors could lay hands on. In this way hundreds of the Frenchmen fell between the ships and were drowned. While the *Bellerophon* was fastened to the enemy on one side, another French man-of-war was at liberty to turn round and fire first one broadside and then another into the English ship. In consequence 300 men were killed or wounded [a vastly exaggerated figure] on board the *Bellerophon*. At last after a very sharp contest, the French ship which was at liberty received such a severe handling that she veered about and sailed away; but still a desultory yet destructive warfare was carried on between the two entangled ships, until out of forty-seven men upon the Quarter Deck, of whom Franklin was one, all were either killed or wounded but seven. Towards the end of the action a very few guns could be fired on either of the ships, the sailors were so disabled. But there remained a man in the foretop of the enemy ship wearing a cocked hat who had during the engagement taken off with his rifle several of the officers and men. Franklin was standing close by, and speaking to a midshipman, his most esteemed friend, when the fellow above shot him and he fell dead at his comrade's feet. Soon after, Franklin and a Sergeant of Marines were carrying down a black seaman to have his wounds dressed, when a ball from the rifleman entered his breast and killed the poor fellow as they carried him along. Franklin said to the sergeant, 'He'll have you next', but the sergeant swore he should not and said that he would go below to a quarter of the ship from which he could command the French rifleman, and would never cease firing at him till he had killed him. As Franklin was going back on deck, keeping his eye on the rifleman he saw the fellow lift his rifle to his shoulder and aim at him; but with an elasticity very common in his family he bounded behind a mast. Rapid as the movement was, the ball from the rifle entered the deck of the ship a few feet behind him. Meantime, so few guns were being discharged he could hear the sergeant firing away with his musket from below, and looking out from behind the mast, he saw the rifleman, whose features he vowed he should never forget so long as he lived, fall over head foremost into the sea. Upon the sergeant coming up, he asked him how many times he fired: 'I killed him', he said, 'at the seventh shot.'

A shot from one of the enemy ships had smashed the rudder, making the ship now impossible to steer or sail. Chain and bar shot were slashing the rigging to shreds, and after one discharge the colours were shot away and came fluttering down to the deck. The Yeoman of Signals, Christopher Beatty, who was standing nearby, said, 'Well, well, that's too bad. The fellows will say we have struck!' Whereupon, seizing the ensign, he began to climb the shrouds to refix them. This was likely to be a most perilous journey, for every seaman who had attempted to fix the rigging before had been killed by the French sharpshooters. No sooner had Beatty begun his climb, than a hail of musket bullets whistled all around him; but none of them hit him, and he stopped about seven feet above the deck and began to fix the flag. At this point the firing suddenly stopped as if the French sharpshooters, appreciating his bravery, had decided to let him carry on with his work unmolested. The ensign fixed, Beatty climbed down to the deck again, completely unharmed.

As related in Franklin's story, the French, seeing that the *Bellerophon*'s gunnery was superior and was beginning to get the upper hand, tried to board. Some of the Frenchmen thought they had found a convenient way to do this by climbing on the spritsail yard and then trying to work their way along to the bowsprit. Their ruse was spotted, and a seaman named MacFarlane quickly released the line holding the yard level, whereupon it canted and tipped the Frenchmen into the sea. Down below the fighting was equally fierce, and the rival gunners were firing at each other through the gun ports, and slashing at each other with cutlasses and rammers. Bombs were thrown in through the ports of the British ship and, as we have seen, one came near to finishing both ships together by blowing up the magazine.

Lieutenant Cumby took time off from his duties on the upper deck to go below and encourage the gunners. He knew that upon them rested their main hope as the upper deck was a complete wreck. Cumby ordered the gunners to elevate their pieces slightly so that the shot was fired upwards through the decks of the Frenchman and injured the people on them.

The French and Spanish ships had now closed the range to a few yards and were all firing into the British ship as fiercely as they could. This was not a one-way affair, for the gunners on the British ship were shooting as well as ever and doing great damage to their opponents. Captain Churraca of the *San Juan Nepomuceno* brought his ship under the stern of the *Bellerophon* and was about to fire a raking broadside into her when the *Dreadnought* loomed up out of the smoke and gave the Spanish ship a very destructive broadside. This was a very fortunate occurrence for the *Bellerophon*, for such an attack from the Spanish ship would probably have greatly damaged if not finished her altogether. Despite this aid, however, the situation was still precarious in the extreme: the *Aigle* was still resisting, the *Monarca* was firing into her port side, and the *Bahama* and French *Swiftsure* were firing into her port and starboard quarters respectively. The *Swiftsure* was an old British ship which had been taken by the French. She had been at the battle of the Nile, where her captain was Benjamin Hallowell, and it had been she who had taken the *Bellerophon*'s place opposite the *Orient* after the latter had drifted damaged out of the action.

Three times during the engagement between the *Bellerophon* and *Aigle* the ship caught fire, but each time the fire was brought under control. The fallen wreckage of sails and spars over the sides of the ships were a great source of danger, for the flashes from the guns could easily have set them alight, and this in fact did happen on the *Bellerophon*, but the wreckage was cut away and the fire extinguished. Lieutenant Cumby, describing the state of the ship at this time, said: 'She was totally unmanageable, the main and mizen topmasts hanging over the side, the jib-boom, spanker-boom and gaff shot away, and not a brace or a bow-line serviceable'. At one-forty when the fight with the *Aigle* had been going on for over an hour, the French ship suddenly broke free and drifted away under a terrific raking fire from the *Bellerophon*. The reason for breaking away was that her captain, Gourrège, had seen the *Revenge* bearing down on the flagship of Admiral Gravina, the *Principe de Asturias*, which was already damaged from previous fighting and he tried to intercept her. He was unsuccessful, however, for after a couple of broadsides Captain Moorsom passed through after other prey.

Aboard the *Bellerophon* it was no time for stock-taking, for three of her original five opponents were still firing into her. These were the *San Juan Nepomuceno*, *Bahama*, and *Monarca*. Of the other two ships which had been engaging her, the fate of *L'Aigle* has already been noted, and the *Swiftsure* had been beaten off by the superb gunnery of the *Bellerophon*. Never before in the war had the sheer superiority and technical excellence of the British gunnery been better demonstrated than at Trafalgar. A number of British ships which had passed the scene had fired into the *San Juan Nepomuceno* to aid the *Bellerophon* and she was now pretty badly damaged. Notwithstanding this, she was still firing and her crew were in reasonably good spirits. This was directly attributable to the influence and example of Captain Churruca on his raw and inexperienced crew. One of her officers said:

Our leader seemed to have infused his heroic spirit into the crew and soldiers, and the ship was handled and her broadsides delivered with wonderful promptitude and accuracy. The new recruits learnt their lesson in courage in no more than a couple of hours' apprenticeship, and our defence struck the English with astonishment.

The resistance terminated with the death of Captain Churruca, who was struck by a cannon ball which took off his leg, of which wound he died soon after. Attempts were made to keep his death a secret from the crew, but the news soon spread and the heart went out of them, so that soon after the *San Juan* struck her flag and was taken possession of by the *Dreadnought*. It was the *Dreadnought* which had drawn the *San Juan* from the *Bellerophon*, and they were last seen from that ship drifting away together in the smoke, firing into each other.

One more of the *Bellerophon*'s opponents was knocked out when the *Monarca* struck her colours at 3 p.m. and was taken possession of by the *Bellerophon*, and it was from that ship that the final fate of the *Aigle* was seen, when she struck to the *Defiance*.

This was virtually the end of the battle as far as the *Bellerophon* was concerned, for as Cumby put it: 'We were now without any opponent within reach of our guns'. Now was the time for assessing the damage and casualties inflicted on the ship during the action. Later Cumby was to write in the log as a final record of the battle:

At 1 the main & mizen topmasts fell over the side. At 1.5 the Master fell. At 1.11 Captain John Cooke (1st) fell. Still foul *L'Aigle*.

[signed]
William Pryce Cumby, Lieutenant.
Captain Killed in Action.

Lieutenant Saunders in his journal recorded the end of the battle as he saw it:

. . . 1.40 *L'Aigle* dropped to leeward under a raking fire from us as she fell off. On the smoke clearing away, several of the enemy's ships had struck. At 3 took possession of the Spanish ship *Monarca*.

Midshipman Walker in his letter also gave his version:

After we had thus got clear of our principal opponent, who did not return a single gun whilst we raked her, and two others of them had been engaged by the *Dreadnought* & *Colossus*, we were now only opposed to two Spanish seventy-fours, one of which, the *Monarca*, shortly afterwards struck and was at 3 o'clock taken possession of by our second lieutenant, myself & 8 men. The remaining one, the *Bahama*, struck to us in about half-an-hour afterwards & was taken possession of by our fourth lieutenant. There was very little firing after this except from five French ships making off to windward, which fired on both the *Bellerophon* and the *Monarca*. One of them was taken by the *Minotaur* and at 7 minutes after 5 the firing ceased.

Walker goes on to describe the casualties:

Our ship as was to be expected from her situation suffered very considerably, having 28 killed outright 127 badly & 40 slightly wounded, 23 are since dead of their wounds

The state of the ship was also very bad:

The *Bellerophon* had her main and mizen topmasts shot away, her fore topmasts, all three lower masts, and most of her yards badly wounded, and her standing rigging nearly cut to pieces. In hull also she was much injured, having had several knees and riders shot away, and part of her lower deck ripped up, besides other damage.

At this point we will leave our description of the damage to the *Bellerophon* and briefly follow the rest of the British ships into action, paying some attention to the ships of Lord Nelson's line.

The next ship in action after the *Bellerophon* was the *Colossus* under the command of Captain James Morris. This ship, as we have seen, had come to the rescue of the *Bellerophon* by engaging the *Swiftsure*. She got into action at about 12.25 p.m., about five minutes after the *Bellerophon*, and after firing a broadside at the *Swiftsure* she passed on into the action until she came up with the French *Argonaute* and both ships collided in the smoke. After ten minutes the guns on the Frenchman were almost silent, and the two ships drifted apart. One of the last shots fired from the *Argonaute* had wounded Captain Morris in the knee, but he stayed on the poop with a tourniquet around the injured limb. The next two opponents of the *Colossus* were the Spanish 74, the *Bahama*, and the French *Swiftsure*. The former was firing from the larboard beam and the latter from the larboard quarter. The *Swiftsure*, already damaged from her encounter with the *Bellerophon*, soon dropped out of the fight under the accuracy of the British fire and drifted away leaving the Spanish ship to face the *Colossus* alone. The men of the *Colossus* were firing superbly, and even though the Spanish captain was setting the most courageous example to his crew it was obvious that the superior gunnery of the British ship would gain the upper hand soon. Captain Galiano fell about three o'clock, just after his coxswain, who was standing next to him, was cut in two by a ball from the *Colossus*. With the fall of the captain resistance crumbled, and as a token of surrender the British flag was run up on the stump of the mainmast, and the *Colossus* took possession of her.

The French *Swiftsure* had now come up astern again and her captain was trying to get into a position to rake the British ship. Captain Morris saw this and gave the order to wear ship, and the *Colossus* gave the *Swiftsure* a broadside which carried away her mizen-mast and main topmast. The discomfiture of this ship was completed some time later when the *Orion* gave her a broadside which took away her mainmast and she surrendered.

The next ship in Collingwood's line was the *Achilles* under the command of Captain Richard King. King took his ship through the enemy line astern of the *Montañés* and ahead of the *San Ildefonso*, firing a raking broadside into the former. He then luffed up the *Achilles* and engaged the *Montañés* for a quarter of an hour, after which time the *Montañés* broke off the engagement with her captain killed and second-in-command wounded, and soon after surrendered. King then took his ship to the rescue of the *Belleisle* which was by that time totally dismasted and with three of the enemy's ships firing into her. Before reaching the crippled ship, however, the *Achilles* was attacked by the *Argonauta* and once again British gunnery proved superior and decisive, and the surrender of the Spanish ship was only averted by the arrival of the French *Achille* which opened fire on the British *Achilles* from the larboard side, and shortly after the French *Berwick*, too, joined in the battle with the British *Achilles*. The French *Achille* soon after went ahead to engage the *Belleisle*, and the British *Achilles* was left engaged with the *Berwick*. The engagement between these two ships lasted just about half an hour, after which the *Berwick* was forced to strike.

The next British ship to engage was the *Revenge* commanded by Captain Robert Moorsom. He entered the action at 12.35 p.m., and instead of driving straight down for the line, his ship was for some time running parallel with the *San Ildefonso* and the French *Achille*. In a running fight between the *Revenge* and the French *Achille* the French ship's mizen-mast was shot away, collapsing over the side and carrying the sharpshooters in its rigging into the sea. This loss slowed the French ship down, and Moorsom took the opportunity of a gap between the French *Achille* and *San Ildefonso* to take his ship through the line. An attempt to board by the crew of the French *Achille* was foiled by the fire of the Marines and the carronades. Moorsom then fired two raking broadsides before luffing his ship to bring his starboard broadside to bear on the stern of the *San Ildefonso*. Gravina, on the *Principe de Asturias*, was just astern of the French *Achille* and turned away to rake the *Revenge* as Moorsom tried to bring his ship on board of the *San Ildefonso*. The situation for the *Revenge* was now highly dangerous for she was being fired into from three sides by three ships, one of them a three-decker. She stayed thus for nearly twenty minutes before help arrived in the form of Captain Durham in the *Defiance*, leading the last ships of Collingwood's column.

Captain Durham tried to take his ship under the stern of the *Principe de Asturias* and ahead of the *Berwick*, but the latter closed the gap and the British ship steered straight for her, carrying away her bowsprit. After extricating his ship from the wreckage of the *Berwick*, Durham went on for the *Principe de Asturias*, but the ship he actually met in the end was *L'Aigle*, which we have earlier seen engaging the *Bellerophon*. Midshipman Colin Campbell of the *Defiance* described the ensuing engagement:

... we now ran alongside her and at 3.10 lashed ourselves to her, where we had it pretty hot till finding we had silenced the guns, we boarded & took possession of her poop & forecastle. One of our men ran to the masthead, hauled down the French pendant and hoisted an English ensign and pendant, but her men still keeping up a heavy fire of musketry from her tops and lower deck, and every now and then firing some guns and throwing stinkpots into the ports, which killed a number of our men, we recalled the boarders, hauled off within pistol shot, and turned to engage her again.

The renewed firing was of short duration and the first lieutenant of the *Aigle*, Asmus Classen, finding himself isolated from the rest of the fleet and with two-thirds of his crew casualties, decided to strike. Soon after, boarders from the *Defiance* arrived and took possession of her, Campbell among them. He was shocked by the heaps of dead and injured he found on board the captured ship.

With the last of the ships of Collingwood's line coming into action, the main strategical plan of Nelson had been achieved; the French and Spanish ships in the rear of the Combined Fleet had been mostly battered and blasted into submission. One of the last British ships to engage was the *Dreadnought* which had been Collingwood's flagship before the arrival of the *Royal Sovereign*. She was a slow sailer, but her gun power was overwhelming and she forced the *San Juan Nepomuceno* to surrender in ten minutes.

Resistance to the British in the rear was rapidly crumbling when the *San Ildefonso* struck to the *Defence*, and the *Berwick* to the British *Achilles*. This left the *Principe de Asturias* as the only ship in the rear division of Gravina which had not yet surrendered. She was pursued by the *Prince* (98) who passed across her stern and fired a raking broadside into her. Gravina had already been wounded and had been taken below during a brief engagement with the *Dreadnought*. The Spanish ship escaped from the *Prince*, but in a very weakened state with her masts tottering, and she had to be taken in tow by the French frigate *Thémis*. Two other allied ships which had been in the vicinity of the *Principe de Asturias*—the French *Neptune* and the Spanish *San Justo*—tried to come to her aid, but were obliged to sheer off by the fire of the British ships.

The *Prince* passed on at about 4 p.m. to engage the French *Achille*, which was lying almost dismasted. The first broadside from the *Prince* brought down the mainmast, which crashed on the deck crushing the boats and only leaving the foremast standing. Somehow a fire started in the foretop of the French ship, and before the French seamen could extinguish it the next broadside from the *Prince* brought it crashing down, setting on fire the wreckage of the other masts which had not yet been cleared away. The fire soon spread, and the *Prince* ordered her boats to be got away to assist the French to escape while she dragged herself clear of the blazing *Achille*, fearing she would go up at any moment. As the flames got a better grip, the crew began jumping into the water and swimming to the British boats clustering around. Among those picked up was a nude young Frenchwoman, wife of one of the maintop-men in the ship, who had been stationed in the powder magazine passing cartridges up to the deck. She was well treated by the British officers, who gave her clothes and a cabin to herself on the *Revenge* to which she was later transferred. Her happiness was complete a few days later when it was found that her husband had been picked up alive and was also on board the *Revenge*. Apparently Jeannette, as she was called, was not the only woman on the *Achille*, for another was picked up by the boats of the *Britannia* and she too was given clothes and a cabin.

Gravina was by now leading the remnants of the rear into Cadiz, while Dumanoir was leading the van, which had taken hardly any part in the battle. The pursuit had been called off by Collingwood, who had gone aboard the *Euryalus* when the *Royal Sovereign* became unmanageable.

As this book is concerned with the story of the *Bellerophon*, which was one of the ships of Collingwood's detachment, this account of Trafalgar naturally concentrates on that section of the battle. However, we cannot leave the battle without a brief description of the attack of the weather column under Nelson. This was led by the three massive three-deckers, *Victory* (100), *Téméraire* (98), and *Neptune* (98), a powerful force which was intended to smash through the allied line. As with Collingwood's line, the ships had to undergo a severe fire from the enemy.

Nelson refused to let the *Téméraire* go ahead and lead the line into battle, and the *Victory* continued in the lead with all sails set. One shot smashed the wheel of the *Victory* and the ship had to be steered from the gunroom, using emergency tackle which had been rigged in advance.

Captain Hardy in the *Victory* had originally intended to head for the gap between the *Bucentaure* and *Santisima Trinidad*, but as he approached the gap closed and he switched his attention to the gap between the *Bucentaure* and the ship immediately astern, the 74-gun *Redoutable*. This gap, too, was closing, but the *Victory* smashed her way through although she was raked by the French *Neptune* when she cleared from the smoke of her own raking broadsides. The British flagship then went alongside the French 74 and commenced a close action with her. The starboard guns of the *Victory* were firing into the *Redoutable*, while the larboard guns fired into the *Bucentaure* and the *Santisima Trinidad*. The French flagship had also been fired into by the leading trio of British ships and was by now pretty badly damaged.

The *Téméraire* had passed astern of the *Redoutable* and raked her, though she too was raked by the French *Neptune*. This broadside put the British ship momentarily out of control, and she crashed into the *Redoutable*. The French ship had been putting up a gallant resistance against the overwhelming mass of the *Victory*, and the fire from her rigging had twice cleared the quarter-deck of the British ship, except for the stately figure of Hardy and the smaller figure of Nelson. In the hail of fire which was sweeping the decks of the British ship it was not possible, however, to escape for long, and such a prominent figure as Nelson was sure to be spotted by the sharpshooters situated in the rigging of the French ship. At 1.35 p.m. the event happened which Hardy and Blackwood and other of Nelson's friends had feared: the admiral was hit by a shot fired from the rigging and collapsed on the deck. He was carried below at once in the hope that his wound might not prove serious, but Beatty the surgeon quickly diagnosed the wound as fatal. Below decks, the superior number of the *Victory*'s guns and the better gunnery of the British ship were knocking her opponent to pieces, and eventually the arrival of the *Téméraire* sealed the fate of the French vessel. French attempts to board were in vain owing to the difference in height of the two ships.

On deck Hardy was left to carry on the operation of the *Victory* in the fight against the *Redoutable*. He was also, in effect, in command of the fleet, as Collingwood had not yet heard of the death of his friend.

The third of the three-deckers, and the third British ship of Nelson's line to go into action, was the *Neptune* commanded by Sir Thomas Fremantle, an old friend of Nelson. This ship, too, passed under the stern of the *Bucentaure*, and then went on through the smoke until she came up against the *Santisima Trinidad* which she also raked with devastating effect. Fremantle then hauled the British ship alongside the Spanish one and commenced a close engagement.

The fourth ship in Nelson's line was the *Leviathan* of 74 guns. A letter from her purser, Sam Rickards, written after the battle, describes events on that ship:

She (the *Leviathan*) was next ship but one to the *Victory* (Lord Nelson's ship). After passing several of the enemies' ships and receiving a dreadful cannonading from them as we passed, amongst the number the *Santissima Trinidad* a Spanish 4-decker of 130 guns which ship we raked and petted in a desperate manner, lying right athwart her stern. We at length singled out our ship, the *San Augustin* of 74 guns, and after giving it her warmly, for about half-an-hour, silenced her, boarded and took possession. At one period of the action, our ship had 6 upon her at once.

The fifth ship in the line was the *Conqueror* under the command of Israel Pellew. Pellew took his ship under the stern of the *Bucentaure*, but instead of passing on as the others had done he brought his ship alongside the French ship and engaged her at close quarters. She had been almost a wreck before, but the attentions of the *Conqueror* completed the process and she was soon entirely dismasted. The captain, Magendie, had already been wounded and Villeneuve was seeking death with a gloomy fatalism but it refused to find him. He ordered a boat to be got ready to transfer him to another ship to continue the fight, but not a whole one could be found. A hail to the *Santisima Trinidad* evoked no response, and Villeneuve gave the order to cease further resistance. Lieutenant Atcherley of the *Conqueror*'s Marines, who came aboard to take possession of the vanquished ship, had no idea that they had just been engaging the flagship of the Combined Fleet. He was rather surprised to be met by a group of three French officers headed by a tall thin man in the uniform of an admiral. The following conversation has been quoted many times, but is worthy of repetition if only for the reasons that it shows the fame of Sir Edward Pellew among his enemies, and the courteous way in which war was still conducted.

'To whom have I the honour of surrendering?' asked Villeneuve in English.

'To Captain Pellew of the *Conqueror*,' replied Atcherley.

'It is a satisfaction to me, that it is to one so fortunate as Sir Edward Pellew that I have lowered my flag,' said Villeneuve.

'It is his brother, sir,' corrected Atcherley.

'His brother? What, are there two of them? Hélas!'

Atcherley then suggested to the group of Frenchmen that they should keep their swords to surrender to an officer of higher rank than himself. After securing the magazine, he returned to the quarter-deck to look for the the *Conqueror* but that ship had passed on in search of other opponents. He therefore took his high ranking prisoners to the nearest British ship which was the battered *Mars*. Here the Captain, Duff, had already been killed, so it was Lieutenant William Hennah who received the swords of Villeneuve, Magendie, and Contamine, who was the representative of the army on the flagship.

The *Conqueror* had in fact passed on to aid in the fight against the *Santisima Trinidad*, and was firing into her on the windward side, while the *Neptune* was firing into her starboard side, and the *Africa* into her larboard quarter. The latter ship had become separated from the British fleet during the previous night and had approached the battle by herself that morning. Although she was only a 64, she had had no hesitation in engaging the biggest ship in the world.

Following the *Conqueror* was the 100-gun *Britannia*, flying the flag of Rear-Admiral the Earl of Northesk, closely followed by the *Agamemnon*, *Orion*, and *Ajax*. The *Britannia* was first engaged by the *San Franciso de Asis* and then by the *Rayo*. This was the final stages of the battle with the result already

decided in favour of the British, although the van of the
Combined Fleet under Dumanoir had tacked and showed some
intention of attacking the cluster of ships around the *Victory*.
Hardy summoned some of the less damaged British ships
around him and was confident of beating off the attack. In
fact, nothing serious was intended, only the *Intrépide* and *San
Augustin* really pressing home the attack; Dumanoir in the
Formidable, followed by the *Duguay-Trouin*, *Scipion*, *Mont-
Blanc*, and *Neptuno* made for Cadiz. The British ships
Spartiate and *Minotaur* engaged the fleeing ships briefly, but
Dumanoir made his escape. Further to the north the *Rayo*,
San Francisco de Asis, and *Héros* were also making their
escape to Cadiz. The only fighting at present taking place in
the vicinity was that between the British ships and the *Intrépide* and *San Augustin*. Captain Infernet of the *Intrépide* was
steering for the centre of the fight to rescue the *Bucentaure*,
and when he informed his crew of this decision his speech was
greeted with loud cheers. Going down with him, but further
to leeward was the *San Augustin* which was also making a
final desperate effort. The *Leviathan*, as previously mentioned
in Rickards's account, was the first to engage the *San Augustin*.
Both ships ran alongside each other firing broadsides and then
the British attempted to board. The Spanish beat off two
attempts, but not having sufficient men left to man the ship
properly and to repel a third boarding, and being surrounded
by British ships, the colours were hauled down.

Infernet in the *Intrépide*, seeing the *Leviathan* engaged in
fighting the *San Agustin*, seized the opportunity to cross her
bows and rake her. He was fired into from a distance by the
Conqueror but no serious damage was done. The next British
ship to fire at him was the *Africa* which luffed across her stern
and raked her. The British ships which were in pursuit of the
fleeing *Rayo*, *San Francisco de Asis*, and *Héros* also fired into
her. Eventually Captain Codrington of the *Orion* brought up
his ship to rake the French ship. As the British ship crossed
the bows of the French 74, a young French officer on the
fo'c's'le of the *Intrépide* sent back a message to Captain
Infernet that he had a chance to lay on board of a British ship.
But suddenly realizing that the ship was not changing course,
he went back himself to find out what was wrong, and found
the young midshipman he had sent with the message lying

flat on the deck frightened by the fire of the *Britannia* which was passing northwards in pursuit of the ships making for Cadiz. By now the opportunity was past and Codrington had raked the *Intrépide*, which was the beginning of the end for the gallant French ship and her crew. At 4.45 p.m. Infernet ordered the men remaining on the upper deck to go and operate the batteries below decks, and continued resistance for another hour or more before he was compelled to strike to the overwhelming mass of ships firing into him.

This was the end of the battle, for the Combined Fleet had all been either sunk, captured, or dispersed. At 4.30 p.m. Gravina had signalled for the remaining ships to rally round him, while at the same time 'a victory having been reported to the Right Honourable Lord Nelson, he died of his wound'. Thus ended the life of Britain's most famous fighting seaman, and thus passed into the hands of the Royal Navy the control of the sea for the next century. Many on both sides felt the loss of this extraordinary man. Rickards of the *Leviathan* records of a Spanish lieutenant, that: 'he did not mind being a prisoner, as he hoped to get a sight of Lord Nelson, and upon being acquainted of his death, expressed his sorrow'.

The death of the Commander-in-Chief was not known yet throughout the British fleet, for instance on the *Bellerophon* Lieutenant Cumby said:

At half past seven we observed that the *Euryalus* to which ship we knew Vice-Admiral Collingwood had shifted his flag, carried the lights of the Commander-in Chief, and that there were no lights on board of the *Victory*, from which we were left to draw the melancholy inference that our gallant, our beloved chief, the incomparable Nelson, had fallen. But so unwilling were we to believe what we could scarcely bring ourselves to doubt, that I actually went on board of the *Euryalus* the next morning and breakfasted with Admiral Collingwood, from whom I received orders without being once told, or even once asking the question, whether Lord Nelson was slain.

The time immediately after the battle was mostly spent on the *Bellerophon*, as on other British ships, in getting the battle damage repaired. The *Bellerophon* had been badly damaged with her main topmast shot away, and her mizen-topmast in a precarious state. Other damage to her hull was less serious, and the leaks were soon under control. The look of the weather more than justified Nelson's warning before the battle to anchor at the close of the day, although such an order was never given by Collingwood. 'Anchor!' he said, 'It is the last thing I should have thought of!'

The log of the *Bellerophon* ceases for a few days after the note of Captain Cooke being killed in action, so we are left only with Cumby for an eye-witness account of what happened on board the ship during those days. It was obviously a time of great trial, for the expected storm blew up next day and soon the British ships and their prizes were fighting to stay afloat. The men of the *Bellerophon* had rigged a jury mizen-topmast and cleared away the wreckage of the battle, and were consequently able to ride out the storm, if not in ease and comfort, at least in a more secure position than their companions on board the shattered prizes. The *Bellerophon* had a prize crew in the *Monarca* where, in efforts to keep the hulk afloat, they had cut away a couple of anchors and cast some of the guns overboard. They succeeded for four days in the most dreadful weather, then with the vessel on the point of sinking they were taken off by the *Leviathan*. Both Spanish and British had worked together for the salvation of the ship and themselves, but their efforts were of no avail and the *Monarca* could not be saved. Midshipman Walker describes the efforts of the combined crews during those hectic days and nights:

... in the ensuing night a storm came on, such as I had never witnessed, and for four following days we had a severer struggle against the elements than we had had against the enemy. You will imagine what has been our suffering in a crippled ship, with 5,000 prisoners on board and only 55 Englishmen, most of whom were in a constant state of intoxication. We rolled away all our masts except the foremast; we were afterwards forced to cut away 2 anchors, heave overboard several guns, shot, etc., to lighten her; and were after all in such imminent danger of sinking that, seeing no one near to assist us, we at length determined to run the ship on shore on the Spanish coast, which we should have done had not the *Leviathan* fortunately fallen in with us & saved us, and all but about 150 Spaniards. The ship then went ashore and was afterwards destroyed.

The *Bellerophon* had the *San Juan* in tow, and eventually managed to reach Gibraltar with her prize on the 28th October. Midshipman Walker, who was on board the *Leviathan*, did not rejoin the ship until the 3rd November, as Collingwood had only sent thirteen of the most battered ships of the fleet to Gibraltar.

This finishes the Trafalgar campaign for the *Bellerophon*; it had been a glorious one for the ships of the Royal Navy. Collingwood, on the death of Nelson, assumed command in the Mediterranean, a command which he was to hold until his death in 1810. He describes the battle in a letter to his sister written on the 25th October:

Off Cadiz,
October 25th, 1805.

My Dear Sister,

We fought a battle on the 21st & obtained a victory such as perhaps there is no instance of. We were 27 ships, the Combined Fleet 33. My dear friend Nelson fell in the middle of the battle. I followed up what he began and in the end took 19 ships of the line. The *Santisima Trinidad* of 130 guns and *Santa Ana* of 120 guns are amongst them. Villeneuve the French Commander-in-Chief is now sitting by my side, Gravina escaped, but I took D'Alava, Spanish Vice Admiral, Cisneros, Spanish Rear Admiral and am told Magon the French Rear Admiral is also among the captives. Four Admirals at a dash is something new.

But they have injured my *Royal Sovereign* very much, so that I was obliged to quit her after the action and come into a frigate to conduct the business of the fleet. The next day a violent gale came on and has continued ever since. Many of the captured ships are sunk, some we have burnt and such is the wrecked state of the whole that I do not expect to get one into port. But the terror of the Combined Fleet is over and the difficulty of making another increased.

The loss in my ship *Sovereign* was very great. I do not know what, but I fear between two and three hundred from all I can hear. When I tell you I have scarce slept or eat since from anxiety of mind, and the extra fatigue of my body, I am sure you will excuse a short letter.

I am ever,
My dear sisters & brother,
Your most affectionate,
Cuthb't Collingwood.

P.S. Tell Thompson's father that his son behaved so admirably in the battle that if he had served his time I would have made him a lieutenant the same day. He is wounded in the arm, but would not quit his duty upon deck until at the very close of the action his leg was broke by a large splinter.

On the 23rd October, the allies had emerged from Cadiz in an effort to recapture some of the eighteen prizes which they had left in British hands on the 21st. They managed to capture four of the eighteen, but lost in doing so the *Rayo, San Francisco de Asis*, and *Indomptable*. The *Santa Ana* was one of those recaptured, as was the *Algésiras*.

A final reckoning for the battle of Trafalgar reads as follows:

Combined Fleet present at battle	33
Captured in battle	18
	—
Total escaped after battle	15
Recaptured by allies on the 23rd	4
	—
	19
Wrecked and captured on the 24th	4
	—
	15
	—
Remaining to Allies: at sea	4
in Cadiz	11
Also taken by Strachan on 4th Nov.	4
	—
Total left to allies in Cadiz	11

Meanwhile what of the officers of the *Bellerophon* who had fought in the battle? The following biographical details may be of some interest.

Captain Cooke: Killed in the battle.

William Pryce Cumby (1st Lt.): Promoted captain after the battle. Later commanded the *Polyphemus*. Made a C.B. in 1831. Died as superintendent of Pembroke dockyard, 27th September, 1837.

Edmund Fanning Thomas: 2nd Lt. Acted as 1st Lt. after the battle. Retired as a commander in 1830. Died at Cleethorpes 28th April, 1842.

David Scott: Wounded in the battle 1st Lt. of the *Bedford* when the Royal Family of Portugal was escorted to Brazil in 1807. Served aboard the *St Domingo* during the Walcheren Expedition of 1809. Captain 1814. Retired rear-admiral 1850. Died 1852.

John Alexander Douglass: 4th Lt. Career not traceable after 1809.

George Lawrence Saunders: 5th Lt. Promoted commander 1814. Died 1834.

Edward Overton: Master. Killed in battle.

Alexander Whyte: Retired in 1824. Died in 1838. Surgeon.

Thomas Jewell: Purser. Died in 1821.

William James Wemyss: Captain of Marines. Wounded in the battle. Major 1812. Lt.-colonel in 1814. Retired 1814. Died 1823.

John Wilson: 1st Lt. of Marines. Brevet captain 1827. Captain 1828. Hon. major in 1854 on retired list.

Peter Connolly: 2nd Lt. of Marines. Placed on half-pay in 1816. Died in 1835.

Luke Higgins: 2nd Lt. of Marines. 1st Lt. in 1806. Placed on half pay 1807.

Thomas Robinson: Boatswain. Died of wounds in Gibraltar hospital 2nd November 1805.

Daniel Woodriff: Master's mate. Lt. in 1807. Commander 1822. Retired captain 1856. Died at Old Charlton, Kent, 1860.

John Franklin: Midshipman. Lt. 1808. Served off America in 1814—wounded. Went to the Arctic in 1818. Commander 1821. Created F.R.S. in 1822. Captain 1822. Commanded Arctic expedition 1825–7. Knighted 1829. Commanded frigate on the coast of Greece 1830–3. K.C.H. in 1836. Lt.-Governor of Van Diemen's Land 1836–44. Commander of the expedition to the Arctic in 1845. Discovered the North West Passage but lost his life on the expedition. Entire expedition perished.

Hugh Patton: Midshipman. Lt. in 1811. Commander 1813. Captain 1819. Retired 1846. Retired rear-admiral 1852. Retired vice-admiral 1857. Retired admiral 1863. Died 1864.

George Hughes: Served as a Volunteer 1st Class, rated as A.B. Promoted after the action to Mid. and Lt. Served in the Copenhagen expedition of 1807. Commander 1811. Served at New Orleans 1814. Captain 1815. Assumed name of d'Aeth in 1808 on succeeding to the estates of his cousin. Retired 1846. Retired rear-admiral 1850. Retired vice-admiral 1857. Retired admiral 1862. J.P. for Kent. Died in 1873.

R. Patton: Cousin of Hugh Patton. Master's mate 1809. Lt. 1810. Commander 1815. Captain 1827. Retired 1847. Retired rear-admiral 1854. Retired vice-admiral 1861. Retired admiral 1864. Died at Daneham, Hants, 1883 aged ninety-two. Daughter Emily died at Wimbledon in 1947.

The last surviving Trafalgar captain was Sir Charles Bullen of the *Britannia* who died as an admiral in 1853, aged eighty-six. The last surviving officer of the battle on the British side was Lieutenant-Colonel James Fynmore, R.M., of the *Africa*, who died in 1887.

The *Bellerophon* was one of those ships sent back to Gibraltar by Collingwood as being too seriously damaged to keep the sea in safety. Among the others was the *Victory* with the body of Lord Nelson on board. She was towed by the *Neptune* and arrived at Gibraltar on the 28th October, the same day as the *Bellerophon*. The ships destined for return to Britain underwent temporary repairs to enable them to make the voyage.

The log of the *Bellerophon* resumes on the 4th November when a new captain was appointed to the ship. He was Edward

Rotheram who had been Collingwood's flag-captain in the *Royal Sovereign* during the battle. They had not got on well together, and had to be reconciled by Nelson before the battle. Collingwood's opinion of Rotheram is made clear in the two following passages. Writing on the 26th October he said:

... but such a captain, such a stick, I wonder very much how such people get forward. I should (I firmly believe) with his nautical ability and knowledge and exertion, have been a bad lieutenant at this day. Was he brought up in the Navy? For he has very much of the stile of the Coal Trade about him, except that they are good seamen!

also, later:

I was sorry to hear of poor Rotheram who, though I think him a stupid man, I was in hope might have gone on in the ship I put him, which I believe was the only chance he had of being in a ship.

Such expressions by Collingwood were very rare, so Rotheram must have been a rather unique specimen among the captains of his acquaintance! Whatever the opinion of Rotheram held by Collingwood, he retained command of the *Bellerophon* for the next three years, until 1809. His subsequent career in the Navy was unremarkable, he was made a C.B. in 1815, Captain of Greenwich Hospital in 1828-30 and died in Suffolk the same year.

The 4th November was a busy day for the men of the *Bellerophon* as well as for the others in the harbour. Captain Rotheram took over the command in the morning, in the afternoon French prisoners from the *Phoebe* were received on board for transportation to Britain, and in the evening they sailed with the *Victory* and *Belleisle* for home.

The three ships weighed anchor at 6.40 p.m. and made their way out of the bay for the long journey back to Britain. They were still not properly repaired, but they were considered seaworthy enough to make the journey home. The body of Lord Nelson was still on board, preserved in a cask of spirits, and was being taken home for burial at St Paul's. The passage was necessarily a slow one, and it was not until the 1st December that the Channel Fleet was sighted, bearing east. Cornwallis was still in command of the Channel Fleet, and was regretting that he had not taken his last opportunity to speak to Nelson when he had passed through the fleet last August on his way home.

The *Bellerophon* moored in Plymouth Sound on the 3rd December, while the *Victory* continued her way up-Channel to Portsmouth and Spithead. Already moored at Spithead were several Trafalgar ships, *Royal Sovereign*, *Spartiate*, *Leviathan*, *Conqueror*, and *Achilles*. Another ship with connections with Nelson was moored there, the *Foudroyant* which had once been his flagship in the Mediterranean.

The *Bellerophon* was warped into the Hamoaze on the 14th December, and on the 15th:

... Mustered ship's company ... read a General Memorandum from Admiral Lord Collingwood, proposing the appropriation of £2,000 out of the Prize Money from the captures made by the squadron on the 21st October 1805 towards the erecting of a monument on Portdown Hill in memory of Lord Nelson, which was assented to by the Captain, officers and ship's company.

The next stage in the repair of the ship was to get her alongside a sheerhulk, which was done on the 20th December, when she was taken alongside the *Medway*. The masts were taken out on the 21st December, and on the 26th Lieutenant Cumby was discharged out of the ship on promotion to captain. Here we will leave the story of the ship until she re-emerges in Cawsand Bay on the 26th February.

8

The Long Blockade

THE log for the 9th March has a footnote in the margin which is of interest: 'P.S. This day's log contains thirty-six hours, thereby it becomes civil time, the Lords of the Admiralty having ordered the alteration.'

The ship was now to join the Channel Fleet which was once again under the command of the Earl St Vincent. Cornwallis had had a disagreement with the Government, and had been relieved of his command on the 22nd February. He had failed to achieve his ambition of a general fleet action while in command, and was never to have another chance for he did not go to sea again. St Vincent was offered and had accepted the command, although he was over seventy years of age, but he pointed out that owing to his age it could only be a temporary measure to calm public alarm at the retirement of Cornwallis. He was no longer as strict as before, although he still kept the close watch on the fleet in Brest which he had begun in 1799.

The *Hibernia*, flying St Vincent's flag, moored in Cawsand Bay on the 13th March while the *Bellerophon* was still there. The next day the *Hibernia* sailed in company with the *Ville de Paris* to join the Channel Fleet. The *Bellerophon* sailed on the 2nd April and joined the Channel Fleet off Cape Finisterre the next day, thus beginning a period of eighteen months which she was to spend with the fleet tossing in the Bay of Biscay, blockading the ports. As the Napoleonic War reached its climax with the Berlin and Milan Decrees and the answering British Orders in Council of 1807, the economic war was at its height, each country trying to defeat the other by strangling her trade having no other means of harming the other.

To the officers and men of the Channel Fleet and of other blockading fleets the war seemed one of endless patrolling, enlivened occasionally by a cutting out duty. The only major action fought was in the West Indies when Sir John Duckworth defeated the squadron of Vice-Admiral Leissegues on 6th February 1806.

The story of the operations of the Channel Fleet in 1806–7 is also the story of the *Bellerophon* for the same period. There were no momentous sea battles, only the quiet pressure of the blockade, and the eternal monotony of patrolling empty seas. We cannot leave the period completely blank, so a brief account of the situation in Europe at that time with particular reference to the role of the Royal Navy in the Channel will be given.

In Brest the French still had a considerable fleet of thirteen of the line, and in Rochefort a further eight of the line. A squadron of eleven of the line had slipped out of Brest on the 13th December of the previous year, and once out had separated into two squadrons. One, comprising the *Impérial* (120), *Alexandre* (80), *Brave* (74), *Diomède* (74), and *Jupiter* (74) under the command of Vice-Admiral Leissegues, unsuccessfully chased a British convoy, then continued to the West Indies where it was destroyed by Sir John Duckworth off Santo Domingo. The other six ships, under Rear-Admiral Willaumez, were the *Foudroyant* (80), *Cassard* (74), *Éole* (74), *Impétueux* (74), *Patriote* (74), and *Veteran* (74), the latter commanded by Jerome Bonaparte, youngest brother of the Emperor. This squadron, too, was sighted and pursued by Duckworth, but no battle took place and it escaped. It shaped its course to the East Indies, but it was too late to prevent the Cape of Good Hope falling into British hands. On hearing this news Willaumez decided to cruise in the South Atlantic, later moving to the West Indies. The squadron suffered from storm damage and was soon reduced to four ships. Of these, the *Impétueux* was run ashore by a British squadron and burned, the *Patriote* and *Éole* sought temporary refuge in the Chesapeake, the *Cassard* sailed back to Rochefort, while the *Foudroyant* had been forced to anchor in Havana after damage received in the storms and after an engagement with the British frigate *Anson* (44).

Of the political situation, Pitt had died in January 1806 after hearing of the disaster at Austerlitz. He was succeeded by a Fox-Grenville ministry which had more leanings towards peace than the previous administrations. Fox tried to start peace negotiations with Napoleon, but was unsuccessful, and on 16th May 1806 the first Orders in Council were issued by the Fox-Grenville ministry. They placed the whole coast of Europe in a state of blockade, from the Elbe to Brest. Particular attention was to be paid to the section of coast between Ostend and the Seine, and no neutral vessel was to be allowed into ports between those two points. Neutral ships could enter providing they had not been loaded at a port belonging to one of Britain's enemies, or if they were leaving the forbidden area they could leave so long as they were not bound for another hostile port.

This was almost the last act of Fox for he died on 13th September, 1806 and was succeeded as Minister of Foreign Affairs by Lord Howick. Blockade restrictions which had previously been imposed on the Elbe and Weser were removed, so that even neutral ships from a port hostile to Great Britain were able to enter. This was an attempt to conciliate opinion in the United States and the still neutral countries in Europe.

On the Continent, Prussia, which had been steering a precarious course of neutrality for the last ten years, at last declared war on France. She was rapidly crushed by Napoleon when her army was completely routed at Jena on the 14th October, and on the 26th Napoleon entered Berlin.

To the people of Britain it seemed as if all hope could be given up for the Continent; in the campaigns of 1805 and 1806 Napoleon had crushed Austria, then Prussia, and forced Russia to retreat. Spain, Holland, and Italy were allies or vassals of France. He dreamed now only of conquering Britain, and this he hoped to do by commercial warfare. He said he would 'conquer the sea by the land', and to this end on the 21st November 1806 he issued his famous Berlin Decrees which placed Great Britain in a state of blockade by closing all the ports of the Continent under the control of France or her allies to British ships.

Having given his Decrees to the world, he still had to enforce them, and Russia was the biggest gap in the Continent by which British goods could enter. He therefore set out to force Russia to adhere to the Continental System, and to close her ports to British trade. Russia was ready to resist and Britain offered monetary and military help. Both came too late and the Russian armies were beaten at Friedland, and the Tsar signed the Treaty of Tilsit with Napoleon. The main object of this treaty was the overthrow of Britain, her trade was to be banned, and her possessions in India invaded. It was thought that then she would see sense and have to sue for peace.

Britain had one nominal ally on the Continent, Portugal, and she had made use of the facilities of the port of Lisbon in the past. Napoleon had threatened to invade the country in 1806, and massed his army for the attempt; and Britain, in support of her ally, had sent the Channel Fleet under Lord St Vincent to Lisbon. This made a great impression, and as the Spanish were also hostile to having French troops on their soil for the invasion of Portugal, Napoleon cancelled his plans for the time being. The fleet returned to its station off Ushant in October 1806, and soon after, on the 27th March 1807, St Vincent struck his flag for the last time.

The year 1807 opened with the French invasion of Russia. While he was engaged in this campaign, Napoleon was unable to spare sufficient time to enforce his edicts against British trade, and Britain placed the whole of the coastline of Europe from the Baltic to the Adriatic in a state of blockade. The new orders were particularly severe on the United States whose trade almost completely disappeared from European waters.

Meanwhile, after his victory at Friedland, Napoleon had made an agreement with the Tsar at Tilsit and had returned to Paris full of plans for the subjugation of Britain. He recognized that the French navy by itself was not powerful enough for the task of gaining mastery of the sea, and tried to form a Grand Coalition of the navies of Europe. The French and Spanish navies were still rebuilding to full strength after the disaster of Trafalgar, while the Dutch navy was still small. He first of all ordered the seizure of the Portuguese navy as had been agreed at Tilsit, but Britain knew of the terms of the Treaty and made plans accordingly. The second stroke planned by Napoleon was the seizure of the Danish navy, but in both plans he was forestalled by the British. An expedition was sent to Copenhagen in August/September, 1807 and when the Danes refused to surrender their ships, the town was bombarded until the Danes surrendered and the British took possession of eighteen sail of the line. In Spain a French army corps under Junot was racing for Lisbon to seize the Portuguese fleet before Britain got word of the plan. He also was too late, for the British had already seized the fleet, the Royal Family, and the treasure, and spirited them all away to Brazil where they formed a government in exile.

In the Mediterranean, a British squadron had been sent to the Dardanelles in November 1806 while Russia was the ally of Britain. The naval command was given to Sir John Duckworth, but without an army on board to attack the forts at the entrance of the straits he hesitated for a week before entering. The Turks made use of the time in strengthening their fortifications and the fleet accomplished nothing and had to withdraw.

Another British expedition sent to Spanish South America, in search of a market for the rapidly piling British goods, was an equal failure. After an unsuccessful attack on Buenos Aires the expedition withdrew with 2,500 killed and wounded on the casualty list.

In other ways, however, the year 1807 was one of disappointment for Britain, and a successful one for Napoleon. He had reached an agreement with the Tsar, the only ruler he really feared on the Continent, added Portugal to his Empire and induced Denmark to come in on his side. His Continental System seemed to be winning the commercial battle, and reports of industrial unrest in the British manufacturing towns were read by him with great joy.

For Britain, she had added to her sea power by the addition of the Danish and Portuguese fleets, but she had failed to find new markets for her goods, and it was obvious that she must soon do so or the country would collapse. Although St Vincent had retired that year, there were still great commanders at sea, but no job for them to do except that of blockade. In the Channel Admiral Lord Gardner had taken over the reins; in the Mediterranean Lord Collingwood was working himself to death for the peace he so ardently desired, though still hoping to meet the French once more; and in the East Indies there was the dashing frigate captain of former days, Sir Edward Pellew.

As for the *Bellerophon* herself, she had become the flagship of Rear-Admiral Sir Albermarle Bertie, while Rotheram was still the captain. No outstanding events had occurred during her service this year, so as for the previous year I have only given a broad outline of international events as a whole.

She was still in home waters, serving in the Channel Fleet under Lord Gardner. Since the disaster of Trafalgar, Napoleon had been rebuilding his fleets for the day when he would once again be able to contest the seas with Britain. By the spring of the year 1808, according to the naval historian James, he possessed a fleet of upwards of eighty sail of the line in commission or building.

In March 1808 Lord Gardner was forced to hand over the command of the Channel Fleet to Lord Gambier, who had led the expedition to Copenhagen in the previous year. He was not a dynamic leader in the mould of Nelson or a popular one in the mould of Howe, Cornwallis, and Collingwood, but he was fit for the job so long as no vital decisions had to be taken and it was only a matter of blockade. Unfortunately, later in his command he was called upon to make a decision, and was unable to act with the required vigour.

The commercial struggle was still continuing and it was anybody's guess as who would be the first to succumb. Both sides realized that only by starvation could the struggle be won and the first side to relax its grip would lose the contest.

The rights of neutrals at sea were frequently violated by the Royal Navy in its search for seamen, and in its efforts to stop any produce from reaching the ports of the French-controlled Continent. The neutral nations, particularly the United States, were becomingly exasperated and it was obvious that this state of affairs could not continue much longer without becoming open war against Great Britain, as Napoleon desired. On the Continent Napoleon was making desperate efforts to stop the flow of British goods and thereby making himself and the French more unpopular than ever. He seemed willing to go to any length to bar British goods from the people of Europe and his exhortations to tighten the blockade were resented by the people of the Continent who were undergoing as much hardship as the people of Britain across the water. It was obvious that the rulers of Russia, Austria, and Prussia were becoming increasingly angry at the attitude of Napoleon and finding his pretensions more and more unbearable, and this time their subjects were with them.

Napoleon conceived the plan in 1808 of trying to make the Mediterranean untenable for the British by taking personal command of Spain, seizing Gibraltar and advancing down the coast of North Africa from which area the British fleet drew most of its supplies. He also planned a joint Franco-Russian-Austrian drive against the Ottoman Empire and then on to India which he considered one of the main sources of British power and wealth. The troops commanded by his brother Joseph in Italy were to cross the Straits of Messina and to invade Sicily, one of the main British bases in the Mediterranean. With their source of supplies gone, and the loss of Gibraltar and Sicily, he knew the British ships would not be able to maintain themselves in the sea and would have to withdraw, thereby allowing the French ships in Toulon to escape. These ships, reinforced by the squadron from Rochefort under Allemand, would draw whatever remained of the British fleet to the eastwards.

He (Napoleon) mentioned his plan to the Tsar in a letter dated 2nd February and said that it would finally force England to make peace. The passage overland to India had been secured by a convention with the Shah, and an army of 50,000 men was all that was needed to destroy the British power in India. The Tsar was invited to invade Sweden and seize Finland, and force the last remaining ally of Britain on the Continent to sue for peace. He also had the double motive of drawing Russian attentions from the Balkans to the Baltic as he had no wish to see a Russian empire established in place of the Turkish one.

The first moves in this Grand Design were made just before writing to the Tsar when French troops retook Reggio from the Neapolitans, and followed this by the capture of Scylla on the 17th February. Admiral Allemand had managed to escape from Rochefort and had reached the Mediterranean, pursued by Sir Richard Strachan. Rough weather had delayed the passage of the pursuing British squadron, but it had also forced Allemand to send back one of his ships to Rochefort as being too badly damaged to continue. Allemand passed through the Straits of Gibraltar on the 26th January, while Strachan did not pass the Rock until the 10th February.

Admiral Ganteaume in Toulon managed to escape on the 7th February, and for some weeks was a great problem to Lord Collingwood, but the united French squadrons never achieved what was hoped by Napoleon, although Collingwood also never achieved his wish of bringing them to battle. The French eventually reanchored in Toulon on the 10th April, having only achieved the revictualling of Corfu which was still held by the French.

On board the *Bellerophon* the blockade of the French Channel ports continued as usual. In April Admiral Bertie had left the ship to hoist his flag in the *Dreadnought* (98), and the previous month Captain Rotheram had also left the ship. They were succeeded by Captain Samuel Warren and Rear-Admiral Alan Hyde Gardner, son of Lord Gardner late commander of the Channel Fleet. In May the ship sailed to the Downs to join the Nore Fleet in which fleet she remained for the next ten months. The fleet they were watching was in the port of Texel which had been ceded by the King of Holland to Napoleon. This transaction had presented no difficulty as the King of Holland was none other than Louis Bonaparte, brother of Napoleon.

The enemy force consisted of ten 74-gun ships and four frigates, while a further six 80-gun ships and three 74s were almost ready for launch. The whole mouth of the Scheldt was now in the hands of the French, and Napoleon considered it as a pistol pointed at the head of England, and had expended 66 million francs on the area since 1805. At Antwerp and Flushing other ships were building or ready to sail, and only waited the disappearance of the British blockading force to put to sea. The French commander was Admiral Missiessy who had played a part in the events leading up to the battle of Trafalgar.

In the Peninsula Napoleon was pushing ahead with his plans for taking over the country and using it more effectively as a weapon against the British. By a secret treaty with the 'Prince of Peace', Godoy, he managed to obtain the French occupation of the towns of Biscay and Navarre. He also managed to get the heir apparent, Prince Ferdinand, arrested for treason by his father the king. This was followed by attacks on Godoy in the government-controlled *Moniteur*, and on 16th February he seized the arsenal at Pampeluna and other important points guarding the entrances to the Pyrenees, and French troops poured into Spain.

Madrid was soon occupied by Murat and for a while the French were received as liberators, and a Spanish mob stopped the escape of the Prince of Peace and the Royal Family to South America. The king was made to abdicate in favour of his son the Crown Prince Ferdinand, who in turn was forced to resign the throne in favour of Napoleon's brother Joseph.

Napoleon, having achieved the first important stage of his plan, with Spain under French control, could now proceed with an attack on Gibraltar. It did not cross his mind that the Spanish people could possibly prefer one of the corrupt and arrogant members of the Spanish Bourbons to his own brother, particularly when he brought in the reforms that he had in mind.

Among the Spanish people, however, a great wave of enthusiasm for the monarchy in the person of Ferdinand swept through the land and they rose against French rule. To help them in their struggle the Spaniards sent representatives to London to beg for arms and money, and the opportunity for which the British had looked for so long had come at last. The Spaniards were promised arms and money as well as the help of a British army, which would be sent to the Peninsula as soon as it could be formed.

So began the long Peninsular War in which the British were able to bring pressure to bear on Napoleon by means of their army as well as their navy. Except for a short period, it was conducted by Wellington, who first of all drove the French from Portugal, then from Spain, and finally he crossed the Pyrenees into France.

The *Bellerophon* had no part in these events, for she was in the cold grey waters of the North Sea maintaining her watch over the ports of the Texel. She saw out the year of 1808 still serving in the North Sea as the flagship of Rear-Admiral Gardner.

9

In Northern Waters

EARLY in the year 1809 the *Bellerophon* returned to Yarmouth for repairs and revictualling preparatory to going to the Baltic to join the fleet of Sir James Saumarez—which she proceeded to do on the 27th March.

The political situation at that time existing in the Baltic was very dangerous and it requires some explanation.

In September 1808 the Tsar had met Napoleon at Erfurt and both Emperors had reaffirmed their previous declarations at Tilsit. France promised not to make a peace until Russia had obtained Finland from Sweden, and Moldavia and Wallachia from Turkey. The Tsar had already declared war on Sweden the previous February on the pretext of her refusing to shut her ports to British trade and refusing to join with Russia and Denmark and close the Baltic to British ships. Denmark and Prussia followed suit with a declaration of war on Sweden, and the Swedes sent an appeal to Britain for help. The Government sent a force of sixty-two sail to the Baltic under the command of Sir James Saumarez. This was followed by an an army of 10,000 men under Sir John Moore, this army was never in action as Moore and the mad king of Sweden, Gustavus IV, could not agree on the way it should be used. Moore was arrested by the king, but made his escape disguised as a peasant and returned to the British ships. The army was then sent back to Britain and from there on to the Peninsula.

Britain's interest in the Baltic stemmed mainly from the fact that it was the source of most of her naval supplies. Once that route was cut off, she would undergo serious difficulties in refitting her fleets. The year 1809 opened with the Russians

already in possession of Finland and preparing to invade
Sweden. It was decided by the government of Sweden that the
safest course lay in forcing the abdication of their king
Gustavus IV on account of his insanity, and then trying to
steer a course of neutrality. It was realized in London that
the Swedes needed Britain as much as Britain needed the
Swedes, and that if by any chance the Swedes were forced
into a declaration of war it would behove the British Government to treat them with great leniency.

Eventually the Swedes were forced into a declaration of
war and instructions were sent from London to Sir James
Saumarez that the rights of Sweden were to be scrupulously
respected. The contrast was often noticed in Sweden that the
country suffered worse treatment from its Russian and
Danish allies than it suffered from its enemy Britain. It was
mainly due to the tact and judgment of Sir James Saumarez
that when the break between Napoleon and the Tsar finally
came, both Sweden and Russia ended up on the same side as
Britain against Napoleon.

This was the position when Captain Warren arrived with
the *Bellerophon* in the spring of 1809. Rear-Admiral Gardner
had not accompanied the ship to the Baltic and had transferred his flag to the *Blake* (74), commanded by Sir Edward
Codrington, a Trafalgar veteran. In this ship he was to see
service during the disastrous Walcheren Expedition of that
year. Just after the arrival of the *Bellerophon*, the British
seized the island of Anholt from the Danes, which had been
used by Danish privateers, and forthwith used it for their
own ends.

The first action for the *Bellerophon* came in June 1809 when
she was cruising off the coast of Russian-occupied Finland
accompanied by the *Minotaur* (74). The *Bellerophon* was
detached off Hango, and at sunset on the 19th discovered an
armed lugger and two other vessels at anchor in the coastal
waters of the numerous islands. There appeared no sign of
life on the vessels or on shore and it was decided to send the
ship's boats with a party of volunteers to cut them out. This
was done and the three vessels were soon taken possession of,
when it was noticed that they were completely dominated by
four Russian batteries. Next a number of Russian gunboats
were spotted, which had not been visible from the *Bellerophon*.

Lieutenant Pilch, who was in charge of the cutting-out operation, realized that it would be impossible to bring away the three captured vessels under fire of the batteries and gunboats, and it was decided to set them on fire. This done, the order was given to row to the island and to storm the battery which would most harass their retreat—not an easy task, for the battery was manned by 103 men armed with muskets and bayonets. Under a fierce but inaccurate fire the *Bellerophon*'s men scrambled ashore and rushed on the battery, and after a short hand-to-hand combat forced the Russians to quit. The Russians were then driven into their own boats, the guns of the battery spiked, and the magazine blown up. Under fire from batteries on other islands the British then re-embarked in their own boats and returned to their ship, which had been unable to manoeuvre to give them covering fire because of the shallowness of the water. The operation had been completed very efficiently and at the small cost of only five wounded, and it gained the ship a mention in the dispatches of Sir James Saumarez to the Admiralty.

On the 7th July the ship was in action again when a British squadron composed of the *Implacable* (74), Captain Thomas Byam-Martin; *Bellerophon* (74); *Melpomene* (38), Captain Peter Parker; and *Prometheus* (18), Captain Thomas Forrest; was once again cruising off the coast of Finland. A Russian flotilla of gunboats and merchant vessels was spotted at anchor under Porcola Point. Martin thought that such a display was insulting to British sea power and determined to try and cut them out or destroy them. The Russians were very strongly placed with their flanks covered by rocks, which narrowed the field of approach to them and enabled the Russians to concentrate their fire. Nevertheless it was decided to make the attempt that night, and for the leader of the enterprise Martin chose Lieutenant Joseph Hawkey of the *Implacable*. He was to have a force of 270 officers and men manning seventeen boats, and the operation was to start at 9 p.m.

At the appointed hour the men filed down into the boats and began the long approach to the moored vessels. They were soon spotted and the boats were subject to a heavy fire; no reply was made by the British until they were alongside the Russian ships, when they swarmed aboard with a great cheer. The first of the gun-boats was soon carried and the British pushed on to the second, when Lieutenant Hawkey was hit and collapsed dying. Lieutenant Charles Allen of the *Bellerophon* took charge of the operation and the British continued to fight their way down the line of Russian gunboats. In the end six of the boats were taken, one sunk and one managed to get away, and all the the twelve vessels composing the merchant convoy were also taken. They were found to be carrying ammunition and other materials for the Russian army in Finland. The ships were brought out to the British squadron, and another smart piece of work by the Royal Navy was completed. Casualties had once again been amazingly light, for the losses were only seventeen killed and thirty-four wounded.

The *Bellerophon* was to remain with the Baltic fleet for another three months before she once again sailed for Britain. The ship anchored in Yarmouth Roads on the 22nd November, and was immediately taken in hand for repairs, which included replacing the running rigging. The whole job was a lengthy process, for the log does not continue with the narration of each day's events until 23rd August of the following year, when the ship is reported at anchor in the Downs.

The Commander-in-Chief in the North Sea during the time the *Bellerophon* was in dock was Sir Edward Pellew, who had been given that post after his return from the chief command in the East Indies. The fleet comprised ten or twelve sail of the line, and the task was to watch the ever growing Dutch fleet in the ports of the Scheldt. This enemy fleet had hardly been damaged by the ill-fated British Walcheren Expedition of the previous year, and remained as always one of Napoleon's main hopes in his bid to take command of the sea from the Roval Navy. Pellew was flying his flag in the *Christian VII* (80), which had been taken from the Danes in 1807 during the expedition to Copenhagen. It was a quiet and uneventful blockade that Pellew maintained, but he stuck to his post off the Scheldt, until the pilots of the fleet sent him a deputation to say that he was keeping the fleet at sea too late in the year. He hung on for a little longer, and then returned to the Downs. It was in the Downs that the *Bellerophon* joined the fleet, but she was not to serve under Pellew for long, for the log records that 'Sir E. Pellew struck his flag' on the 21st October 1810, although it was not until

April of the following year that he finally relinquished the command and went to the Mediterranean.

The *Bellerophon* had evidently not been fully repaired at Yarmouth, for in November she moved down to Spithead, and then into Portsmouth harbour where she underwent a proper refit. There had been changes in her command, for Warren left her on his return from the Baltic, and was succeeded by Lucius Hardyman in August 1810, and then he was replaced by John Halstead in November 1810. Morale, which had been high under Warren, had dropped with the frequent changes in command and the long periods of inactivity while the ship was in dock. No doubt the thought of home, so near and yet unattainable, contributed; life had probably become one long hard round of unremitting toil with very few intervals of action to relieve the boredom. Whatever the cause, the crew were becoming increasingly restless, and matters came to a head on the night of the 27th/28th November while the ship was still at Portsmouth.

It had been another day of the usual routine: the log mentions 'scraping masts, spars and decks' and 'people employed as necessary'. That night the crew must have had more than their usual ration of liquor for the log continues:

. . . at 6.30 from the disorderly state of the ship's company, arising from drunkenness, the lights were put out by the command of the Commanding Officer. At 7 they lighted their candles, contrary to the above order. The Commanding Officer with several other officers sent on the Lower Deck to put the lights out. A general shout was heard from the ship's company, with several mutinous expressions. The Marines were ordered under arms to enforce the order, and a guard kept arms the remainder of the night.

For a moment the situation was tense, but the Marines followed the lead of their officers and the danger was averted. The candles were extinguished, and Captain Halstead returned on deck with the other officers, no doubt thankful that the Marines had been loyal.

The following day some punishment would have to be meted out to those who had been prominent in the disturbance, but evidently the thoughts of Halstead turned on leniency, for although the twenty-four lashes inflicted on the worst offenders sounds severe to modern ears, the punishment in those times could have been much worse. Below is a list of the floggings which took place the following morning:

Saml. Hennessy	
John Parker	
John Elliott	—24 lashes each, for abstaining from duty
Jas. Hancock	and drunkenness.
Chas. Bowie	
John Birmingham	—12 lashes each for abstaining from duty
John Parry	and drunkenness.
Daniel McCann (Marine)—24 lashes for disobedience of orders.	

Three seamen only were sent for trial by court martial; these were Jacob Fambane (?), Emanuel Rotherings, and James Maguire, who had been the most forward in the 'mutinous expressions' which the log records. They were tried on the 18th aboard the *Royal William* and the charge was found proved. Fambane and Rotherings were each to receive 100 lashes and Maguire fifty lashes. This sentence was carried out on the 26th December on board the *Bellerophon*, and was duly recorded in the log.

On the 21st December the ship was moored at Spithead when what the log calls 'strong gales and squally weather' struck the port. The *Bellerophon* had her cutter away from the ship fetching stores for the sailmaker. The cutter had just started the return journey when the gales blew up, and she was unable to reach the ship. As the wind heightened, the cutter became unmanageable, and she was eventually driven ashore near Southsea castle, and all her sails and sail gear lost, as well as suffering structural damage herself. No member of the crew is recorded as killed, so one can assume that they all got ashore safely.

The weather prevented the *Bellerophon* from leaving Spithead until the new year of 1811 was two weeks old, and it was not until the 16th of January that she rejoined the fleet in the Downs. The following day she was honoured by becoming the flagship of Rear-Admiral Ferrier, who hoisted his flag on the 17th. The season was still too early and the weather too rough for the main ships to be risked at sea off the shoals of the Texel, and it was not until the 9th March that the *Bellerophon* and the rest of the fleet got to sea.

For the rest of the year the work continued normally for such blockades, with only the grey of the North sea and the

long flat coastline of Holland to look at. They passed places
with names famous in British naval history, such as Camperdown, and Scheveningen, scenes of battles against the Dutch
in previous years. The blockade must have been wearing
work on both men and ships on any station, and occasionally a
man would be driven too far. This was the case with William
Barrett, a seaman of the *Bellerophon* who was found hanging
by his neck in the mizen rigging on the 10th September.

The rest of the year 1811 continued uneventfully, and 1812
was seen in by the ship while she was anchored at The Nore.
She was still the flagship of Rear-Admiral Ferrier, and
Halstead was still her captain, and her station was still the
grey waters of the North Sea. Possibly none of the officers or
crew, or indeed anybody in Britain or Europe, realized that
they were entering on the most vital year of the war, the war
which seemed to have been going on for as long as most of
them could remember. The events of this year were eventually to lead to the surrendering of Napoleon to the British
people in the form of the officers and crew of the *Bellerophon*,
but although that event was still three years off, the seeds of it
were laid at this time.

For Britain it saw the outbreak of a new war with the
United States, which added a further strain on British
resources. On neither side was it creditable that a war should
have begun, but the Americans conducted their war with
success and vigour, lending the full weight of their power to
Napoleon, although not by a formal treaty, in his efforts to
enslave Europe. On the British side it was only regarded as
a minor affair, until several lost frigates and other ships, and
letters from the Duke of Wellington complaining of the loss of
supplies bound for the army in the Peninsula to American
privateers, stirred the Government to greater efforts.

The Duke continued to conduct the Peninsular War with
success, since the loss of Sir John Moore at Corunna, and the
clearing of his own name after the Convention of Cintra.

In Europe the position of the French seemed as firm as ever,
although the spies of the British Government reported
increasing tension between Russia and Napoleon. Many of
the statesmen of the Continent although openly friendly to
Napoleon were still in contact with London, and looking for
promises of subsidies should they renew the war. All Europe

was beginning to feel the effects of the British blockade, particularly the merchants of the middle classes. It was on this class that Napoleon was most dependent for the success of his schemes to remodel Europe.

Outside Europe the Royal Navy still ruled the sea. Although Nelson had been dead for seven years, Collingwood for two, and St Vincent retired along with Cornwallis, the Navy still retained leaders of experience and ability. In the Mediterranean, Collingwood had been succeeded first by Sir Charles Cotton then by Sir Edward Pellew. In the Channel, St Vincent had been followed by Lords Gardner, Gambier, and now Sir Charles Cotton. Sir James Saumarez was in his final year in the Baltic, Sir Samuel Hood was in the East Indies and Sir John Borlase Warren was soon to be given the command of the North American station.

As for the *Bellerophon* herself, she continued in the North Sea fleet until she was detached to Portsmouth to await the arrival of Sir Richard Keats. She was then to proceed to the North American station with a large convoy of merchantmen. It was not until the 17th December that she sailed from the Downs and proceeded to Portsmouth, but once there she went into the harbour and underwent a further refit, which included the removing of her lower deck guns for repairs and replacement. On the 20th March 1813 two new officers joined the ship, Mr McClaverty as master, and the Hon. Charles Orlando Bridgeman as one of the junior lieutenants.

By the end of March the ship had moved out of the inner harbour, and was beginning to take on stores for the long journey to Canada. Lighters were coming and going between the ship and the shore with all the varied supplies which a ship of the line would need. On the 7th April the signal was flown for the convoy for North America to start assembling. Altogether the merchantmen would total over seventy sail, and at sea other ships would join who had got separated from their own convoys or who had been sailing alone.

Sir Richard Keats came on board on the 22nd and hoisted his flag as a Vice-Admiral. He was a well known figure in the Navy, and one very popular with the men. He had been a friend of Nelson, and had been with him on the long chase across the Atlantic after Villeneuve. He had just missed the Battle of Trafalgar, being met in the Channel by the

Entreprenante as he was hurrying to join Nelson. Possibly his most distinguished action had been that on the 12th July 1801, when he was under the command of Sir James Saumarez who had defeated a superior French and Spanish force off Gibraltar.

No sooner was Admiral Keats on board than the signal was given for the convoy and its escort to get under way. Making up the escort with the *Bellerophon* were the *Niobe*, *Loire*, and *Contest*, frigates; while the convoy numbered seventy-two sail, which was later raised to seventy-seven when five late-comers joined, and then to seventy-eight when yet one more ship appeared. They were also to pick up a smaller convoy sailing from Torbay, which would bring the total to eighty-four sail, and also add the *Comet* as extra protection.

Progress with any convoy is bound to be slow as the speed has to be adjusted to that of the slowest ship. Also there was not much love lost between the Navy and the Merchant Service and it was extremely difficult to keep a close formation as was desired by all naval officers. If a civilian master felt he had a good chance of proceeding by himself he would often leave the convoy and travel at his own speed. The progress of this convoy was marked by the entries in the log: on the 25th they were twenty leagues west of Cork, on the 26th three leagues north of the Old Head of Kinsale. The convoy was now going before the wind into northern waters, and the temperature began to drop. By the middle of May they were in the region where they were likely to come across icebergs, or 'islands of ice' as they were referred to in the log. Several were sighted on the 17th May, and again on the 18th, and with the intermittent fog which was prevailing a sharp look-out had to be kept. In fog there was not only the danger of colliding with icebergs, but also with each other, as well as the possibility of American privateers sneaking in under its cover and making a quick capture. Signal guns were ordered to be sounded at regular intervals as the ships groped their way through the cold mists towards the coast of Newfoundland. The convoy finally anchored at St John's, Newfoundland, on the 31st May.

The *Bellerophon* was to remain on the North American station for the next six months. Her main duty was helping in the blockade of the coast of the United States and escorting convoys to the southward. Sir Richard Keats had been sent to the colony as Governor and Commander-in-Chief, at his own request for a more peaceable post than those he had occupied before, to give his health a chance to recover. He was promised more active employment by the Admiralty as soon as the state of his health permitted it.

During November, a convoy began to assemble at St John's awaiting escort to England, and as the *Bellerophon* was still in need of a complete and thorough overhaul, Keats decided to take her to England as part of the escort. This convoy, composed of thirty-three merchant vessels and escorted by the *Bellerophon*, *Rosamon*, and *Adonis*, sailed from St John's on the 22nd November. There was no trouble on the passage across the Atlantic, and the convoy arrived safely at Spithead on the 19th December. The following day Keats went ashore to begin his leave, and on the 22nd his flag was struck.

There was no vacancy for the *Bellerophon* to be moved into the inner basin immediately, and the new year of 1814 still finds her at anchor at Spithead. Once she had moved into the harbour, the process of dismantling her began. The work went as follows:

28th January: Took down running rigging. Returned anchors to dockyard.

29th January: Got out lower deck guns. Began removing provisions.

30th January: Got out main deck guns.

31st January: Removed remainder of guns and topmasts.

1st February: Unrigged masts and returned sails. Moved out stores and shot.

2nd February: Began clearing hold.

3rd February: Began getting out ballast. Returned gunners' stores.

4th February: Returned rigging to dockyard

5th February: Cleared ballast and holds and tiers.

8th February: Moved alongside sheerhulk. Removed mainmast. Moved alongside wharf and removed rest of ballast.

9th February: Hauled into dry dock.

25th February: Left dock. Got ballast on board.

3rd March: Set up masts and lower rigging.

30th March: Left harbour and moored at Spithead.

While the *Bellerophon* was in harbour, the war was rapidly coming to a close. Some of the last French ships taken by the Royal Navy came into harbour. The 40-gun frigate *Clorinde*, taken by the *Eurotas* and *Dryad*, came in on the 17th. *La Sultanne* of 40-guns, captured by the *Hannibal* (74), came in on the 30th March, the very day the *Bellerophon* left the harbour and moved to Spithead.

On the Continent, the régime of Napoleon was rapidly drawing to its end. The previous year Wellington had entered the south of France, and the Allies had come in from the east and north. Napoleon was having the greatest difficulty in raising men and money to continue the campaign, and eventually after several battles the allies entered Paris.

Napoleon arrived at Fontainbleau, too late, when the allies were already in occupation of the capital, and after some negotiation he offered to abdicate in favour of his son. He finally signed his abdication on the 6th April, and the Senate under Talleyrand voted for the recall of Louis XVIII. In the Treaty of Fontainebleau, signed on the 11th April, Napoleon was given the island of Elba as a place of exile and a revenue of 2 million francs, with the title of Emperor.

This ended the long Napoleonic Wars for Europe, but Britain was still at war with America. It was for this reason that Sir Richard Keats once again hoisted his flag on the 8th April and began to assemble another convoy for North America. A sign of the new friendship between Britain and France appeared when a French battleship came into Spithead flying the flag of a Rear-Admiral and was cheered by the crew of the *Bellerophon*.

On the 26th April, a signal gun was fired from the *Bellerophon* for the convoy to unmoor, and that afternoon Sir Richard Keats came on board and the convoy sailed from Spithead as escort to thirty-five sail of merchant vessels. The other vessels of the escort were *Perseus*, *Medusa*, and *Wolverine*. The convoy ran down the south coast, but was forced by the wind to put into Torbay. Here a few more ships were added before they finally sailed on the 2nd May. It was another uneventful passage across the North Atlantic and land was sighted through gaps in the fog on the 4th June. Signal guns were fired which were answered from the shore and that afternoon the convoy anchored at St John's.

The *Bellerophon* resumed the duties she had formerly pursued on this station, and cruised for two months off Cape Race, sighting several American ships which were intercepted and boarded. She left St John's for the last time on the 14th December and made a rapid crossing of the Atlantic, anchoring at Spithead on the 31st December. By this time the 'War of 1812' had been over for a week, although the news had not reached the other side of the Atlantic.

With the end of the war the British began to think of economy and of paying off most of the massive fleet which they had accumulated for the defeat of Napoleon. The *Bellerophon* was one of those so selected, and it seemed that her active career was over. Captain Hawker left the ship, most of the crew were paid off, and the ship herself was left moored at Spithead. Her career, although outstanding, did not distinguish her from other ships of her type and period. The *Orion* had fought in four major actions to the *Bellerophon*'s three, and already had been broken up that year. The most famous of them all, the *Victory*, had fought under most of the famous admirals of the time, from Keppel to Saumarez, but she too was to be laid up, and a few years later was in danger of being broken up by the Admiralty until saved by the personal intervention of Sir Thomas Hardy, then an admiral.

It was fortunate, therefore, that the year of 1815 was to give the ship a final chance of writing her name in the pages of history.

10

Surrender of Napoleon

WITH the signing of the peace treaty between Britain and the United States the whole world seemed to be at peace. The statesmen of Europe converged on Vienna to arrange the settlement of Europe; the terms to be forced on France were not as harsh as the French had a right to expect, and this was mainly due to the influence of the British delegation led by Lord Castlereagh and supported by the government of Lord Liverpool, and the considerable influence of the Duke of Wellington. Only the British delegation stood between France and the fierce reparations which were demanded by Prussia and to a lesser degree by Austria. Russia under the Tsar Alexander veered from side to side but mainly was on the side of moderation although she did not fancy the Bourbons on the throne. It was Castlereagh, Liverpool, Camden, Bathurst, and their colleagues who obtained such moderate terms for France, men whose names, according to Lord Rosebery, 'do not shine bright in History', and called by Thiers 'the creatures of Pitt' with no talent, genius or humanity!

Then the whole course of the Congress was thrown into confusion by the escape of Napoleon from Elba where he had been for almost a year. The allowance promised to him by the Bourbons had not been paid, and he could not live on the island without such means. Napoleon ordered his only warship, the brig *Inconstant*, to be made ready and sailed in her on the 26th February while the British Commissioner, Sir Neil Campbell, was visiting Italy. He landed at Antibes on the 1st March with only a few hundred faithful followers. The march on Paris was a fantastic success, with the troops which were sent to capture him coming over to his side, and, most valuable of all, he gained the support of Marshal Ney as well as the acclamations of a large part of the populace of the Dauphine. Louis XVIII fled from Paris on the 19th March, and the following evening Napoleon arrived at the Tuileries and the French Empire was established once again.

While these events were taking place the *Bellerophon* had remained at Spithead, but on the 21st March she was moved to Sheerness where she was once again prepared for commission. The nation was again preparing for war with the French, but there was a feeling in the country which let it be known that if the French could eject the Bourbons so easily it was not worth the British nation fighting for them, and that subject to certain guarantees Napoleon should be allowed to stay. It was certain that unless the war was short and victorious, public opinion would not support it. Opinion in France was much the same and Napoleon realized that his former power was gone and that a short and victorious war was needed. He was prepared to grant a liberal constitution and to give promises to Europe not to extend the French borders. All hopes which Napoleon had had of living at peace with Europe without having to fight a war were shattered by the declaration of outlawry made by the Congress of Vienna which placed him 'beyond the pale of civil and social relations'. All sides then began to gather their arms and armies for the coming struggle. The Duke of Wellington was appointed commander of the 100,000 British, Hanoverian, Dutch and Belgian troops, and Blucher of the 120,000 Prussians. Napoleon was in a stronger position than in 1814 for he had at hand the old veterans of the invasion of Russia who had been prisoners of war the previous year and was able to raise a force of 300,000 by June, but many of these were tied up in fortress duty or in guarding the various other frontiers of France.

On the naval side, Lord Keith was appointed to the command of the Channel Fleet and was to have a force of twenty-four sail of the line prepared for him, while Sir Edward Pellew was to be reappointed to the Mediterranean command.

A new captain was appointed to the *Bellerophon*—Captain Frederick Lewis Maitland, a relation of Lord Lauderdale who had been sent to France by Fox in 1806 during the abortive peace negotiations between Napoleon and Lord Yarmouth. Maitland had been born in 1777 and had joined the Navy at an early age. His career had been fairly distinguished, as he was present at the battles of the 'Glorious First of June' and the Nile, as well as at the action at Basque Roads. He had been flag-lieutenant to Lord St Vincent on the Mediterranean station before being detached for the battle of the Nile. Before the peace of the previous year he had been captain of the *Boyne* (98) which had been destined for the North American station, but while sheltering from gales at Cork the news of the peace with the United States arrived and the *Boyne* was recalled home. When he did get back he found the ships in port once again getting ready for war upon the news of the escape of Napoleon, and the *Boyne* was to be the flagship of Sir Edward Pellew with another captain, while Maitland was to be reappointed to the *Bellerophon*.

It was originally intended that the *Bellerophon* should accompany Rear-Admiral Sir Henry Hotham in the *Superb* to the blockade of France, but at the last moment the *York* (64) took her place, and the *Bellerophon* was to wait for further orders. She eventually sailed on the 24th May, and Captain Maitland had sealed instructions to be opened at sea, and a further order not to be opened unless he found himself separated from Rear-Admiral Hotham. The first instructions were to detain and send into port all armed vessels which he found trying to enter or leave French ports.

In France itself the Royalists had risen once again in La Vendée, and Sir Henry Hotham was under orders to support them with the squadron under his command. When Maitland sailed from Torbay he had received no formal intelligence of a declaration of war by Britain on France, nor did he receive any until the 27th June, over a week after the battle of Waterloo had been fought.

Maitland reached his station on the 28th May, and there he joined the frigates *Astrea* and *Telegraph*. These ships were stationed off the Isle Dieu and were charged with watching the French Biscay ports. The following day the *Helicon* arrived with three transports loaded with arms for the Royalists in Vendée. On the 30th May Maitland received orders from Hotham to take the *Eridanus* and proceed to watch the port of Rochefort. He was to watch particularly for a corvette which intelligence rumoured was being sent by Napoleon to the restored French West Indian colonies to induce them to declare in his favour. He anchored in Basque Roads on the 31st May, and found anchored there under cover of the guns of the Isle D'Aix two frigates, a corvette, and a large brig, all ready for sea.

Maitland and his squadron were unable to prevent a French corvette, the *Vésuve* from entering the port on the 9th June. His ships had been blown to the southward during the night, and were unable to regain their station in time to stop her. On the 18th June he stopped a French ship loaded with timber for Rochefort and sent her to Hotham, but the admiral released her as he did not think she came under his instructions to detain only armed vessels. On the 21st June he made a useful capture when he took the *Marianne*, a French transport from Martinique with 220 troops on board returning to join Napoleon. She was sent to England under the escort of the *Eridanus*, and the latter ship did not return to him, being sent on some other service by Lord Keith.

The Royalists were the object of much attention by the Government, even after the news of Waterloo. Lord Melville, writing to Lord Keith on the 23rd June, said:

Captain Nicholls' accounts of the Royalists are very favourable, and to a certain extent are confirmed by Fouché which you will see in the newspapers of today; but we must soon know for certain whether Bordeaux is really in possession of the Royalists. It remains to be seen what effect the Duke of Wellington's efforts may have on affairs in France, this last [Waterloo] is a staggering blow to Bonaparte; and will require a great deal [of effort] on his part as well as much enthusiasm in the country to recover.

On the 28th June the news of Waterloo reached Maitland from one of the vessels he had taken. Even more interesting news reached him on the 30th by a boat which had come from Bordeaux. It was written on thin paper in English and concealed within a quill. This letter read as follows:

With great degree of certainty, being informed that Buonaparte might have come last night through this city from Paris, with the new Mayor of Bordeaux, with a view to flight, by the mouth of this river, or La Teste, the author of the last note sent by Mr— hastily drops these few lines to give the British Admiral advice of such intention, that he may instantly take the necessary steps, in order to seize the man. His ideas will certainly have brought him to think it natural, that the British stations will be less upon their guard in this quarter than anywhere else. The writer benefits by this opportunity to inform the Admiral that, since the last note, some alteration has taken place with regard to the troops spread in these two Divisions; in lieu of 800 to 1000 in this city, there are now 5000, which is supposed owing to the intention of compressing the minds of this populace in this decisive instant.

It is supposed that the British Admiral is already informed of the Grand Army being totally defeated and destroyed, the abdication of Buonaparte, &c. and the arrival of the allies near the Capital.

An attempt should be made on this coast, with no less than 8000 men altogether. Immediate steps are wanted to put a stop to the supposed flight.

Should the attempt be made on the coast from La Teste to Bordeaux, an immediate diversion should be made on this side; the success is beyond any doubt.

A sharp eye must be kept on all American vessels, and particularly on the *Susquehannah* of Philadelphia, Captain Caleb Cushing; General Bertrand and other goes with him. The two entrances of Bordeaux and La Teste must be kept close; a line or two is expected, on the return of the bearer, from the Admiral or Chief Officer on the Station. As this is writing, the news is spread generally, that the Duc de Berri and Lord Wellington are in Paris.

Earlier rumours had already reached London of the possible escape of Napoleon to America, and on the 27th June Lord Melville wrote to Lord Keith:

Reports have reached His Majesty's Government from various quarters that in the event of adverse fortune it was the intention of Bonaparte to escape to America. If there is any truth in these statements he will in all probability make the attempt now, unless he should be forcibly detained in Paris. If he should embark in a small vessel from one of the numerous ports along the coast of France, it may be scarcely possible to prevent his escape; but if he should wait till a Frigate or a Sloop-of-War can be fitted out for him, you may perhaps receive information of such preparations and may thereby be enabled to watch and intercept her. At any rate it is desirable that you should take every precaution in your power with a view to his seizure and detention should he endeavour to quit France by sea.

A couple of days later the Secretary to the Board of Admiralty wrote:

. . . the reports on this subject have been daily assuming more creditable shape, and that the likelihood of such an event is much increased by the advice received from Paris this morning wherein it is stated that Bonaparte with some members of his family, had actually set out for Havre there to embark for England.

Although the note he had received had directed his attention to Bordeaux, Maitland's own opinion was that the attempt to escape was more likely to be made from Rochefort. However, he could not entirely neglect Bordeaux and he sent the *Myrmidon* off to that port, the *Cephalus* to the Arcasson, and remained with the *Bellerophon* off Rochefort. With no further ships at his disposal he sent his own barge to seek Admiral Hotham and to give him the note, he also wrote an order for the captains of any of the British ships which the barge might fall in with to proceed with the news to Quiberon Bay. The barge was lucky enough to fall in with the frigate *Cyrus*, which ship hoisted the barge and its crew on board and made full speed to Quiberon Bay.

At Torbay Admiral Keith had received two pieces of telegraphic information from London. The first said: 'French papers confess Bonaparte totally defeated', and the second: 'Bonaparte abdicated'. Both of these he forwarded to Admiral Hotham on the next day. On the 30th June he wrote to Hotham from the *Ville de Paris* with more definite information:

As it is possible that Bonaparte may attempt to leave France you will be pleased to direct the officers under your orders to examine strictly all vessels they may meet and to use their best endeavours to detain him if fallen in with.

By intelligence from Brest dated the 19th instant it appears that the *Hortense* the fastest sailing frigate in France has been suddenly ordered to be prepared for sea for the purpose, as has been said, of receiving him in the event of his defeat.

Napoleon had reached Paris on the 21st June, still believing that all was not lost. The very same day the two Chambers met and agreed that they would not be dissolved by the wish of Napoleon. After twenty-four hours of a tense political manoeuvre Napoleon signed his second abdication and his career was over. On the following day he asked the Minister of Marine, Decres, to order two frigates at Rochefort to be put in a state of readiness to carry him and the members of his family to America. Fouché, hearing of this, at first refused to release the frigates unless the Allies promised them safe conduct, but he later dropped this condition. Napoleon moved to Malmaison on the 25th June, and was still having second thoughts about carrying on the war. He offered on the 29th June, in his capacity as general, to attempt to throw back the Allies before quitting the country for America, but the government refused his offer. Therefore, after saying farewell to his family and friends, he left Malmaison for the coast, and reached Rochefort on the 2nd July.

The Provisional Government in Paris had asked the British Government for safe conduct passes for Napoleon to America, and were refused. Croker, writing to Keith, said:

... I am commissioned by my Lords Commissioners of the Admiralty to acquaint your Lordship that a proposition reached His Majesty's Government last night from the present ruler of France demanding a passport and safe conduct to America. To this proposition His Majesty's Government have returned a negative answer and it now seems more probable than ever that Bonaparte will endeavour to escape either to England, or what is much more likely to America.

At Rochefort Napoleon hesitated between the several schemes for escape which presented themselves to him. The American consul was willing to place a fast sailing vessel at the disposal of the ex-Emperor; Joseph offered to act as his double while Napoleon escaped from some other part of the coast; and there were also the French naval vessels in the port who were still loyal. At the time of his arrival at Rochefort any one of these schemes could probably have got him away, but he hesitated as to which course to take, and each day lost allowed the British to close in nearer with their blockade.

Meanwhile the *Bellerophon* was still in the Basque Roads, where one day she picked up a small punt with two boys in it who had drifted too far from the shore and were unable to get back. Maitland took them on board where he rested and fed them for a few days before returning them to the shore.

Information was received on the 1st July that the frigates in Aix Roads had taken powder on board and were all ready for sea, and that several civilians had arrived on the Isle D'Aix who were rumoured to be members of Napoleon's suite. This seemed to indicate to Maitland that the time of the attempted escape was near, and that it was most likely to be made by the frigates which were in that port. He therefore brought his

ship in as close as the French batteries on the island would
allow, and ordered guard boats to row all night. As it was probable that the *Bellerophon* would have to face at least two
frigates when the attempt was made, Maitland trained his men
in the type of action which he thought most likely to bring
success.

His idea was to cripple one ship by firing into her, then
close with her and board her with a party of 100 men; then
he was going to cast off from that ship and proceed in pursuit
of the other. This plan would seem to have a good chance of
success, for the narrowness of the Roads made them comparatively easy to cover by the fire of a single ship. In his *Consulate
and Empire* Thiers describes the *Bellerophon* as an old slow
ship armed with only 74 guns, and says that she would have
been no match for two fast well-armed frigates; but one
well directed broadside from a 74 could sink a frigate, as
Saumarez proved at the battle of the Nile.

That evening Maitland was joined by the *Phoebe*, and he
also sent orders for the recall of the *Myrmidon*, intending to
replace it off Bordeaux by the *Phoebe*.

On the 7th July Maitland received an order from Hotham
telling him that if he had any frigates with him he was to
retain them so as to increase his chances of catching Napoleon.
This letter and also an order to the same effect was brought by
the *Slaney*, which ship Maitland duly detained for his service.
The next day he received a further order from Hotham, this
time delivered by a Chasse Marée, which notified him of the
receipt by the British Government at the end of June of a
request from Fouché's Government for passports for Napoleon, and which consequently ordered him to keep a closer
watch than before.

There was no news on the 9th July, but on the 10th Maitland was informed by the watch that a small schooner was
standing out from the French squadron towards the *Bellerophon*. Thinking that this might possibly be the attempted
escape, Maitland ordered all preparations to be made for
sailing. As the vessel drew nearer she hoisted a flag of truce,
and by 7 a.m. was alongside. She proved to be the *Mouche*, a
tender to the ships of war, and was carrying the Duke de
Rovigo (Savary) and Count Las Cases. They were charged to
deliver a letter to the officer commanding the British ships off

Rochefort from Count Bertrand, Grand Marshal of the Palace to Napoleon.

Soon another vessel was spotted approaching from the other side, this proved to be a Chasse Marée from Hotham with further news of Napoleon which had been gleaned from the French Press, and telling Maitland that if he was so lucky as to fall in with him he was to take him on board and to sail to the nearest British port.

When Savary and Las Cases came on board they presented their letter, which was dated the 9th July:

Sir,

The Emperor Napoleon having abdicated the throne of France, and chosen the United States of America as a retreat, is, with his suite, at present embarked on board of the two frigates which are in this port, for the purpose of proceeding to his destination. He expects a passport from the British Government, which has been promised to him, and which induces me to send the present flag of truce, to demand of you, Sir, if you have any knowledge of the above mentioned passport, or if you think it is the intention of the British Government to throw any impediment in the way of our voyage to the United States. I shall feel much obliged by your giving me any information you may possess on the subject.

I have directed the bearers of this letter to present you my thanks, and to apologise for the trouble it may cause.

I have the honour to be,
Your Excellency's most obedient, &c. &c.,
Grand Marshal Count Bertrand

The task of the negotiators was to find out whether Maitland had orders to prevent a neutral vessel leaving the port if he could not allow the frigates to go. Maitland said that he would write a reply for them which would make his position perfectly clear to their master. In this reply he said that as the two countries were still in a state of war it would be impossible for him to allow any vessel to leave the port of Rochefort. He also said that the authority of Hotham would be required for permission for the Emperor to proceed in a merchant ship. He had forwarded the letter he had received to Hotham in Quiberon Bay, and until he received a reply he would be bound to stop any ship leaving port. Having now accomplished the ostensible object of their mission, the two Frenchmen stayed a further time on the *Bellerophon* discussing the state of affairs in France, and trying to impress on Maitland that Napoleon was not in as bad a situation as the papers made out, that he desired to quit Europe only in order to prevent further bloodshed.

Maitland was unable to make any definite replies to these arguments, having been without news since the battle of Waterloo. He did, however, inquire what pledge would be given, if the British Government allowed Napoleon to go to America, that he would not return to disturb Europe again. Savary replied that the power of Napoleon over the French public was now broken by his second abdication, therefore it was in the Emperor's own interest to retire to America. At this point Maitland saw the possibility of making the greatest coup of his career. Why not, he suggested to the Frenchmen, persuade Napoleon to accept asylum in England? Having now brought Maitland to the point which they required, the two began to discourage him. They said that the climate was too cold and damp; that the country was too near to France, and that he would be looked on as the source of any revolutionary disturbance which took place; that the English had been his enemies too long, and so it would be impossible to live amicably with them.

With this the interview ended, and the Frenchmen left. In his book written after the war, Maitland says that the efforts the two Frenchmen made to impress on him that the situation of Napoleon was not as bad as it was painted, made him the more inclined to take the opposite view.

Maitland had sent the letter from Bertrand to Hotham, who in turn had forwarded it to Lord Keith at Plymouth, who in his turn forwarded it to the Admiralty in London.

Further news was obtained on the 11th when a small boat was seen coming off from the island of Oléron. It was rowed by four men, and carried two other men as passengers. They asked to speak to the captain of the *Bellerophon* and were shown down into Maitland's cabin. The information they had to give was that a request had been received that morning from the Isle D'Aix for the best pilot for the Mamusson passage, and that a large sum of money had been offered to him to pilot a vessel to sea from that passage. They further averred that it was now certain that it was Napoleon's intention to escape either in a corvette or in a Danish brig which was lying at anchor in the port. On receipt of this information

Maitland ordered the *Myrmidon* closer in as soon as the weather would permit, while the *Bellerophon* and *Slaney* remained under way further out. The following day the *Cyrus* was sighted in the offing, and was signalled to close in with the Baleine lighthouse, and to search every vessel leaving the Pertuis de Breton.

Observation from the ship on the 13th July showed the white flag of the Bourbons to be flying from every tower in La Rochelle, as well as on the isle of Oléron. Maitland communicated this information to Hotham, saying that he would bring the *Bellerophon* into Basque Roads again that evening. That same day Croker, the secretary to the Admiralty, was writing to Hotham from Paris.

The French Government has received information that Bonaparte has embarked at Rochefort on board one of the small squadron which the Provisional Government had placed at his disposal, and it is understood that this squadron is anchored under forts of the Isle D'Aix ready to escape by the first opportunity. . . .

Lord Castlereagh feels that it is of the most urgent importance to seize Bonaparte . . . and if the ship in which Bonaparte may be, should by an obstinate resistance, drive you to extremities, he feels that you ought not for the sake of saving her or any one on board her, to take any line of conduct which should increase any degree of your own risk. The consequences of the resistance will be chargeable on those who make it . . .

If Bonaparte for himself, or the Governor of the Forts or Commander of the Squadron for him should propose to surrender on TERMS, Lord Castlereagh is of the opinion that you should reply, as the fact really is, that you are not authorized to enter into any engagement of that nature that your orders are to seize the person of Napoleon and his family and to hold them for the disposal of the Allied Powers.

It is unnecessary to say anything as to the safe custody of Bonaparte if you should be so fortunate as to take him, as your orders on that head are sufficiently ample. But that particular of your present orders which enjoins you to convey Bonaparte without any delay to a British port in the event of his capture, Lord Castlereagh thinks should not be literally followed under the circumstances in which you would obtain possession of him, and his Lordship wishes therefore that you should delay sending him to England till you shall have had a communication with him on the subject.

In Basque Roads Maitland was still able to see from the *Bellerophon* that the white flag of the Bourbons was flying from the buildings of La Rochelle, as well as on the isle of Oléron. It was also noticed that the frigates had all the signs

of being ready to put to sea. He therefore kept his squadron
ready to make all sail at a moment's notice.

On the 14th July another small boat bearing a flag of truce
was seen coming from the shore. It was identified as the
Mouche, which had been out a few days earlier, and was carrying Las Cases, Lallemand, and Savary. This was not Maitland's first meeting with Lallemand, for the Frenchman had
been his prisoner for three weeks when Maitland was in command of the *Camelion* off Egypt. At the same time he had also
met General Savary, then a guest of Sir Sidney Smith.

Maitland signalled to Captain Sartorious of the *Slaney* to
come on board the *Bellerophon* in order to have a witness of
anything which he might say to the French. This was vitally
important in view of the calumnies which have been cast on
Maitland by Bonapartists and others, accusing him of getting
Napoleon on board by a trick. The truth was that Napoleon
had already made up his mind to go on board the British
ship, and hoped, once there, to use his powerful personal
attraction to get himself released to live in England.

When Las Cases arrived on the quarter-deck, he asked
Maitland if he had received a reply to the letter which he had
delivered on the 10th. Maitland said that he had had no reply,
but was confident that the admiral would be here as soon as
possible after reading the letter which Maitland had sent him.
Maitland then added:

If that was the only reason you had for sending off a flag of truce, it was
quite unnecessary, as I informed you when last here that the Admiral's
answer, when it arrived, should be forwarded to the frigates by one of the
Bellerophon's boats; and I do not approve of frequent communications
with an enemy by means of a flag of truce.

Having stated his views, Maitland invited the Frenchmen
into his cabin for breakfast. This enabled them to pass the
time until Captain Sartorious had arrived on board. When
breakfast was over the negotiations proceeded; Las Cases
said once again that Napoleon was anxious to stop any further
shedding of blood, and that he would proceed to America in
any way the British Government allowed. To this Maitland
answered that he had no authority to agree to any arrangement
of that sort, believing that his Government would not approve
of it. Then he produced the idea which the Frenchmen had
half planted in his mind at the previous interview.

I think I may venture to receive him into this ship, and convey him to England: if, however, he adopts that plan, I cannot enter into any promise, as to the reception he may meet with, as, even in the case I have mentioned I shall be acting on my own responsibility, and cannot be sure that it would meet with the approbation of the British Government.

To this proposition, Maitland says, Las Cases replied that under those conditions he had no doubt that Napoleon would come on board the *Bellerophon*. Later, when Maitland's conduct was questioned by numerous Frenchmen and English radicals, he was asked to write a full account of his actions, which he did, and which he asked Captain Sartorius to read and verify, which the latter did. There seems to be no foundation for the remark by Claude Manceron that Maitland had tricked the three Frenchmen, that in fact he had 'done much more than lie'.

Napoleon himself could have had no real hope of ever being allowed to live in England. No one can ever say what he really thought his future would be once he had surrendered to the British. He himself had come to the conclusion that this course was safer than surrender to any of the other allies. The Prussians would have shot him without a doubt, the Emperor of Austria wanted to lock him away in a castle for the rest of his life, and when asked later why he did not surrender to his one-time friend the Emperor Alexander of Russia, he replied, 'La Russe! Dieu garde!'

When Las Cases inquired whether Napoleon would be well received in England, Maitland replied that he did not know the intention of the British Government, but had no reason to suppose he would not be well received. This remark has been seized on to indicate that Maitland stated that he would be well received in England, which, say his detractors, means that he *would* be received in England. This might apply if Maitland had not prefixed his remark with the statement that he did not know the intention of his Government. Asked where Napoleon was at present, Las Cases replied that he was at Rochefort, which proved to be untrue, and which Maitland knew to be untrue. This is also seized on by Manceron as further evidence of Maitland's deceit. On the French side, too, all was not straightforward honesty; Las Cases, apart from his lie about the Emperor being at Rochefort, pretended not to speak English, which language he knew well. In this way he hoped to pick up an unguarded word from Maitland which would give him some information to take back to his master. A further question was whether there was any risk of the people who accompanied Napoleon being handed over to the French Government if he decided to surrender. To this Maitland was able to give a definite 'No', which in fact proved to be the case.

At 9.30 a.m. the Frenchmen left, saying that they would go and see the Emperor and give him all the facts which Maitland had stated to them. Maitland was surprised when the boat with a flag of truce appeared later in the day, and he hastened to recall Captain Sartorius, and also Captain Gambier. The boat was alongside by 7 p.m., and this time contained Las Cases and Gourgaud, one of Napoleon's A.D.Cs. On their coming on deck, Maitland asked if they had been to Rochefort, to which Las Cases replied that there had been no need as they had found the Emperor had already arrived at Isle D'Aix when they got back from the first trip. Las Cases then presented the letter which he was carrying from Bertrand to Captain Maitland, which stated quite definitely Napoleon's intention to proceed on board the *Bellerophon* at the first opportunity the next morning. The letter read as follows:

Sir,

Count Las Cases has reported to the Emperor the conversation which he had with you this morning. His Majesty will proceed on board your ship with the ebb tide tomorrow morning, between four and five o'clock.

I send Count Las Cases, Counsellor of State, doing the duty of Maréchal de Logis, with the list of persons composing His Majesty's suite.

If the Admiral, in consequence of the despatch you forwarded to him, should send the passport for the United States therein demanded, His Majesty will be happy to repair to America; but should the passport be witheld, he will willingly proceed to England, as a private individual, there to enjoy the protection of the laws of your country.

His Majesty has despatched Major-General Baron Gourgaud to the Prince Regent with a letter, a copy of which I have the honour to enclose, requesting that you will forward it to such one of the ministers as you may think it necessary to send that general officer, that he may have the honour of delivering the letter with which he is charged to the Prince Regent.

I have the honour to be sir,

Your very humble servant,

Count Bertrand.

To the Officer commanding the
Cruizers off Rochefort.

Enclosed with the letter was a list of the persons whom Napoleon wished to have accompany him, a list totalling fifty people, from Grand Marshal Bertrand to the lowest footman. Also enclosed was a copy of the famous letter to the Prince Regent:

Rochefort, July 13th, 1815.

Your Royal Highness,

A victim to the factions which distract my country, and to the enmity of the greatest powers of Europe, I have terminated my political career, and I come, like Themistocles, to throw myself upon the hospitality of the British people. I put myself under the protection of their laws; which I claim from your Royal Highness, as the most powerful, the most constant, and the most generous of my enemies.

Napoleon.

This letter, it will be seen, is dated the 13th July, which seems to make it plain that Napoleon had at that time already made up his mind to surrender to the British.

Having read the two letters, Maitland said that he would be pleased to receive Napoleon on board the next morning, and in the meanwhile he would forward General Gourgaud to England in the *Slaney* when he sent his dispatches to the Admiralty. Maitland added, however, that Gourgaud would not be allowed to land until permission was received either from London or from the port admiral. Las Cases then asked for paper that he might write to Bertrand of the acceptance of his proposal for the surrender of Napoleon. As a final safeguard, as though he could see all the trouble ahead, Maitland said to Las Cases, 'Monsieur Las Cases, you will recollect that I am not authorized to stipulate as to the reception of Buonaparte in England, but that he must consider himself entirely at the disposal of his Royal Highness, the Prince Regent'. To which Las Cases answered, 'I am perfectly aware of that, and have already acquainted the Emperor with what you said on the subject'. Maitland afterwards regretted that this declaration was not given in a written form, but at the time he was satisfied with receiving it in front of witnesses.

The letter written by Las Cases was sent ashore by the boat in which he arrived, while the Frenchman stayed on board. Captain Maitland then wrote to the Admiralty about the whole affair. He told them that he had received a proposal to receive on board Napoleon Bonaparte and had agreed to it, and that

Napoleon was to consider himself at the mercy of the Prince Regent. He reported that he had dispatched Gourgaud in the *Slaney*, and also enclosed a copy of the letter to the Prince Regent.

With these formalities over, he discussed with Las Cases proposals for the accommodation of Napoleon and his suite on the *Bellerophon*. His idea was to divide the after-cabin in two, one part for the ladies, the other for Napoleon. Las Cases interrupted at this point to say that it would be better if the whole after-cabin was given to the Emperor as he liked to have plenty of room to walk about. Wishing his 'guests' to be as comfortable as possible, Maitland agreed to this proposal. Maitland then gave orders for the erection of the bulkheads to make up cabins. These bulkheads had been removed when the ship was cleared for action, and it took some time to erect them and to get all the necessary cabins fixed.

In the middle of this preparation Maitland had another visitor from the shore. This was yet one more person with news of Napoleon, this time that he had passed through La Rochelle with the intention of escaping to sea from the Pertuis de Breton, and that being now in that passage he intended to sail that night. Maitland told the man openly that he doubted his information as he had one of Napoleon's chief assistants on board at that very moment. What proof could he give of his story? The man answered that a boat had passed close to the one which he was in, and that a man wrapped in a sailor's greatcoat was pointed out to him as the ex-Emperor.

Despite the presence of Las Cases on board, Maitland still feared that he might have been tricked, and he had already sent dispatches to the Admiralty containing the news that he had captured Napoleon! He faced Las Cases with the new information, but the Frenchman was completely unruffled by the news. He asked at what time the man had said that Napoleon had passed through La Rochelle, and when told it was 10 a.m. he said that that was impossible as he had only left him at half-past five that very evening. Maitland accepted this denial and concluded that the information had resulted from a mistaken identity. The following morning, however, he again received information that the ex-Emperor had passed through La Rochelle. He decided to stick by Las Cases's assurance, and later learnt that both the stories he had heard had had a certain amount of truth in them. Two Chasses Marées had been prepared for Napoleon in case the mission to the *Bellerophon* was unsuccessful, in which case it was planned to cross the Atlantic in them. Maitland stated in his account later that he doubted whether Napoleon, in the condition in which he then was, and in the style in which he was used to travelling would have been able to make the journey. He did inquire, however, from the man who brought the intelligence, as to the state of La Rochelle, and whether it would be safe for him to send a boat there to purchase supplies. He was told that although the townspeople were well disposed towards the Bourbons, there were a fair number of soldiers in town who were still faithful to Napoleon, and that it would not be advisable to send such a boat.

The dawn of the 15th came at last, and with it the end of the career of Napoleon in Europe:

... observed a French Brig & Schooner coming out with Flags of Truce. Answered Ditto. At 6 sent boats to Ditto. At 7 received on board Napoleon Bonaparte (late Emperor of France) and his suite.

Almost as soon as the boats were sighted coming from the shore, two more were sighted coming in from the open sea. It did not need a telescope to see that it was the *Superb* with Hotham on board. With the prevailing direction of the wind, the *Superb* was making better progress than the two boats coming out, and for some minutes there was consternation on the *Bellerophon* in case Hotham should arrive first and get all the credit by actually receiving Napoleon. This was the reason why Maitland sent his own boats away to pick up Napoleon and bring him to the *Bellerophon* before the *Superb* arrived. His barge, with First Lieutenant Mott in charge, returned with Napoleon soon after 6 p.m. according to Maitland's account, but as will be seen in the extract from the log above, different times are recorded.

Maitland had received no instructions as to how Napoleon was to be received by any vessel into which he should be taken, and decided to abide by the rules of the service. The particular rule which applied in this case was that honours were not to be paid to anyone coming on board before the flag was hoisted at 8 a.m., and it was now only between 6 and 7 a.m. The Marines were drawn up on the poop, but they did not salute as Napoleon came over the side to be met by Maitland. A witness to the occasion was Midshipman George Home, who left his own description of the scene. In his account he places the guard of Marines as drawn up aft on the quarter-deck.

The lieutenants stood grouped first on the quarter-deck, and we more humble middies behind them; while the Captain, evidently in much anxiety, kept trudging backwards and forwards between the gangway and his own cabin, sometimes peeping out of one of the quarter-deck ports to see if the barge were drawing nearer.

Midshipman Home then relates a story of Manning the boatswain, and of one of the midshipmen, who

walked very demurely up to Manning, . . . who was standing all import-ance at the gangway, and after comically eyeing his squat figure and bronzed countenance, . . . gently laid hold of one of his whiskers to which the boatswain good naturedly submitted, as the youngster was a great favourite with him.

'Manning!' said he, most sentimentally, 'this is the proudest day of your life! You are this day to do the honours of the side to the greatest man the world ever produced, or ever will produce!'

Here the boatswain eyed him with proud delight. 'And along with the great Napoleon, the name of Manning, the boatswain of the *Bellerophon*, will go down to the latest posterity; and, as a relic of that great man, permit me my dear Manning, to preserve a lock of your hair!'

On that he made an infernal tug at the boatswain's immense whiskers, and fairly carried away part of it, making his way through the crowd and down below with the speed of an arrow. The infuriated boatswain finding he had passed so rapidly from the sublime to the ridiculous, through the instrumentality of this imp a of youngster, could vent his rage in no way but by making his glazed hat spin full force after his tantalizer, with an expletive consigning his young eyes and limbs to perdition. The hat, however, fell far short of young Bruce (the Midshipman), and the noise and half-burst of laughter that the trick occasioned drew the attention of the Captain, who coming up, with a 'What—what's all this?' the poor boatswain was glad to draw to his hat and resume his position.

For an actual description of Napoleon boarding the *Bellero-phon* we have the accounts of Midshipman Home and of Captain Maitland. In his book Maitland describes the scene thus:

General Bertrand came first up the ship's side, and said to me, 'The Emperor is in the boat.' He then ascended, and, when he came on the quarter-deck, pulled off his hat, and, addressing me in a firm tone of voice said, 'I am come to throw myself on the protection of your Prince and laws.' When I showed him into the cabin, he looked round and said, 'Une belle chambre. This is a handsome cabin.' I answered, 'Such as it is Sir, it is at your service while you remain on board the ship I command'. He then looked at a portrait that was hanging up, and said, 'Who is that young lady?' 'My wife', I replied. 'Ah! She is both young and pretty.' He then asked if I had any children, and put a number of questions respecting my country, and the service I had seen. He next requested I would send for the officers, and introduce them to him: which was done according to their rank. He asked several questions of each, as to the place of his birth, the situation he held in the ship, the length of time he had served, and the actions he had been in. He then expressed a desire to go round the ship; but as the men had not done cleaning, I told him it was customary to clean the lower decks immediately after their breakfast, that they were then so employed, and if he would defer visiting the ship until they had finished, he would see her to more advantage.

Midshipman Home tells of the arrival on board as follows:

The barge approached, and ranged alongside. The first lieutenant came up the side, and to Maitland's eager and blunt question, 'Have you got him?' he answered in the affirmative. After the lieutenant came Savary, followed by Marshal Bertrand, who bowed and fell back a pace on the gangway, to await the ascent of their master. And now came the little great man himself, wrapped up in his grey greatcoat buttoned up to the chin, three cocked hat and Hussar boots, without any sword; I suppose as emblematical of his changed condition. Maitland received him with every mark of respect due to a crowned head, which was afterwards insidiously thrown out against Maitland. So far from that, the Captain, on Napoleon's addressing him, only removed his hat, as to a general officer, and remained covered while the Emperor spoke to him. His expressions were brief, I believe only reiterating what he had stated the day previous in his letter to the Prince Regent, 'That he placed himself under the protection of the British nation, and under that of the British commander as the representative of his sovereign.' The captain again removed his hat, and turned to conduct the Emperor to the cabin. As he passed through the officers assembled on the quarter-deck, he repeatedly bowed slightly to us, and smiled. What an ineffable beauty there was in that smile; his teeth were finely set, and as white as ivory, and his mouth had a charm about it that I have never seen in any other human countenance. I marked his fine robust figure as he followed Captain Maitland into the cabin, and, boy as I was, I said to myself, 'Now have I a tale for futurity!'

It will be seen by this passage that Napoleon had soon made his first conquest, for the mind of Midshipman Home was completely dominated by the glory of Napoleon. It would be hard to reconcile 'a fine and robust figure' with the drawing of Napoleon made by an officer of the *Bellerophon* while he was on board, but his power was such that he made people see in him things which he never really was.

His dress seems to be a matter of some controversy. Captain Maitland differs from Midshipman Home in describing it as:

An olive coloured greatcoat over a green uniform, with scarlet cape and cuffs, green lapels turned back and edged with scarlet, skirts hooked back with bugle horns embroidered in gold, plain sugar-loaf buttons and gold epaulettes; being the uniform of the Chasseur à Cheval of the Imperial Guard. He wore the star of Grand Cross of the Legion of Honour, and the small cross of that order; the Iron Crown; and the Union, appended to the buttonhole of his left lapel. He had on a small cocked hat with a tri-coloured cockade; plain gold hilted sword, military boots and white waistcoat and breeches.

Now that he was on board the *Bellerophon* Napoleon began to fight his last battle. This was the battle to win the good opinions of those around him; he had, in fact, already conquered Midshipman Home! When he made his tour of the ship, he asked many questions and made remarks designed to influence his hearers in his favour. How much cleaner British ships were than French! How much quieter they were! He admired the men, remarking that they must be the reason why the British were so great at sea, which no doubt a few of the men would have agreed with if they could have spoken French. Maitland told him that, without detracting from the merit of the men, he thought the major share of the credit was due to the excellence of the officers. Napoleon agreed that probably he was right, and then changed the subject to the conduct of several famous naval actions. He said that many times he had been dissatisfied with certain French officers, and that in particular he had tried to get two men punished for misconduct. One, he said, ought to have suffered the death penalty, but being tried by a naval court martial was only dismissed the service. At this point Maitland remarked that he thought the sentence of death passed on the officer who commanded the *Calcutta* in the action in Basque Roads in 1809 particularly unjust, as the ship had been defended to the last extremity. Napoleon answered that Maitland did not know the full circumstances, that the captain in question had been the first to leave his ship, and the ship had been then defended by the rest of the officers and crew.

He next commented on the remarkable successes of the Royal Navy throughout the war:

> I can see no sufficient reason why your ships should beat the French with so much ease. The finest men of war in your service are French; a French ship is heavier in every respect than one of yours, she carries more guns, those guns of a larger calibre, and has a great many more men.

Maitland replied that the difference was explained by the excellence of the officers and men of the British ships, which was attained by their always being at sea. Napoleon remarked then that he understood from French prisoners released from the *Bellerophon* a few days previously, that a great deal of time was spent at gun practice. Maitland replied that he considered that accuracy of fire was essential for victory. Napoleon then asked what chance a ship of 74 guns had of stopping two frigates, as if for instance he had tried to force a passage in the ships at Isle D'Aix. Maitland said that the superior weight of the fire of the larger ship, combined with the difficulty of getting the two frigates into an effective fighting position, would make the odds in favour of the larger ship, but much would still depend on chance. Napoleon then returned to what he had said before, remarking that he had once wanted to introduce firing at targets into the French Navy, but the expense of the powder was so great that the country was never able to afford it. He examined the guns in detail, remarking that he thought the mixing of the various calibres on the quarter-deck and forecastle must make for much inconvenience.

As soon as the inspection was finished, breakfast was taken, English style, consisting of 'tea, coffee, cold meat, etc.' Napoleon did not appear to enjoy this meal, and on Maitland inquiring if there was anything he would prefer, he was told that the Emperor always had a hot meal in the morning, so Maitland gave instructions for his steward to follow the orders of Napoleon's maître d'hôtel and prepare a hot breakfast for Napoleon. The morning meal became a custom for the rest of Napoleon's time on the *Bellerophon* so that he could feel as much at home as possible. The conversation during breakfast mainly consisted of Napoleon's queries as to customs in England: 'I must learn to conform myself to them, as I shall probably pass the remainder of my life in England.' The approach of the *Superb* was also an object of comment, and Napoleon asked how soon she would be anchored. Would Hotham approve of Maitland having received him, and when Maitland went to report to Hotham, would he tell the admiral that Napoleon was desirous of seeing him.

As soon as the *Superb* had anchored Maitland went on board, and gave a full explanation of his conduct to Hotham. He added that he trusted that he had done right, as he considered it to be the wish of the Government to prevent Napoleon's escape to America. Hotham reassured him in this, by saying that it was great luck to have got hold of him, but to have accomplished it without accepting any conditions was doubly fortunate, and he did not doubt that the Government would approve of what he had done. Hotham asked Maitland how he felt about keeping him, would he like to hand him over to the *Superb*? This offer Maitland refused, saying that as he had had all the trouble of getting him he would have all the credit of taking him to England. He would not, however, detain Napoleon in his ship if he expressed a desire to move to the *Superb*. Maitland then delivered Napoleon's message. Hotham replied that he would look forward to a meeting with pleasure.

When Maitland returned to the *Bellerophon* he told Napoleon that Hotham would be calling on him later that day. Napoleon desired Count Bertrand to go and pay his respects to Hotham, which he did, being shown over the *Superb* by Captain Senhouse. In the afternoon, Hotham and Captain Senhouse came on board the *Bellerophon*, and the two officers, accompanied by the admiral's secretary Irving, were introduced to Bonaparte in the after-cabin. Captain Senhouse wrote to his wife later telling her of the meeting:

We were received by the ex-Emperor with all his former dignity; and the party consisting of Napoleon, Bertrand, Sir Henry Hotham, Captain Maitland, Mr Irving, and myself, were kept standing the whole time.

Napoleon's person I was very desirous of seeing, but on doing so, I was disappointed. His figure is bad, he is short with a large head, his hands and legs small, and his body so corpulent as to project very considerably, his coat made very plain, as you see it in most prints, and from being very short in the back it gives his figure a more ridiculous appearance than it has naturally. His profile is good and is exactly what his busts and portraits represent him, but his full face is bad. His eyes are a light blue, heavy and totally contrary to what I had expected, his teeth are bad, but the expression of his countenance is versatile, and expressive beyond measure of the quick and varying passions of the mind. His face at one moment bears the stamp of good humour and again immediately changes to a dark, penetrating, thoughtful scowl denoting the character of the thought that excites it. He speaks quick, and runs from one subject to another, with great rapidity. His knowledge is extensive and very various, and he surprised me much by his remembrance of men of every character in England. He spoke much of America and asked many questions concerning Spanish and British America, and also of the United States.

He plays the Emperor in everything, and has taken possession of Maitland's after-cabin. As a specimen, he sent this morning to Captain Maitland to request the pleasure of his company to breakfast at Maitland's own table. In consequence of this assumption Napoleon walked into the dinner cabin as into his own palace, and Marshal Bertrand was left to usher in the strangers and staff. Dinner was served entirely in the French style by Napoleon's domestics. Without any ceremony, he commenced eating, no notice was taken of any individual, and we had all only to eat and drink as fast as the servants plied out plates and glasses with food and wine. Directly after dinner we had coffee and then adjourned to the after-cabin; very little conversation took place; afterwards we were principally amused by seeing a very compact bed of Napoleon's set up, and his bed made by 3 or 4 of his valets.

Soon after this we went to the Quarter Deck, by Napoleon's desire, with the ladies, and remained until ½ past 7, when Sir Henry Hotham, Mr Irving and I returned on board. At dinner Napoleon said little, but ate heartily; as little was said afterwards, and on going on deck he amused himself much in talking with the subordinate officers and midshipmen by turns, and in walking the deck with Bertrand. At an early hour he retired to bed apparently much fatigued.

The description of Napoleon in this passage is almost precisely opposite to that of Midshipman Home, and evidently by one who had not yet fallen under the spell of the ex-Emperor. In his account of the meal, Maitland said that Napoleon conversed 'a great deal' and was not at all depressed. He asked Maitland many personal questions, where was he born, had he any property? When he found that Lord Lauderdale was the head of the Maitland family he said that Captain Maitland resembled him a little, though Maitland was fair and Lauderdale was dark. Lord Lauderdale had been sent to France by Fox to join Lord Yarmouth in the peace negotiations of 1806, and Napoleon remarked that had Fox lived it 'would never have come to this', but that the death of Fox had ended all hopes of peace.

Napoleon was invited to the *Superb* to take breakfast with Hotham the next day, the 16th, and that morning when Maitland came on deck he saw that the *Superb* had removed the tompions from her guns and had fixed man ropes on her yards, as if they meant to salute Napoleon when he came on board. Maitland was rather worried by this as he had received Napoleon with no form of salute at all, and was afraid that if the admiral saluted him as he went on board the *Superb* his own action would be construed as a form of insult. He therefore sent to Hotham to ask whether he had any intention of saluting Napoleon, and if this was the intention should the same be done on his leaving the *Bellerophon*? Hotham replied that he had no intention of saluting Napoleon—only of manning the yards; but that Maitland was not to do so on Napoleon's leaving the *Bellerophon* though he was at liberty to do so when he returned. Maitland also received directions to hoist a signal when the visitors were ready to leave to give Hotham time to make his preparations.

The barge was ready and manned by 10 a.m. and a captain's guard was turned out. When Napoleon came on deck he looked at the body of Marines drawn up and remarked on their fine appearance. He went through their ranks, inspecting their arms, and said to Bertrand that with '100,000 such soldiers as these' much could have been accomplished. He asked which was the longest serving member of the guard, and when the man was pointed out he put many questions to him which Maitland interpreted. When he found out that the man had been serving ten years, he asked if it was not the custom in the British service to reward long service. Maitland replied that the man had been a sergeant, but had been reduced to the ranks for some sort of misconduct. Napoleon then put the guard through a few manoeuvres with the help of Maitland as interpreter. He said that he did not like the British bayonet, as he thought it would be easier to twist off when seized by an enemy than the French one.

Napoleon then climbed down to the barge, and once again made some remarks on the fine appearance of the barge's crew. Las Cases, who was wearing the uniform of a naval officer to which he was entitled by his early service in the navy, was teased by Napoleon about his appearance. Las Cases replied that he was wearing the uniform because he thought that a uniform would evoke more consideration in a foreign country. As the barge covered the distance between the two ships, his attention was drawn to the men on the *Superb*'s yards, and to the general appearance of the ship. He asked whether she was French, and how old she was, and how many guns she carried.

On arrival at the *Superb* Bertrand went up the side first to announce to Hotham that Napoleon was in the boat. Napoleon then went up and was received by Hotham. For details of his visit to the *Superb* we cannot do better than return to the letter of Captain Senhouse to his wife:

Napoleon came to breakfast on the 16th at the hour appointed, with the officers and Ladies of his suite, and was received with our yards manned and with every attention customary to Generals-Commanding-in-Chief. As usual he immediately went into the after-cabin and requested that the officers of the ship might be presented to him. He had many little remarks to make during the presentation, and the moment it was concluded he requested to see the interior of the *Superb*. I was fully prepared for this and had everything in good order for him. The Admiral attended when I showed Napoleon round, who asked a thousand questions, and made numerous observations, which showed him to be well versed in everything relative to the Naval Service. He was particularly struck with the healthy and youthful appearance of the Ship's Company, Officers as well as the Men, and continually gave his opinion of the good order the Ship was in, crying out constantly 'Bon ordre', 'Bien soigné', as he passed on. He expressed himself very sensible of the superiority of the British Navy at present, but considered the French Navy were increasing rapidly in good discipline and in number of vessels. He went through the whole of the Ship, even the Store Rooms, but seemed to move with painful sensations as if he were afflicted with gout! I was obliged to assist him up and down ladders with the Count de Montholon, and his weight was rather more than convenient.

I afterwards accompanied Mme Bertrand round the ship; on reaching the lower deck, she stopped me to make some enquiries (which I think the Marshal, her husband, had desired her to do). They were relative to Napoleon, and she was very desirous of knowing what would be done with him, where he would be sent, how provided for, etc.—and she entered into a very long history of all their circumstances and transactions for some time before. Napoleon, she told me, had only with him a million of

Francs, a mere nothing to support him, that he had not a sou in any other country, that Talleyrand had large sums in different places, but that Napoleon had not; that the ex-Emperor had lost a large portion of his property at the Battle of Waterloo.

We were now summoned to breakfast. Napoleon was perfectly the Emperor, I assure you. He eats very heartily, but talk little at meals, very soon retires, and it is astonishing the respect and attention paid him by those who were about him.

I could not avoid remarking his apparent sovereign contempt for females. They had no part in his attention. They did not even presume to intrude themselves into the same apartment where he was, and when, on going away, I asked whether the Ladies would proceed, or get into the boat afterwards, he answered very coolly that the Ladies might come afterwards in another boat and so they did with only one gentleman, who would not have remained if I had not given him a hint to do so.

Napoleon on this occasion showed no dark clouded looks—his face was the picture of good-humour, conciliation and pleasantry, and his spirits were surprisingly good for the circumstances under which he was placed. I cannot enter into all that was said—everything was interesting, and in the contemplation of so great a man fallen from so high a station, paying so handsome a compliment to the Country we belong to, conciliating the minds of all around him, it was impossible not to forget, in some degree, the darker shades of his character through life, and feel nothing but benevolence towards him and his followers *at the moment*: though had he been opposed to us again, not a sword but would have sprung from its scabbard to annihilate him. It is strange that anyone should suppose that this man would not win the hearts of his old soldiers who so frequently were victorious with him, when he makes such impressions on his enemies.

The comments in this part of the letter show that Napoleon was impressing Captain Senhouse in spite of himself. Hotham, when writing to his cousin Admiral Sir William Hotham, thought differently:

. . . he was not natural, and that he had very little the manners of what we should call a gentleman. He was civil, and, under existing and very trying circumstances, good-humoured; but not a gentleman.

The party all returned to the *Bellerophon* about noon, when the yards were manned as the party came on board. In obedience to orders received from Hotham, Maitland immediately got under way for Torbay accompanied by the *Myrmidon*. On arrival at Torbay he was to send two officers to London with the dispatches which Hotham had written, and to inform Lord Keith of the full facts of the situation.

A boat from the shore had approached with a load of fresh vegetables for the use of Napoleon, which were accepted on board, and then the two British ships continued on their way. Napoleon asked, as the *Bellerophon* was passing a cable's length from the *Superb*, whether that was close for a naval engagement, and Maitland replied that the habit in the British Navy was to close to half that distance.

The Emperor remained on deck all the time the ship was beating out of the passage, but went below at 6 p.m. for dinner. He seemed at this meal to be in very good spirits, and related several stories about himself. As Maitland had served in the Egyptian campaign, it was inevitable that sooner or later the subject should turn to that campaign, and probably to Sir Sidney Smith. This officer and Napoleon had always had a violent dislike of each other, more violent on Napoleon's side than on Sir Sidney's, and on hearing that Maitland did not know the cause of the quarrel, Napoleon proceeded to enlighten him.

When the French Army was before St Jean d'Acre, he had a paper privately distributed among the officers and soldiers, tending to induce them to revolt and quit me; on which I issued a proclamation, denouncing the English commanding officer as a madman, and prohibiting all intercourse with him. This nettled Sir Sidney so much, that he sent me a challenge to meet him in single combat on the beach at Caiffa. My reply was, that when Marlborough appeared for that purpose, I should be at his service; but that I had other duties to fulfil besides fighting a duel with an English commodore.

Napoleon talked further of Syria, and then made his famous remark: 'If it had not been for you English, I should have been Emperor of the East; but wherever there is water to float a ship, we are sure to find you in our way.'

The weather for the next few days was good, and Napoleon spent much of his time on deck. He also played cards frequently, particularly vingt-et-un, and he invited Maitland to play a hand, but the Captain declined.

Maitland had written to Lord Keith on the 18th recounting the whole process of the negotiations up until the surrender of Napoleon, and hoping that his conduct met with the approbation of the Admiralty. Lord Melville also wrote to Keith on the 21st July stipulating measures to be taken for the greater security of the prisoner:

... if he should come to Plymouth, he should remain in the Sound in a line of battle ship, and the most positive orders should be given to prevent any person whatever, except the officers and men who form the complement of the ship, from going on board. No person, whether in His Majesty's Service or not, who does not belong to the ship, should be suffered to go on board either for the purpose of visiting the officers, or on any pretence whatever, without permission from the Admirality.

General Gourgaud, who had left some days earlier in the *Slaney* for England, arrived late at night on the 22nd July, and Lord Keith immediately wrote to the Admiralty reporting the *Slaney*'s arrival and the news she carried:

There is a General Gourgaud on board the *Slaney* who is charged with a letter to the Prince Regent of which a copy is inclosed in Captain Maitland's Dispatch; and as I understand from the Captain of the *Slaney* that he refuses to deliver that letter to any other person than His Royal Highness, I have directed that he is to remain on board the *Slaney*, and ordered her to Torbay there to wait their Lordships' Command.

Three days later Sir John Barrow wrote to Keith giving the Admiralty's reply:

... I am commanded by their Lordships to acquaint you that they have ordered that ship [*Slaney*], as also the *Bellerophon*, to proceed immediately from Torbay to Plymouth Sound.

... I am to signify their Lordships' directions to you to give the most positive orders to Captain Maitland to prevent all communications whatever with the shore but through him, and by him through your Lordship, and on no account to permit any person whatever to go on board the ship without your Lordship's permission given in writing for that purpose.

The next day Melville himself was writing to Keith:

... we have since had a Cabinet on the whole business. I am afraid that the result will not come in the shape of an official letter from Lord Bathurst in time to send off by this post, but I can state for your *private* information that in all probability the Ex-Emperor will be sent to some foreign Colony, and in the mean time he will not be allowed to land or to have any communication whatever with the shore, and we shall not apprize him immediately of his future destination.

Melville also had a few words to say regarding Gourgaud:

The Aide-de-Campe in the *Slaney* will be sent back to the *Bellerophon*, there to remain and he will be told that he must send this and all other letters through you, as no others will be allowed to come ashore. I am afraid we find Bonaparte and his suite troublesome guests while they remain here; but we have no cause to grumble on the whole very much the reverse.

Melville also heard of the manning of the yards for the visit to the *Superb*, and laid down some instructions for the future:

It would appear that the yards were manned when Bonaparte visited the *Superb* (which was an unnecessary visit) that he insists upon being treated with Royal Respect, that he invited Captain Maitland and other officers to dine with him, and in short, that if we do not interfere, the same follies in this respect are likely to be committed as were exhibited last year by some of the officers in the Mediterranean. I have written the enclosed which may assist you in putting a stop to anything of that kind, and which you can show where it may be necessary.

And also a word as to the final destination of the ex-Emperor:

I think we shall send Bonaparte to St Helena, and that Sir George Cockburn's appointment as Commander-in-Chief on the Cape Station which was suspended will now go forward, and that he will convey this Prisoner to St Helena and remain there for some time. We must take it (St Helena) under the King's Authority, to which the Court of Directors I believe will not object.

In the enclosure mentioned above, Melville stated that Napoleon could only be allowed the rank of a general officer, and that no further salutes were to be made to him as a royal personage. He was sure that no British officer would be guilty of inhumanity towards the prisoner, and that he would be grateful if Lord Keith would circulate his (Melville's) ideas to the various officers concerned.

The *Bellerophon* was continuing her way to Torbay, and on the 20th July met the *Swiftsure* which Captain Maitland boarded. The *Swiftsure* was commanded by another Nile veteran, Captain Webley, who had been first lieutenant to Sir Samuel Hood of the *Zealous*. Webley was astonished when Maitland remarked, 'Well, I have got him.'

'Got him! Got whom?'

'Why Bonaparte; the man that has been keeping all Europe in a ferment these last twenty years.'

'Is it possible?' asked Webley, 'Well, you are a lucky fellow.'

On the 22nd signals were exchanged with the *Prometheus*, and Napoleon asked Maitland when they were at dinner if he could inquire from her whether the ships at Brest had hoisted the white flag or not. Maitland sent for the officer of the watch and asked him to make the question, and when Napoleon heard that they had, he digested the information without comment, changing the subject to the technicalities of signalling.

During the trip across the Channel Napoleon watched a play performed by members of the crew. It was called *The Poor Gentleman*, and the female parts were played by the youngest of the midshipmen. Lady Bertrand acted as interpreter, which arrangement seemed to afford him some opportunity of enjoying the play, particularly the female parts!

At daybreak on the 24th the *Bellerophon* was off Dartmouth and Count Bertrand sent to inform Napoleon of the fact. Napoleon did not come on deck until 4.30 p.m., but then he stopped until the ship was brought to anchor in Torbay. He admired the beauty of the coast, remarking on the advantage of the coasts of England over those of France which were surrounded by rocks. On coming into Torbay he exclaimed, 'What a beautiful country! It very much resembles the bay of Porto Ferrajo, in Elba.'

No sooner was the ship at anchor than an officer came on board with orders from Lord Keith which explained the measures to be taken for the better security of Napoleon. Keith also sent a personal letter to Maitland in which he underlined the need for the greatest security to be enforced, and as a way of introducing himself to Napoleon he asked Captain Maitland to thank the Emperor for the attention he had paid to Lord Keith's nephew, who had been wounded at Waterloo and had been brought before Napoleon. He said that Napoleon was not to want for anything, those items which could not be obtained at Brixham were to be ordered from Lord Keith. Napoleon was much gratified by this friendly approach from Lord Keith, and recollected the circumstances to which he was referring. Napoleon also expressed a desire to read as many newspapers as possible to gain some idea of his future destination. It was here that he saw the first reports of his being sent to St Helena, which considerably worried him.

No sooner had Maitland dropped anchor and the news spread that Napoleon was on board, than the ship was surrounded by dozens of little boats full of inquisitive passengers. Maitland therefore ordered the ship's boats to row round the ship on guard to keep the other boats at a decent distance. Being the object of such attention was pleasing to the Emperor and he appeared often on deck, showing himself to the crowds around. He observed to Maitland that the English seemed to have more than their fair share of curiosity! One of those who went out to see Napoleon while the ship was in the bay was the Rev. R. H. Froude, Archdeacon of Totnes, who wrote the following letter to his friend J. P. Taylor, who had originally intended to accompany him:

My Dear Sir,

I was very sorry to read that you came to Livermead with a full expectation of finding a boat ready to take you out to the *Bellerophon*, the fact was we went out on Monday but returned without the least expectation that Bonaparte would show himself during his stay in the bay. Kitness and I hired a small boat . . . rather for the purpose of spending a day on the water than of paying a second visit to the ship, but had determined, however, if you had been down to give up our places to your party, but as you were not here at ½ past eleven I really had not the least expectation of you at all. However, when we landed at 2 o'clock at Meadfort Sands to get our dinner we heard of your arrival. John Kitness set off an hour back to Torquay to offer our boat, there he learnt you had gone out with Sir H. Carew, and we were glad that you had not been eventually disappointed.

Having come to anchor ahead of every boat astern of the *Bellerophon* for half an hour, we had a full view of this extraordinary personage for full half the time. I could not help admiring his totally [?] air, seeming to be a spectator of some show, rather than an object of curiosity under such circumstances to so many spectators. They are off this morning.

An officer of the *Bellerophon* gave us a copy of a letter from Bonaparte to the Prince, which I will give you as I received it.

(Here followed a copy of the letter to the Prince Regent)

I transcribed my copy in pencil whilst in the boat and must have made a mistake where I have left a blank. It is a word expressive of enmity, *inimité* if there is such a word. If I see [?] this morning he will give it me right.

What an interesting day it was. I really am very sorry that you were not together. An officer of the ship said they all expected to be ordered as far up the river as their ship could go.

R. H. FROUDE.

The *Bellerophon* received orders to go to Plymouth on the 26th by the hand of Captain Sartorius. Maitland got under way, accompanied by the *Myrmidon* and *Slaney*, asking Las Cases to report the fact to his master.

Maitland had a slight brush with Madame Bertrand, who attacked him for neglecting Napoleon by not telling him personally of the fresh orders which had been received about him, and said he was offended by this. Maitland made his own inquiries as to whether Napoleon had expressed any annoyance, but Las Cases assured the captain that no such thing had happened. However, the progress of the ship westward was by no means designed to please Napoleon, for it removed him farther from London. Maitland had many opportunities for conversations with Madame Bertrand during her stay on the *Bellerophon*. As she spoke English well there was no difficulty over language. On one occasion she asked if Maitland was acquainted with Captain Ussher, of the frigate *Undaunted* which had conveyed Napoleon to Elba. The Emperor, she said, had become very friendly with him, and had presented him with his portrait set in diamonds; he had another portrait which he wished to present to Captain Maitland. Maitland replied that he could not accept it in the circumstances in which he was placed at that moment. She insisted that Napoleon would be very offended if he did not accept the gift, to which Maitland replied that he would be grateful in that case if Madame Bertrand would intercede for him with the Emperor to save him the pain of having to refuse personally.

Another conversation concerned the course which events might have taken had Napoleon won the battle of Waterloo. Had he won, Madame Bertrand asserted, he would have been firmly seated on the throne of France. Maitland replied that it would probably have protracted his downfall, but he would assuredly have been overwhelmed by the advancing Russians and Austrians. Madame Bertrand replied that if the British army had been defeated the Russians would never have dared to act against Napoleon. Maitland pointed out that that was hard to believe as they (the Russians) had been making every effort to join the allies. Madame Bertrand assured him that in the event of Wellington's defeat it had never been the intention of the Tsar Alexander to cross the frontier of France in opposition to Napoleon.

As soon as the ship was at anchor in Plymouth, Maitland informed Napoleon that he was going to call on the Commander-in-Chief, and asked if there were any messages which he wished to have conveyed. Napoleon said that he wanted to express his thanks to Lord Keith for his kind intentions and was anxious to see him at the first available opportunity. On receipt of this message Lord Keith replied that he would be glad to visit Napoleon, but had as yet no instructions as to how the prisoner was to be treated.

As a security precaution the frigates *Liffey* and *Eurotas* were ordered to anchor on either side of the *Bellerophon*, not only for the purpose of preventing the escape of Napoleon, but also to keep back the crowds of sightseers which were expected.

Napoleon listened to Maitland's account of the meeting, and then said that he was desirous of meeting Lord Keith and hoped that the admiral would not stand on ceremony. He would, he said, be satisfied to be treated as a private person until the Government had decided in what light he was to be considered. The presence of the two frigates was taken exception to, as he said that he was perfectly secure on the *Bellerophon*, and a further complaint was made of the musketry which had been going on all afternoon to keep off the shore boats, Napoleon would be very grateful if Maitland could stop it. This last request Maitland acceded to.

Melville wrote to Keith on the 26th July, giving further news of the preparations which the Government were making for the departure of Napoleon from Britain:

The *Northumberland*, Sir George Cockburn's flagship, is in the Medway, and being fully manned is ready to proceed: but if she should be detained by contrary winds, we may possibly on that account to lay our hands on the *Tonnant* which I believe is also ready. The sooner that Bonaparte is disposed of and despatched to his destination, the better for all concerned.

When we communicate to Bonaparte our final intentions respecting him, I think it probable you may have to visit him; at least I do not expect that we shall be able to come to a conclusion on all matters without your having a personal communication with him.

The following day Maitland received a letter from the Admiralty which told him that the Lords of the Admiralty approved of all his actions, which was a considerable load off his mind.

Lord Keith also wrote to Maitland on the subject of the reports which Napoleon had read in the papers about his being sent to St Helena. Lord Keith thought it most likely that, with the possibility of being sent to St Helena looming in front of him, Napoleon would try to escape, and that in consequence all guards should be doubled.

In London it had been decided to send Sir Henry Bunbury down to Plymouth with full instructions to deal with Napoleon. He was to accompany Lord Keith on board the *Bellerophon* so that he could explain any points of policy which were not known by Lord Keith. Lord Melville wrote a private letter to Lord Keith from his home at Wimbledon letting him know the time at which Bunbury had left London. He also warned Keith to keep a 'vigilant eye' on Savary and Lallemand as they were on the list of proscribed persons made out by the French Government, as was Bertrand. Melville also wrote a more official letter to Keith which set out the reasons for the decision arrived at by the Government:

.. It would be inconsistent with our duty to this country and to His Majesty's Allies, if we were to give General Bonaparte the means to again disturb the peace of Europe and renewing the calamities of War....

The Island of St Helena has been selected for his future residence; the climate is healthy, and its local situation will admit of his being treated with more indulgence than would be compatible with adequate security elsewhere.

Meanwhile Napoleon was still the centre of attraction in Plymouth Sound, and every day there were scores of boats. Among those refused access to the *Bellerophon* was a boat containing Maitland's wife and Vice-Admiral Sir Richard and Lady Strachan. On Mrs Maitland being pointed out to him, Napoleon made a slight bow in her direction, and also remarked that Sir Richard Strachan looked rather young to hold such a post as Second-in-Command of the Channel Fleet. Among other visitors was the artist J. J. Chalon, who happened to be in Plymouth on the day of the *Bellerophon*'s arrival. That evening Chalon made a rough sketch of the scene, and later converted it into a painting which now hangs in the Maritime Museum. Another artist, Charles Eastlake, also happened to be in the crowd, and made several sketches of Napoleon; in fact he said later that he was sure that Napoleon saw him, and specially posed for him.

Lord Keith made his first trip to the *Bellerophon* on the 28th July, coming on board between eleven and twelve o'clock. He was shown into the after-cabin by Captain Maitland, where Count Bertrand introduced him to Napoleon. Lord Keith had not yet received his final instructions from the Government so he could give Napoleon no definite information of his final destination, and it was more in the nature of a social call. As Lord Keith was leaving he was caught by Madame Bertrand, who drew him aside to tell him that it would be 'the height of injustice to send them to St Helena,' and endeavoured to persuade the admiral to interfere with his Government.

The 29th was a day of continuous rain, consequently there were no visitors to the waters around the ship. On the following day, however, the crush of boats was greater than ever and the guard boats had the greatest difficulty in keeping them off. Some of the Frenchmen were upset by the rough methods employed, particularly against those boats containing ladies. On this day Maitland was informed that Sir Henry Bunbury was due in Plymouth with the decision of the British Government regarding Napoleon's final destination. Maitland already knew that Napoleon was to go to St Helena, but he had been asked by Keith not to disclose this fact to him.

The following day, the 31st, Lord Keith and Sir Henry Bunbury came on board to give the official Government decision. Both Bunbury and Keith made out reports of the meeting, so there is no difficulty in following the exact course of the conversation. In his report Sir Henry Bunbury said:

We were announced and admitted immediately. After I had been introduced and Buonaparte had put a few trivial questions Lord Keith produced a copy of the letter from Lord Melville containing the Orders of His Majesty's Government and tendered it to Buonaparte. He enquired if it was in French, and on being told that it was in English, he observed that it would be useless to him, and that it would be necessary to translate it. Upon this Lord Keith began to read the paper aloud in French, but Buonaparte appeared not to hear distinctly, or not to comprehend, and after a line or two had been read he took the paper from Lord Keith's hands and proposed to me that I should translate it. I believe that he meant that I should make a written translation, but I preferred reading it aloud in French.

Napoleon listened attentively to the whole without interrupting me, and appeared as if he had been previously aware of what was to be communicated to him. At the conclusion Lord Keith asked Buonaparte if he wished to have a written translation made, but he answered no, that he comprehended the substance perfectly that the translation had been sufficiently good. He received the paper and laid it upon the table; and after a pause he began declaiming his solemn protest against this proceeding of the British Government: that they had not the right to dispose of him in that manner, and he appealed to the British people, and to the laws of the country. Buonaparte asked what was the Tribunal or if there was not a Tribunal, where he might prefer his appeal against the illegality and injustice of the decision taken by the British Government—'I am come here voluntarily' said he, 'to seek a place at the fireside of your nation, and to claim the rights of hospitality, I am not even a Prisoner of War, if I were a Prisoner of War you would be bound to heed me, according to the rights of Prisoners, but I am come to this country a passenger on board one of your ships of war after a previous negotiation with its Commander. If he had told me that I was to be a prisoner I should not have come, I asked him if he was willing to receive me and my suite on board and to carry me to England. *Admiral* Maitland answered that he would, and this after having received and telling me that he had received the special orders of his Government concerning me. . . . in coming on board a British ship of War I confided myself to the Hospitality of the British nation as much as if I had entered one of their towns, a ship, a town, it is all the same. To send me to St Helena is to sign my death warrant. I protest against being sent thither and I protest against being imprisoned in a Fortress in this country. I demand to be received as an English Citizen. I know indeed that I cannot be admitted to the rights of an Englishman at first, some years are requisite to entitle one to be domesticated. Well let the Prince Regent place me during that time under any surveillance he may think proper. Let me be put in a Country House in the center of the island, 30 leagues from any sea. Place a Commissioner about me to examine my correspondence and report my actions, and if the Prince Regent should require my Parole, perhaps I would give it. There I might have a certain degree of personal liberty, and I could enjoy the liberty of literature, in St Helena I should not live three months, with my habits and constitution it would be immediate death. I am used to ride 20 leagues a day what am I to do on this little Rock at the end of the World ? The climate is too hot for me, no I will not go to St Helena.

If your Government wishes to put me to death, they may kill me here, it is not worth while to send me to St Helena, I prefer death to St Helena, and what good is my death to you ? I can do you no harm, I am no longer a Sovereign, I am a simple individual, besides times and affairs are altered. What danger could result from my living as a private person in the heart of England, under any surveillance and restricted in any way the Government might imagine necessary. . . .

Why should I not have gone to my father-in-law (the Emperor of Austria), or to the Emperor Alexander who is my personal friend. We have become enemies because he wanted to annex Poland to his dominions, and my popularity among the Poles was in his way, but otherwise he was my friend, and he would not have treated me in this manner. If your Government acts thus, it will disgrace itself in the eyes of Europe, and even your own people will disapprove and blame its conduct. Besides you do not know perhaps what a feeling my death will create both in France and Italy, and how greatly the character of England will suffer if my blood rests here. There is a high opinion of the Justice and Honour of England, if you kill me your reputation will be low in France and Italy, and it will cost the lives of many Englishmen. There never has been a similar instance in the History of the World. What was there to force me to the step I took? The Tricolour flag was still flying at Bordeaux, at Nantes, at Rochefort, the Army has not submitted at this hour. I could have joined them, or if I had chosen to remain in France, what could have prevented my remaining concealed for years among a people who were all attached to me, but I preferred to settle as a private individual in England.

. . . and after all this a snare has been laid for me. If you kill me it will be an eternal disgrace to the Prince Regent, to your Government, and to the Nation. It is an unexampled act of cowardice. I offered the Prince Regent the most glorious page in his history! I am his enemy and I place myself at his direction. I have been the greatest enemy of your country, I have made War upon you for 20 years and I do you the highest honour and give you the greatest proof of my confidence by placing myself voluntarily in the hands of my most inveterate enemies! Remember what I have been, and how I stood among the Sovereigns of Europe. This courted my protection. That gave me his Daughter. All sought my friendship. I was Emperor, acknowledged so by all the powers of Europe except Great Britain, and she had acknowledged me and treated with me as Chief Consul of France.

Your Government have not the right to style me General Buonaparte, I am at least First Consul, and I ought to be treated as such if treated with at all. When I was at Elba, I was as much a Sovereign as when I was on the throne of France. I was as much a Sovereign in Elba as the King was in France. We each had our flag, I had my flag, he repeated, 'We had each our troops, to be sure [He said smiling] mine were on a small scale. I had 600 soldiers and he had 200,000 . . . but there was nothing in all this to alter my position or to deprive me of my rank as one of the Sovereigns of Europe.'

At this point Napoleon paused as if for a reply, but Bunbury could only tell him that all his objections would be forwarded to the Government, but that he was sure that the Government had only decided on St Helena because it would afford him a greater degree of personal liberty than could be allowed him in any part of Europe. Napoleon again protested at being sent to St Helena, saying that he would not go. He asked Bunbury and Keith whether, if they were in his position, they would go. He would rather die than go to St Helena.

You found me free, send me back again, replace me in the state in which you found me, and which I quitted only under the impression that your

Admiral was to land me in England. If your Government will not do this, and will not permit me to reside there, let me go to the United States. But I appeal to your laws, and throw myself on their protection to prevent my being sent to St Helena or being shut up in a Fortress.

Napoleon then inquired from Lord Keith as to when the *Northumberland* was due to arrive and would be ready to sail. He pressed the admiral to agree that no step should be taken towards his removal before the result of his appeal to the Government had been made known. Lord Keith was ready to grant this point. Napoleon then urged Bunbury to acquaint the Government with what he had said, to which Bunbury replied that he would be making a full report of the interview to the Government immediately he left the *Bellerophon*. On Lord Keith asking if he wished to put his answer in writing, Napoleon replied that he was sure that he could trust Bunbury to report faithfully everything he had said. Napoleon then went back over the same ground again, laying stress on the fact that he would never have surrendered if Captain Maitland had not led him to believe that he was acting in accordance with the instructions of his Government, and finished with the statement that he would never go to St Helena. The interview then being over, the two British officers made their bows and retired. They had not been outside more than a few minutes when a message was sent by Napoleon for Lord Keith to return. Napoleon then asked him for advice as to how he should proceed:

I replied, 'I am an officer and have discharged my duty. I have left the heads of my instructions with you in order that you may observe them if you consider it necessary.' I added, 'Sir, if you have anything more to say I must beg to call in Sir Henry Bunbury', to which he replied 'Oh no, it is not necessary.'

The Emperor then enquired if Keith had the power to detain him until he had heard from London?

... to which I answered 'that will depend upon the arrival of the other Admiral of whose instructions I am ignorant.'

Napoleon then returned to the subject of his appeal; did Lord Keith know of any Tribunal to which he could appeal?

... to which I replied, 'I am no Lawyer, but I believe none. I am satisfied there is every disposition on the part of the British Government to render your situation as comfortable as is consistent with prudence.' He immediately took up the paper from the Table and said with animation, 'How So! St. Helena?' to which I observed, 'Sir it is surely preferable to being confined in a small space in England, or being sent to France, or perhaps to Russia.' 'Russia! Dieu garde' was his reply. I then withdrew.

The interview with Napoleon was over in half an hour, after which Lord Keith called Captain Maitland to the fore-cabin where all the suite of Napoleon was assembled. They were all presented to Lord Keith and Hotham, and were seemingly much distressed by the news which Lord Keith had delivered. Savary and Lallemand in particular were most pressing for knowledge as to how they were to be disposed of. Madame Bertrand tried to use her charm on Lord Keith to prevent the Government sending Count Bertrand to St Helena with Napoleon.

As soon as the two admirals had left the ship, Napoleon sent for Captain Maitland and showed him the paper which Lord Keith had brought. He also delivered yet another of his protests about being sent to St Helena:

The idea of it is perfect horror to me. To be placed for life on an island within the Tropics, at an immense distance from any land, cut off from all communications with the world, and everything that I hold dear . . . I would prefer to be delivered up to the Bourbons . . . they style me General! they can have no right to call me General; they may as well call me Archbishop, for I was head of the Church, as well as the army. If they do not acknowledge me as Emperor, they ought as First Consul; they have sent Ambassadors to me as such; and your King in his letters, styled me brother. Had they confined me in the Tower of London, or one of the fortresses of England, (though not what I had hoped from the generosity of the English people) I should not have so much cause of complaint; but to banish me to an island within the Tropics! They might as well have signed my death-warrant at once as it is impossible a man of my habit of body can live long in such a climate.

Napoleon then asked for writing materials to write another letter to the Prince Regent, which Captain Maitland forwarded to Lord Keith the same afternoon, who immediately sent it to London.

Napoleon was not the only one who was worried about his future, Savary and Lallemand were both afraid that the British Government would deliver them up to France, or else why should they not be allowed to accompany Napoleon? Neither had any real desire to cut himself off from the world by following him to St Helena, but they both thought such a fate better than being handed back to France to be shot by the Bourbons. Both wrote similar letters to Lord Keith protesting at their exclusion from the list of persons to accompany Napoleon, both said that they had come with the initial intention of living in England, and they appealed to Keith as a husband and a father to think of the unhappiness of their two families. Maitland assured them that as he had received them on board the *Bellerophon* he considered himself responsible for their personal safety, but to satisfy them he would write to Lord Melville to obtain an express intention of Government policy with regard to their future. Dating his letter 'H.M.S. *Bellerophon*, Plymouth Sound, 31st July, 1815', Maitland wrote the letter before retiring to bed that night.

My Lord,

I am induced to address your Lordship in consequence of having observed, in the intimation delivered to Napoleon Buonaparte of the number of persons allowed to accompany him to St Helena, that the names of Savary and L'Allemand are expressly excepted, which, together with their being proscribed in the French newspapers, has created in them a belief that it is the intention of His Majesty's Government to deliver them up to the King of France. Far be it from me to assume such an idea; but I hope your Lordship will make allowance for the feelings of an officer who has nothing so dear to him as his honour, and who could not bear that a stain should be affixed to a name he has ever endeavoured to bear unblemished. These two men, Savary and L'Allemand (what their characters or conduct in their own country may be I know not), threw themselves under the protection of the British flag; that protection was granted them with the sanction of my name. It is true, no conditions were stipulated for; but I acted in the full confidence that their lives would be held sacred, or they should never have put foot in the ship I command, without being made acquainted that it was for the purpose of delivering them over to the laws of their own country.

I again beg leave to repeat to your Lordship, that I am far from supposing it to be the intention of His Majesty's Government to deliver these men over to the laws of their country; but they are strongly impressed with that belief, and I look upon myself as the cause of their being in their present situation, I most earnestly beg your Lordship's influence may be exerted that the two men may not be brought to the scaffold who claimed and obtained at my hands the protection of the British flag.

I have the honour to be,

&c. &c. &c.

Fred L. Maitland.

Napoleon seemed to be no longer upset by the news he had received of his future, and appeared on deck the following day to show himself to the crowds on the water. Maitland had already sent to some friends of his, who had come with the hope of seeing the Emperor, saying that he would probably not be appearing that day as he was rather distressed by the news he had received. The people in the boats were kept abreast of the Emperor's movements by the crew, who hung out signs which would read: 'He is coming on deck', 'Asleep in the cabin', 'Gone to dinner', 'Talking with his officers', or 'In the cabin with Capt. Maitland'. However, most people managed to get a glimpse of him, dressed in his olive green coat, with a scarlet collar and epaulettes, white waistcoat, breeches, silk stockings, shoes with gold buckles, and with a large star on his left breast. One such eye-witness, who died at the end of the last century, gave his remembrance of the scene:

I have a distinct recollection of the scene at the moment Napoleon presented himself at the gangway, and received the respectful homage of the thousands, men, women, and children, that stood up in their boats and gave expression to their feelings by a subdued roar, not approaching to a huzzah, not partaking in the least of reproach. I fancy I see him now—short in person, stiff, upright, rather stout. He graciously saluted the assembled crowd, stayed a few minutes, and then retired. This was continued day after day as long as the ship remained in the sound.

Although Napoleon appeared outwardly unaffected by the news he had received, the same could not be said of Madame Bertrand. One day she tried to throw herself out of the stern windows and was only stopped by the intervention of Montholon. She was in hysterics for some time after, and used the strongest language, both English and French, about the actions of the British Government and nation. Lallemand too joined in this tirade, saying that it was horrible that they should have been tricked on board for the purpose of butchering them. Maitland ignored the outburst of Madame Bertrand, but told Lallemand that he could not stand by and hear such expressions used of his Government and country, and that if he did not moderate his language he would be obliged to use unpleasant measures to enforce respect. This, says Maitland, had the effect of silencing him. Napoleon's three A.D.Cs. came to Maitland later and told him that Napoleon would never go to St Helena, that he would rather put himself to death. Under questioning they finally admitted that Napoleon himself had never used such a phrase as 'he would put himself to death', but that he had said that he would not go, which was the same thing. Also, they said, there were three of them who were determined that Napoleon should not go; whereupon Maitland warned them that such an event would be looked on as murder by the laws of England, and they would undoubtedly be hanged.

On 1st August, after returning from a visit to Lord Keith and Sir Henry Bunbury, Maitland had a few words with Dr O'Meara, the surgeon of the ship, and Montholon as to the health of Madame Bertrand, and whether she did in effect attempt to drown herself. He then went into the room where Madame Bertrand was resting to see how she was.

When asked how she could try to destroy herself, she replied that she was driven to desperation. She had failed to persuade her husband to remain behind instead of accompanying Napoleon to St Helena. She spoke abusively of Napoleon, saying that if his ends were served he did not care what became of other people. This was not the last interview which Maitland had with Madame Bertrand on the subject of stopping her husband going to St Helena; on another occasion she called on Maitland and endeavoured to persuade him to write to Lord Keith to get him to interfere. Maitland replied that it would not be right for him to write, but that he would be pleased to deliver to the admiral anything she cared to put down on paper. Madame Bertrand did write a letter to Lord Keith, but the admiral replied that he could not interfere in the matter, saying that it was the duty of every good wife to follow her husband wherever he might go.

The feelings of Madame Bertrand had by now become common knowledge all over the ship, and the three A.D.C.s felt it their duty to deny one of the remarks of Madame Bertrand that there was not one of them who would not gladly quit him. They would, they asserted, follow him with pleasure; they would lay down their lives to serve him. They asked Maitland to keep quiet about the conversation they had just had, to which the captain replied that he could not really keep quiet about their conversation when they themselves professed to know all about a private conversation he had had with Madame Bertrand, and that he must know how they had heard about it. One of them replied that he had been on the quarter-gallery and had overheard the conversation.

Napoleon did not appear on deck on the 2nd August, but remained in his cabin. He had so far refused to nominate the list of people who were to go with him to St Helena, and appeared to Maitland still to have some hope that his appeal to the Prince Regent would save him. His non-appearance did not discourage the crowd of sightseers, and the crush was so great that some boats were upset and their occupants cast into the water. In fact during the time that the *Bellerophon* was in Plymouth Sound some people were drowned in their attempts to obtain a good position. The captains of the guard boats were under orders to make out a list of people who did not keep their distance, and to submit it to Lord Keith each day. The list made out for the 1st August by Captain Lillicrap of the *Eurotas* reads as follows:

> Dockyard Boat No. 3, who refused to give his name.
> Mr Arnold belonging to the Dockyard.
> Mr Wallace belonging to the Dockyard (Shipwright).
> Mr May belonging to the Dockyard (Shipwright).
> Lieut. Gold of H.M.S. *Rhin*
> Lieut. Johnson of H.M.S. *Ville de Paris.*
> Lieut. Justice of H.M.S. *Caledonia.*
> The *Ganges* boat.
> Mr William Vickers of the Dockyard.
> Colonel Rivers, Quarter-Master-General.
> Mr Boardman, Midshipman in Sir J. Duckworth's barge.
> Charles Hole, *Elizabeth* Sloop of Plymouth.
> Mr Thompson, Midshipman of H.M.S. *York*

The 3rd of August brought a rumour of an attempted escape by Napoleon. Maitland was informed of this by Sir William Lemmon, whom he met on board the *Ville de Paris* while visiting the admiral. He was told that there was a rumour going around that there would be a boat under the stern of the *Bellerophon* just before ten that night for the purpose of removing Napoleon from the ship. Maitland says that he gave 'no credit to the report', but as soon as he got back on board he asked if Napoleon had been seen on deck that morning, and was informed that he had not been seen, and that he had not attended breakfast. He sent a message to the *Eurotas*, which was astern of the *Bellerophon*, to ask if she had seen the prisoner at the stern windows, but was again disappointed. He then sent one of his midshipmen out on the spanker-boom to try and see into the cabin in which Napoleon was, but the boy returned with nothing to report. Maitland was by now 'extremely uneasy' and on a minor pretence sent his servant into the cabin to fetch a paper. This man returned with the news that Napoleon lay on his bed with the curtains drawn around him, and apparently unwell. That night Napoleon deviated from his usual habit of retiring to bed early, for Maitland heard him walking up and down his cabin in conversation with Bertrand until 11.30 p.m. Maitland gave orders that extra care was to be taken that night, and that a boat was to be under the stern of the ship all night. Nothing happened, however, and the night passed peacefully.

Before daybreak on the 4th August, Maitland had a letter from Lord Keith which warned him to be ready to put to sea at any moment. Therefore at daylight he unmoored, bent the top-gallant sails and made all other preparations for a speedy departure for sea. The French officers who watched these preparations were alarmed, but Maitland only told them that he had received orders to prepare for sea, but had as yet no orders actually to make sail. That morning Maitland waited on Lord Keith in the *Ville de Paris*, where Keith told him that he had received information that a lawyer was on his way down from London with a writ of Habeas Corpus to serve on Napoleon. This was in connection with a libel suit which Vice-Admiral Cochrane was bringing against a certain Alexander Mackenrot on the grounds that he had libelled him in a book he had written. This book criticized the conduct of Cochrane when in command of the West Indies station. He said that Cochrane had not done all in his power to bring the French fleet of Admiral Willaumez to action in 1807 when it had made its excursion to the West Indies. The writ also named Jerome Bonaparte and Admiral Willaumez, the former having been a captain in the fleet at the time. These two officers were needed to testify to the state of the French fleet at that period, as was Napoleon himself. Mackenrot went further in his book and connected Admiral Cochrane with the Stock Exchange scandal which had caused his nephew Lord Cochrane to flee the country in 1814. It was the intention of the

Government to get Napoleon to sea as quickly as possible to prevent the writ being served. Keith was to shift his flag from the *Ville de Paris* to the *Tonnant* for the easier achievement of this, as the latter ship was more ready to sail.

Keith told Maitland that he had received the final instructions of the Government on the matter of Napoleon's future, and that they had not changed their minds in the slightest degree, and that therefore Napoleon was to furnish the names of those that were to accompany him so that preparations could be made to receive him and them.

That day Mackenrot arrived in Plymouth from London, and made several attempts to get in touch with Keith. Failing in this he returned to the King's Arms tavern where he was staying, and wrote the following letter to the admiral:

My Lord,
   I arrived this morning from London with a writ issued by the Court of the King's Bench to subpoena Napoleon Bonaparte as a witness in a trial impending in that court.

   I was extremely anxious of waiting on your Lordship, most humbly to solicit your permission to serve such process on your said prisoner, but unfortunately could not obtain any admission into your presence, neither at your house, nor at the two offices, nor on board H.M.S. *Tonnant* where your Lordship was said to be.

   I humbly entreat your Lordship to consider that an evasion of my process would amount to a High Contempt against that Honble. Court from whence it issues and that under the continuance of such circumstances I shall be under the painful necessity of making my return accordingly.

   Leaving the issue to your Lordship's direction I shall remain here until tomorrow night, but to remove all doubt from your mind I beg leave to enclose a copy of the Writ for your perusal, having already exhibited the original to Sir Thomas John Duckworth [sic] as likewise to your secretary, and have the honour to subscribe myself with greatest respect,

My Lord,
Your Lordships,
most obedient and
most humble servant,
A. MACKENROT.

Keith was not entirely unmoved by the threat in this letter, and he wrote to the Government to clarify his legal position. He was assured by the Lord Chancellor that he could not be touched, but to make perfectly sure a new law was in the process of being passed. Keith had forwarded Mackenrot's letter to the Government, and a few days later received the following comforting reply from Lord Melville.

My Dear Lord,

I return herewith Mr. Mackenrot's letter to your Lordship. His menace is silly and impudent and empty; it is not worth an answer. Sir A. Cochrane is prosecuting him for a scurrilous libel, and the most charitable opinion which can be formed respecting him is that his intellects are not altogether sound.

Mackenrot's intellects may not have been altogether sound, but he was nothing if not persistent, and wrote the following letter to Napoleon himself, although the latter never received it.

Plymouth Dock,
August, 6th 1815.

Sire,

I have been at Plymouth Dock since Friday morning, being the bearer of a summons from the Court of King's Bench for Your Majesty, demanding your presence at London on November 10th next.

Although I desire to deliver this authentic document into Your Majesty's hands personally, Admiral Lord Keith has constantly escaped the presentation of this writ emanating from a Superior Court, although he should be obliged to submit to it, in spite of that I have not ceased to follow his movements on board the *Tonnant* where he denied me access twice, before quitting Plymouth Sound. However, I shall make every possible effort to obtain the ends of justice both public and constitutional, in order to make Your Majesty appear in the said Court to bear witness on my behalf in a 'cause célèbre', and as long as law reigns in England I shall not despair.

In any case I beg Your Majesty to do me the honour of entrusting me with your orders, or with your correspondence, if that is practicable, in return for which I dare to offer my commercial services in London.

I have also a private letter for Count Bertrand, but at the moment I dare only send these few words by means of the ordinary post to assure Your Majesty of my sentiments of respect and admiration, and I have the honour to be Sire, the Humble servant of Your Majesty,

A. MACKENROT.

We must go back now to the morning of the 4th August, when the *Bellerophon* received orders to prepare to put to sea. This meant an explanation by Maitland to Napoleon, and he told him that it was the intention of the British Government that the transfer of the prisoners to the *Northumberland* should take place at sea. Napoleon made one more appeal to Lord Keith, but the admiral refused to see him, writing to Maitland that he had no authority to alter the resolution of the Government in one degree. When Maitland pressed Bertrand to get the Emperor to make out the list of persons to accompany him to St Helena, Bertrand only replied again that the Emperor would never go to St Helena.

At 9 a.m. on the 4th August, the signal was made for the *Bellerophon* to prepare to weigh, and half an hour later to weigh anchor and to get to sea. The wind was contrary for putting to sea, so Maitland ordered the guard boats to tow the ship out until she met a favourable wind. While this operation was in progress, a suspicious looking boat was spotted coming up astern, and Maitland ordered the boats to cast off their tow and move round to the stern of the *Bellerophon*, and not to allow the boats to come any nearer. It proved later to be Mackenrot with his writ, making a last attempt to serve it, but he had to go away foiled. Another boat also kept close company with the *Bellerophon* as she was making her way out of the Sound. This contained two well-dressed women, who stood up and waved their handkerchiefs every time that Napoleon appeared at the stern windows.

Off Ramhead, the *Bellerophon* was joined by the *Prometheus* flying the flag of Lord Keith. Why he was not flying his flag in the *Tonnant* was because he had been chased out of that ship by Mackenrot. The lawyer had first driven him from his house, then followed him to the *Tonnant*, which ship he attempted to board on one side as Lord Keith was leaving on the other! He afterwards pursued Lord Keith towards Cawsand Bay, but the barge in which Lord Keith was travelling outrowed Mackenrot's boat and he gave up the chase. It was on his return from this chase that he spotted the *Bellerophon* and tried to board her, but in this he was also unsuccessful.

Napoleon now appeared to realize that his game was up, if he ever really thought that he stood any chance of success. He kept to his cabin for the rest of the day, often being closetted with Bertrand and Las Cases. He was preparing his final protest which was to be yet another shot in the propaganda war he was carrying on against the British Government. This protest was delivered to Maitland on the 5th August, and he in turn sent it to Keith. It was full of the usual phrases which Napoleon was so fond of using at that time. What was happening to him was a violation of his rights. He came on board the *Bellerophon* only because her captain had assured him that he had orders from his Government to conduct him to England.

If the Government, in giving orders to the Captain of the *Bellerophon* to receive me as well as my suite, only intended to lay a snare for me, it has forfeited its honour and disgraced its flag.

If this act be consummated, the English will in vain boast to Europe of their integrity, their Laws, and their Liberty. British good faith will be lost in the hospitality of the *Bellerophon*.

I appeal to History; it will say that an enemy, who for twenty years waged war against the English people, came voluntarily, in his misfortunes, to seek an asylum under their laws. What more brilliant proof could he give of his esteem and his confidence? But what return did England make for so much magnanimity? They feigned to stretch a friendly hand to that enemy; and when he delivered himself up in good faith, they sacrificed him.

In his narrative, written later, Maitland said that

no snare had been laid, either on the part of His Majesty's Government or mine. I was placed before Rochefort for the open purpose of preventing Buonaparte from making his escape from that port; and the exertions of myself and those under my command had been so completely successful, that the intention of forcing past the ships under my orders, as well as every other plan proposed, of which there appear to have been several, were abandoned as utterly hopeless.

He further stated that he discouraged all contact with Napoleon by means of white flags 'as improper except in extraordinary cases' until he had received the news in Lord Keith's letter of the 23rd July that Napoleon's arrest had been ordered in Paris.

Las Cases raised the subject of the promises made to the Emperor, as they were walking on the deck on the morning of the 6th August. Las Cases said that he understood that Napoleon had only come on board on the assurance that he would be well received in England. To this Maitland replied that he could not imagine how such a misunderstanding could have come about, as he had in all his letters and communications stated that he could make no promises whatever as to the reception Napoleon would meet with from the British Government, and all he was able to say was that he had no reason to think that he would not be well treated *if* he was received in England.

That afternoon Maitland had another conversation with Napoleon, in which the latter once again complained of the conduct of the British Government. In fact his mind was already made up about going to St Helena; however many times he might say 'I will not go to St Helena', he knew that there was no option. He had actually proposed to the surgeon of the *Bellerophon* that he should go with him as his personal physician, as the doctor whom Napoleon had brought from France was averse to making the trip which would mean cutting himself off from Europe. Apart from that he was a bad sailor and suffered from sea-sickness! The surgeon, O'Meara, was attracted by the offer, and approached Maitland on the 6th August for permission to take it up. Maitland replied that if he, O'Meara, thought it would be suitable for him he should accept, dependent upon the consent of the British Government. He had better write to Lord Keith, and Captain Maitland would pass on the letter the next time he went to see the admiral. O'Meara therefore penned the following letter, which Maitland forwarded:

My Lord,

Application having been made to me yesterday by Count Bertrand to accompany General Napoleon Bonaparte to St Helena ... I beg to inform your Lordship that I am willing to accept that situation (provided it meets with your Lordship's approbation) and also on the following conditions; Viz. that it shall be permitted me to resign the above situation should I find it not consonant to my wishes on giving due notice of my intentions thereof. That such time as I shall serve in that situation shall be allowed to count as so much time served on full pay in His Majesty's Navy; or to be indemnified in some way for such loss of time as Surgeon of full pay as it may occasion to me. That I am not to be considered in any way depending upon or to be subservient to, or paid by the aforesaid Napoleon Bonaparte; but as a British Officer employed by the British Government; and lastly that I may be informed as soon as circumstances will admit, of what salary I am to have, and in what manner and from whom I am to receive it.

I have &c. &c.

Barry C. O'Meara.

Lord Keith gave his consent to the proposal, and O'Meara took up his position at St Helena, to become one of the perpetrators of the Napoleonic legend.

By now Lord Keith had moved his flag into the *Tonnant* and that ship and the *Bellerophon* were cruising together off Berry Head. At 9 a.m. on the 7th the *Northumberland* was in sight from the two ships, and they made to close with each other. On board the *Northumberland* was Rear-Admiral Sir George Cockburn, famous for his burning of Washington, and his later remark that since steam had been introduced into the Navy he could not send for any captain without his arriving looking like a chimney sweep! He was not known for his tact or moderation, but seems to have handled his delicate position as the first 'jailer' of Napoleon with considerable success.

Once the squadron was joined, the three ships stood in together and came to anchor off Berry Head. On board the *Northumberland* were two civilians, Viscount Lowther, and the Honourable Mr Lyttleton, a Whig Member of Parliament for Worcestershire. When the squadron had come to anchor, Maitland went on board the *Tonnant* and told Lord Keith that he thought that Napoleon would consent to his removal from the *Bellerophon* without force. He then returned to his ship and sent Bertrand across to the flagship on the instructions of Lord Keith, where he was joined by Sir George Cockburn, and the three of them spent some time together in the admiral's cabin.

After dinner on the *Tonnant* the three of them went back to the *Bellerophon*, where preparations had been going on for the transfer of the members of the suite who were to go to St Helena. All arms had been confiscated from all the Frenchmen except Napoleon, who, as a mark of respect by Lord Keith, was not asked to give up his sword—which respect Napoleon made no effort to repay by any similar courtesy to the admiral. Bertrand and Montholon were employed in making out the list of persons who were to accompany the Emperor, and the necessaries which they would require to make life comfortable.

When Lord Keith and Cockburn came on board the *Bellerophon*, Napoleon was on deck to greet them dressed in his usual green coat with red facings. On being told of his immediate transfer from the *Bellerophon* to the *Northumberland*, he once again protested his indignation at the action of the British Government. A British officer standing near observed that if he had been handed over to the Russians he would probably have been shot, whereupon Napoleon replied 'Dieu me garde des Russes!' and looking at Bertrand he shrugged his shoulders. Cockburn asked at what time *General* Bonaparte would be ready to be received on board the *Northumberland*; Napoleon, rather surprised at being styled only General, replied that ten o'clock would be convenient to him. Cockburn then asked if he or his suite wanted anything further on board the *Northumberland*, to which Bertrand replied, twenty packs of cards, a backgammon board, and a domino table, and Madame Bertrand also required some necessary articles of furniture.

Maitland gives a slightly different version of how Napoleon learned of his removal to the *Northumberland*, the next day. He says that Bertrand sent for Maitland and told him that Napoleon wished to see him, this Maitland says was about 9.30 p.m. In the cabin, Napoleon said that he had *just been informed* by Bertrand that he was to be transferred to the *Northumberland* the next morning. This was followed by another of the now familiar tirades against the British abuse of hospitality.

Early the next morning Cockburn came on board the *Bellerophon* to order the search of Napoleon's baggage, which was fairly extensive and included such items as two services of plate, a travelling library, and several gold articles. Many of Napoleon's personal servants had to be cut from the list of persons going to St Helena, and of the original total of about forty, two-thirds were sent to the *Eurotas* for transport back to France. Las Cases came to Maitland and asked if he could have an interview with Lord Keith. This Captain Maitland obtained for him, and Las Cases told Keith that Napoleon had been promised by Maitland that he would be well received in England. Lord Keith was unable to ignore such a statement and wrote to Maitland to make a written record of the whole affair.

Bertrand was late for breakfast that morning and when he arrived only his wife and Captain Maitland were left at the table. Madame Bertrand at once attacked him for not leaving Napoleon and going to live in England, but Bertrand re-

mained silent under this verbal onslaught. She again tried to
get Maitland to interfere on her behalf, but he told her that if
Count Bertrand were to leave Napoleon he 'will forfeit the very
high character he now bears in this country.' With these
words he left the table. Madame Bertrand followed him to the
deck, but this time she was attacking on behalf of Napoleon.
She had heard that he was not to have the whole of the after-
cabin of the *Northumberland*, which Maitland agreed, as he
had heard that Cockburn had orders to that effect. 'They had
better treat him like a dog at once,' said Madame Bertrand
'and put him down in the hold.' At this point Maitland says
that what remained of his self-possession gave way under the
strain of the past few days, to which Madame Bertrand had
contributed more than her fair share. 'Madam,' he replied,
'you talk like a very foolish woman; and if you cannot speak
more to the purpose, or with more respect of the Government
I have the honour to serve, I request you will not address
yourself to me.'

Soon after this outburst, Marchand, Napoleon's principal
valet, came to see Maitland and told him that Napoleon
wished to see him in his cabin. When he went in, Napoleon
said to him:

I have requested to see you Captain to return my thanks for your kindness
and attention to me whilst I have been on board the *Bellerophon* and
likewise to beg you will convey them to the officers and ship's company you
command. My reception in England has been very different from what I
expected; but it gives me much satisfaction to assure you that I feel your
conduct to me throughout has been that of a gentleman and a man of
honour.

When Cockburn came to make the search of the baggage,
Bertrand was so indignant that it should be searched at all
that he refused to attend or to order anyone else to do so.
However, Savary was present, as was Marchand, who was
permitted to take enough money out of one of the cases for the
payment of the wages of the servants. One box of 4,000 gold
napoleons was handed over to Maitland to take back with him
to London, and he later handed this over to Sir Hudson Lowe
when he was about to leave as Governor of St Helena.

Lord Keith arrived in the *Tonnant*'s barge at eleven, and of
this last act in the scene we have several witnesses. All are
agreed that Napoleon kept Lord Keith, nearly seventy years

old, waiting in his barge for two hours before he appeared on deck. When Cockburn began to get annoyed at the delay, and said that Napoleon ought to be reminded of his position, Keith replied: 'No, no, much greater men than either you or I have waited longer for him ere now; let him take his time.' Midshipman Home thought that this was 'nobly said of the old Scotchman'.

As Napoleon left his cabin and crossed the quarter-deck to leave the ship, the captain's guard which had been turned out presented arms, by the special direction of Lord Keith, and three ruffles of the drum were beat for a general officer. He stopped to thank Captain Maitland once more for his treatment of him while on board the *Bellerophon*, then he thanked the officers and then the men, to whom he bowed two or three times. Napoleon was the first to step into the barge; he was followed by General and Madame Bertrand and their children, Count and Countess Montholon and child, General Gourgaud, nine men and three women servants, and the surgeon O'Meara. Last to come was Lord Keith himself. The barge then moved about thirty yards from the ship and Napoleon stood up and bowed to the officers and men of the *Bellerophon*.

About a quarter an hour before Napoleon had left the ship, Montholon had come to Maitland and said that Napoleon regretted that he had not been able to obtain an interview with the Prince Regent as he was sure that he could have got Maitland appointed Rear-Admiral! Maitland, rather shocked by such a suggestion, replied that although he did not feel ungrateful for the idea which had been entertained, he regretted that it was contrary to the rules of the service. Montholon then said that Napoleon had wanted to present him with a box containing his portrait, but he was given to understand that, owing to the delicate position in which Maitland was situated, he would not be able to accept. Maitland took the opportunity to say that he 'was much hurt' that Las Cases should have mentioned to Lord Keith that Maitland had promised Napoleon would be well received in England. To this Montholon replied, 'Oh! Las Cases negotiated this business; it has turned out very differently from what he and all of us expected. He attributes the Emperor's situation to himself, and is therefore desirous of giving it the best countenance he can; but I assure you, the Emperor is convinced your conduct has been most honourable, and that is my opinion also.'

Savary and Lallemand had been left behind on the *Bellerophon*, which at first caused them some fears for their fate, but they were repeatedly assured that the British Government would not hand them over to the French. They did go on board the *Northumberland* for a last visit to Napoleon, and spent some time with him in the after-cabin; then they were both embraced by Napoleon and left to return to the *Bellerophon*.

This was the end of the story of the Emperor Napoleon as far as the *Bellerophon* was concerned, for the ship, with the *Tonnant* and *Eurotas*, returned to Plymouth Sound, while the following day the *Northumberland*, with two troop ships, a frigate, and several sloops of war, made sail to the westwards. At last the 'Eagle' was chained to the rock, and was to die there.

This service was the last that Lord Keith rendered to his country, hauling down his flag soon after reaching Plymouth. In a letter to his daughter on the 13th August, he describes the transfer of Napoleon to the *Northumberland*:

He was anxious no doubt about his fate, but always temperate & civil, even funny and jocose at times. Asked my advice about the law etc., etc. Not pleased at being styled General.

'If not Emperor, I am First Consul. You made treaties with me as such.'

'Yes, sir, but when you crushed the Commonwealth you sank the title in Emperor.

He said he would not quit England alive. I laughed.' He said 'Would you go to St Helena, Admiral? Oh, no, plutôt la mort! I will not leave this ship, you must take me by force. Surely you would not reduce an officer like me to a measure so disagreeable?'

'Oh no! but you shall order me,' and at the door of the outer cabin he said: 'Admiral I have given you my solemn protest in writing, I now repeat I will not go out of this ship but by force, you must order me.'

'My barge is ready for your reception, and if you choose to go in her, please to warn them and the ladies. It depends on you and I order you to go.'

He went to the gangway, thanked Maitland and the officers and then the men; bowed to all and went to the boat. Bertrand and Madame, Montholon and Madame, Gourgaud and Las Cases I fetched and put beside him, but he said, 'What! do you take the trouble to come too? Sit by me, we shall talk.'

He talked of St Helena, laughed at the ladies being sea-sick, asked if that was the *Tonnant* of Aboukir? If the *Bellerophon* was old? Why I changed my name from Elphinstone which he knew me by ever since Toulon? When on board the *Northumberland* he talked to all, and asked questions very quick and said, 'Let us look at the cabin.' Took me with him and said: 'This is very good, better than the *Bellerophon* for my little green bed is in it.'

We then came on deck, he began to talk to the land officers, and I took my leave of him and Sir George Cockburn and in an hour made the signal to weigh and part company—it was then dark.

Europe had now finished with Napoleon, although stories of him were to filter through for the next six years. Traditional Europe had now conquered the incarnate spirit of the French Revolution.

For the next six years Napoleon waged his last campaign, his targets were the British Government and their representative on St Helena. Most people would agree that the treatment of Napoleon on St Helena was less than charitable, full of many petty slights which might have been avoided; and for all this the responsibility lies directly with the British Government. It may also be said that the treatment of France at the peace which followed the Hundred Days was extraordinary for its leniency; and the responsibility for this lies again with the British Government. Though it was incapable of magnanimity and generosity to a defeated individual, it did show it to a defeated nation.

The period of Napoleon's life which he spent on St Helena was probably one of great interest. There was hardly a topic upon which he did not speak his mind, but of the men who sent him there he never said a good word, although he did once protest to Lady Malcolm, wife of Admiral Sir Pulteney Malcolm, that he did not hate the English. There is no actual record of any favourable opinions of the Duke of Wellington, who was responsible for his final fall, although one of his aides once reported to Maitland that he, Napoleon, considered the Duke, 'in the management of an army, is fully equal to myself, with the advantage of possessing more prudence.'

Of his charm there can be no doubt; we have already heard the opinion of Mishipman Home. Lord Keith was so alarmed about it that he once exclaimed, 'Damn the fellow, if he had obtained an interview with his Royal Highness, in half an

hour they would have been the best friends in England'.
Maitland reported:

He possessed, to a wonderful degree, a facility in making a favourable
impression upon those with whom he entered into conversation: this
appeared to me to be accomplished by turning the subject to matters he
supposed the person he was addressing was well acquainted with, and on
which he could show himself to good advantage. This had the effect of
putting him in good humour with himself; after which it was not a very
difficult matter to transfer a part of that feeling to the person who had
occasioned it.

This is also the end of the active serving life of the *Bellerophon*, for within five weeks of her return to Plymouth she was
taken out of commission. Maitland wrote the last words in the
log on the 13th September, 1815: 'Light airs and fine weather.
Washed decks. At 11 came on board the Pay Captain and
Clerk and paid the Ship's Company. Sunset—hauled down
the pendant.'

Soon afterwards the *Bellerophon* was handed over by the
Admiralty to the Transport Board for use as a convict hulk;
so the old ship, which had spent most of her life trying to keep
Britons free, ended by keeping them in thrall. At first she was
employed in this duty under her old name, but in 1826 this
was changed to the more suitable one of *Captivity*. She
continued thus until 1836, when she was sold to a ship breaker
for £4,030. As a lucky coincidence, Captain Maitland, then
Sir Frederick, was Admiral Superintendent of Portsmouth
dockyard, and was able to save one or two relics of the old
ship, and the figurehead and stern ornaments are now on
view in the Victory Museum at Portsmouth.

Other *Bellerophon*s followed her; the second was an 80-gun
ship, originally called *Talavera*, changed to *Waterloo* before
launching, but changed again in 1824 to *Bellerophon*. This
name was adopted on the recommendation of Admiral Sir
William Johnstone Hope who had been the captain of the
original *Bellerophon* at the 'First of June'.

The second *Bellerophon* served at the bombardment of
Acre, and later at that of Sebastopol, and ended her existence
in 1892 when she was broken up after thirty-six years as a
harbour hulk.

The third *Bellerophon* was laid down in 1863, and was an
armoured ship of 7,550 tons, steam driven. She was present

when the ill-fated *Captain* went down in a storm in the Bay of Biscay. The *Bellerophon* ran directly over the spot where the *Captain* went down, but with the storm and the darkness of the night she saw none of the survivors and passed on.

The fourth *Bellerophon* was a 'Dreadnought' class battle-ship which fought at Jutland in 1916, and was broken up between the wars. The name was considered again during the Second World War, but it was thought too difficult for the modern sailor to get his tongue around, or at least that is how the story goes! At the present day *Bellerophon* is a shore base at Portsmouth, but what more fitting name could there be for one of the new nuclear submarines than this?

APPENDIX I

CAPTAINS AND FLAG OFFICERS WHO SERVED ON THE *Bellerophon*
1791–1815

Captain Thomas Pasley	1791–93
Rear-Admiral Pasley ⎱ Captain William Hope ⎰	1794
Captain Lord Cranstoun	1795
Captain John Loring (acting)	May–Oct. 1796
Captain Henry Darby	1796–1801
Captain Lord Garlies	May–Dec. 1801
Captain John Loring ⎱ Admiral Sir John Duckworth ⎰	1803–5 July 1803
Captain John Cooke	April–Oct. 1805
Captain Edward Rotheram ⎱ Admiral Albermarle Bertie ⎰	1805–8 Nov. 1807–March 1808
Admiral Lord Alan Hyde Gardner ⎱ Captain Samuel Warren ⎰	March 1808 1808–10
Captain Lucius Hardyman	Aug.–Nov. 1810
Captain John Halstead ⎱ Admiral Ferrier ⎰	1810–13 1811
Captain Augustus Brine	Feb.–March 1813
Captain Edward Hawker ⎱ Admiral Sir Richard Keats ⎰	1813–15
Captain Frederick Maitland	Mar.–Sept. 1815

II LIST OF SOURCES

BARROW, Sir John, *Life of Howe* (1838).

BERRY, Sir Edward, *A Narrative of the Proceedings*, etc.

BRENTON, Captain Edward, *A Life of Lord St Vincent*.

BRYANT, Sir Arthur, *The Years of Endurance*; *Years of Victory*; *The Age of Elegance*.

CHARNOCK, *Naval Architecture*.

CORBETT, Sir Julian, *The Campaign of Trafalgar* (1910).

CLARKE and M'ARTHUR, *Life of Nelson* (1809).

CORNWALLIS-WEST, G., *A Life and Letters of Admiral Cornwallis*.

DE POGGI, *A Narrative of the Proceedings of the British Fleet*, etc. (1796).

DESBRIERE, Col. E., *The Trafalgar Campaign*.

FRASER, Edward, *The Enemy at Trafalgar* (1806).

JAMES, Admiral Sir William, *Old Oak*.

LONGRIDGE, Nepean, *Anatomy of Nelson's Ships* (1961).

LEWIS, M. A., *A Social History of the Navy, 1793–1815*.

MACKENZIE, Col. R. H., *The Trafalgar Roll* (1913).

MAHAN, A. T., *Life of Nelson*, Vols. I and II.

MAITLAND, Capt. Frederick, *A Narrative of the Proceedings Onboard*, etc. (1826).

MANCERON, Claude, *Which Way to Turn, Napoleon's Last Choice*.

MARCUS, G. J., *A Naval History of England*, Vol. I (1962).

MARKHAM, Felix, *Life of Napoleon* (1963).

MASEFIELD, John, *Sea Life in Nelson's Time*.

NAVAL CHRONICLE, THE (Published 1799–1819).

NAVY RECORDS SOCIETY, *Logs of the Great Sea Fights*, Vols. I and II; Keith Papers (Ed. C. Lloyd).

NICOL, John, *Adventures of John Nicol, Mariner* (1822).

OMAN, Carola, *Nelson* (1947).

PARKINSON, C. Northcote, *Edward Pellew, Viscount Exmouth* (1934).

POPE, Dudley, *England Expects* (1959).

PUBLIC RECORD OFFICE SOURCES: The following material was used from the records of the Public Record Office, and extracts appear by permission of the Controller of Her Majesty's Stationery Office.

> *Bellerophon*, Captains' Logs: ADM. 51/99, 100, 1142, 1162, 1190, 1262, 1281, 1359, 1414, 1463, 1478, 1517, 1522, 1608, 1727, 1749, 1925, 2024, 4417; ADM. 53/189, 190, 191, 192; Master's Journals: ADM. 52/2752, 2755, 2756, 2779, 2780, 3359, 3568, 3734, 4044; Cornwallis's Journal: ADM. 50/40.

ROSEBERY, Lord, *Napoleon, The Last Phase* (1906).

ROSS, Sir John, *Life of Lord de Saumarez* (1838).

SOCIETY FOR NAUTICAL RESEARCH, *The Mariner's Mirror*.

STIRLING, A. M. W., *Pages and Portraits from the Past* (1919).

THIERS, Adolphe, *A History of the Consulate and Empire* (1845).

THOMPSON, J. M., *A Life of Napoleon*.

WARNER, Oliver, *The Glorious First of June*; *The Nile*; *Trafalgar*. (Batsford, British Battles Series).

III GLOSSARY

ABACK A ship is said to be taken aback when the wind blows against the front of the sails and flattens them against the mast.

BAR-SHOT Two round shots connected by an iron rod, used for the destruction of rigging.

BEAK-HEAD A platform immediately below the forecastle, railed in and used for setting up the rigging of the bowsprit.

BEAM The measurement of a ship at its greatest breadth.

BEAR (down or up) To keep farther away from the point of the wind. To 'bear down' was to perform the same manoeuvre, but to use it to close with the enemy.

BEAT, To To try to make headway against the wind by the use of various tacks.

BEND, To To fasten a knot or to fasten a sail to the yard.

BOMB The shortened version of 'bomb-ship'; 'bomb-ketch'; or 'bomb-vessel' etc. A two-masted vessel fitted with a large mortar in the bows.

BROADSIDE The discharge of all weapons on one side of a ship.

CANISTER A type of shot, consisting of a number of small iron balls packed in a cylindrical tin case, and used at close quarters.

CAULK, To To cover the bottom of a ship with oakum and pitch to make it watertight.

CHAIN-SHOT Two cannon-balls linked with a chain.

CLOSE-HAULED Sailing as close to the wind as possible.

COURSES All sails which hang from the lower yards.

CRANK   The condition of a ship in which it is dangerous to carry all sail.

DOLPHIN-STRIKER   A short perpendicular spar under the bowsprit to secure the jib-boom.

FLAG RANK   An officer with the rank of Rear-Admiral or above.

FREEBOARD   The extent of a ship's side from waterline to gunwale.

FURL, TO   To wrap or roll a sail close to the yard.

JIB   The fore topmast staysail.

JURY MASTS   Masts set up to replace those lost in action or storm.

LANYARD   A short piece of rope used for several purposes.

LEEWAY   The drift of a ship to leeward, i.e. the side of the ship away from the wind.

LUFF, TO   To bring a vessel closer to the wind.

MIZEN   The aftermost mast of a ship.

ORLOP   The uppermost portion of a ship's hold.

POOP   The highest and aftermost deck of a ship.

POST RANK   A Captain of one of H.M. Ships, usually a frigate or above.

QUARTER-DECK   The deck situated between the poop and mainmast and used by officers.

RAKE, TO   To fire into a vessel from ahead or astern so that the shots pass from end to end.

REEF, TO   To reduce sail in case of higher winds.

SHEER   The longitudinal curve of a ship's decks or sides.

TACK   A rope attached to the lower corner of a sail on the weather side, used when the vessel sails on a wind.

TACK, TO   To turn a ship's head in opposition to the wind.

TOMPION   A plug of wood used to keep the water out of the muzzle of a gun.

TRIM   The set of a ship on the water.

WARP, TO   To move a ship from one place to another by pulling on hawsers attached to buoys or anchors.

WEAR, TO   To turn a ship on to a new course but retaining the wind.

YAW, TO   To vary the amount of deviation in the course of a ship from a straight line.

Index

Italic numbers indicate illustrations.